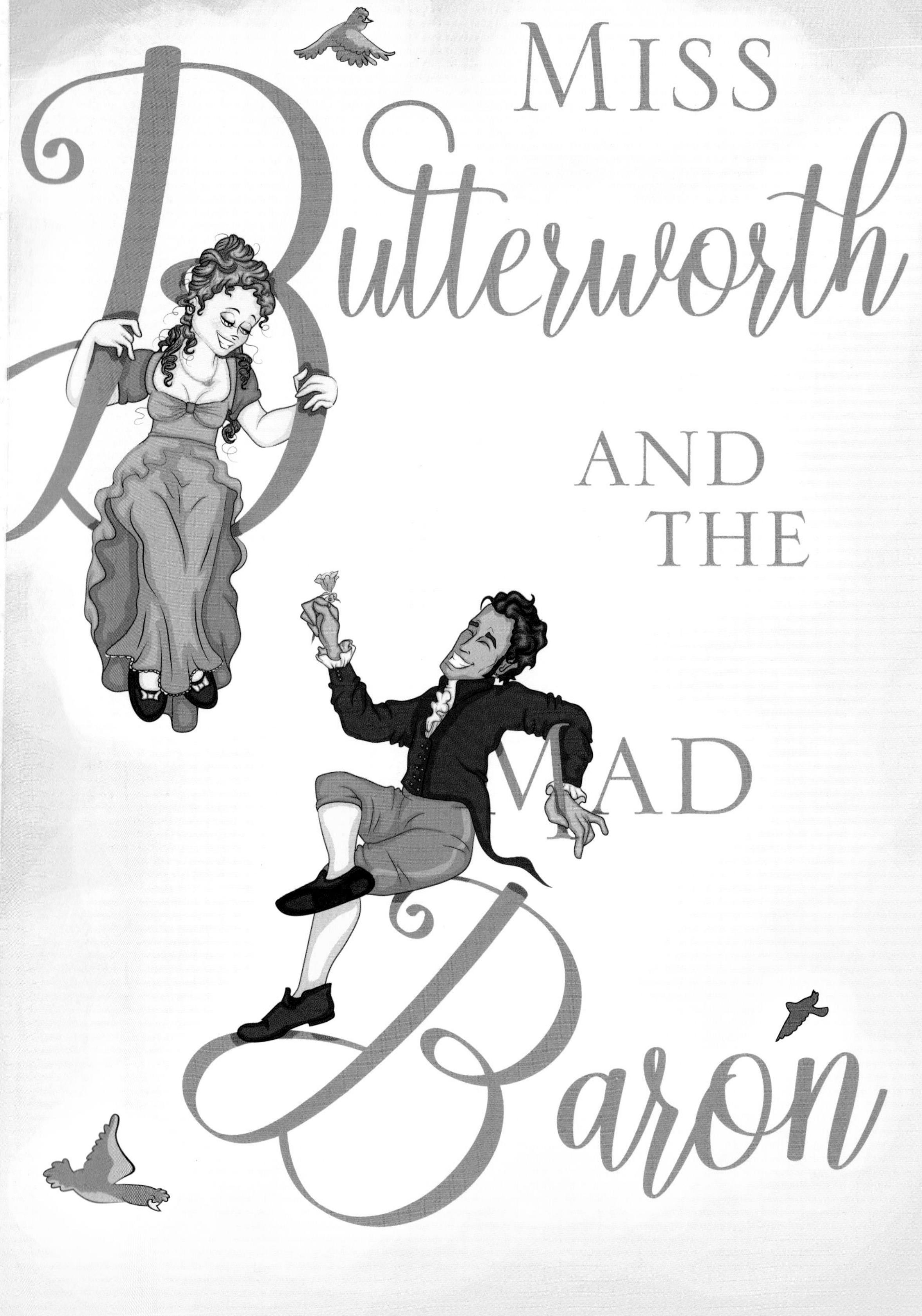
MISS
Butterworth
AND
THE
MAD
Baron

# Also by Julia Quinn

## THE BRIDGERTON PREQUELS
*Because of Miss Bridgerton*
*The Girl With the Make-Believe Husband*
*The Other Miss Bridgerton*
*First Comes Scandal*

## THE BRIDGERTON SERIES
*The Duke and I*
*The Viscount Who Loved Me*
*An Offer From a Gentleman*
*Romancing Mister Bridgerton*
*To Sir Phillip, With Love*
*When He Was Wicked*
*It's In His Kiss*
*On the Way to the Wedding*
*The Bridgertons: Happily Ever After*
*The Wit and Wisdom of Bridgerton*

## THE SMYTHE-SMITH QUARTET
*Just Like Heaven*
*A Night Like This*
*The Sum of All Kisses*
*The Secrets of Sir Richard Kenworthy*

THE BEVELSTOKE SERIES

*The Secret Diaries of Miss Miranda Cheever*

*What Happens in London*

*Ten Things I Love About You*

TWO DUKES OF WYNDHAM

*The Lost Duke of Wyndham*

*Mr. Cavendish, I Presume*

AGENTS OF THE CROWN

*To Catch An Heiress*

*How To Marry a Marquis*

THE LYNDON SISTERS

*Everything and the Moon*

*Brighter Than the Sun*

THE SPLENDID TRILOGY

*Splendid*

*Dancing at Midnight*

*Minx*

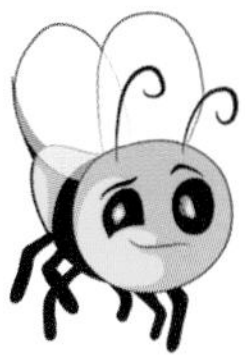

THE BEVELSTOKE SERIES
*The Secret Diaries of Miss Miranda Cheever*
*What Happens in London*
*Ten Things I Love About You*

TWO DUKES OF WYNDHAM
*The Lost Duke of Wyndham*
*Mr. Cavendish, I Presume*

AGENTS OF THE CROWN
*To Catch An Heiress*
*How To Marry a Marquis*

THE LYNDON SISTERS
*Everything and the Moon*
*Brighter Than the Sun*

THE SPLENDID TRILOGY
*Splendid*
*Dancing at Midnight*
*Minx*

For Dad*
~JQ

For Pobz*
~VIOLET

*(same person)

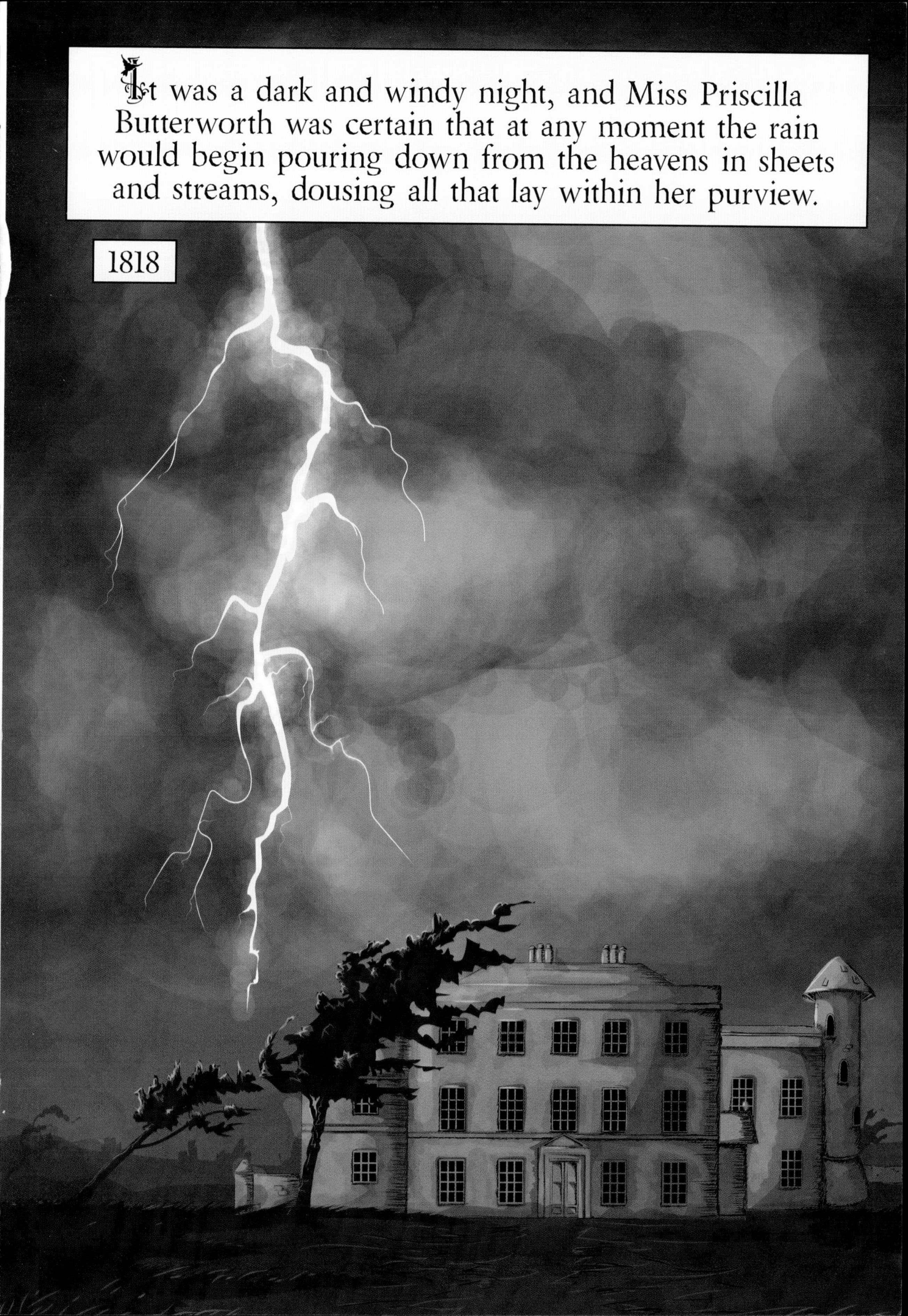
It was a dark and windy night, and Miss Priscilla Butterworth was certain that at any moment the rain would begin pouring down from the heavens in sheets and streams, dousing all that lay within her purview.
1818

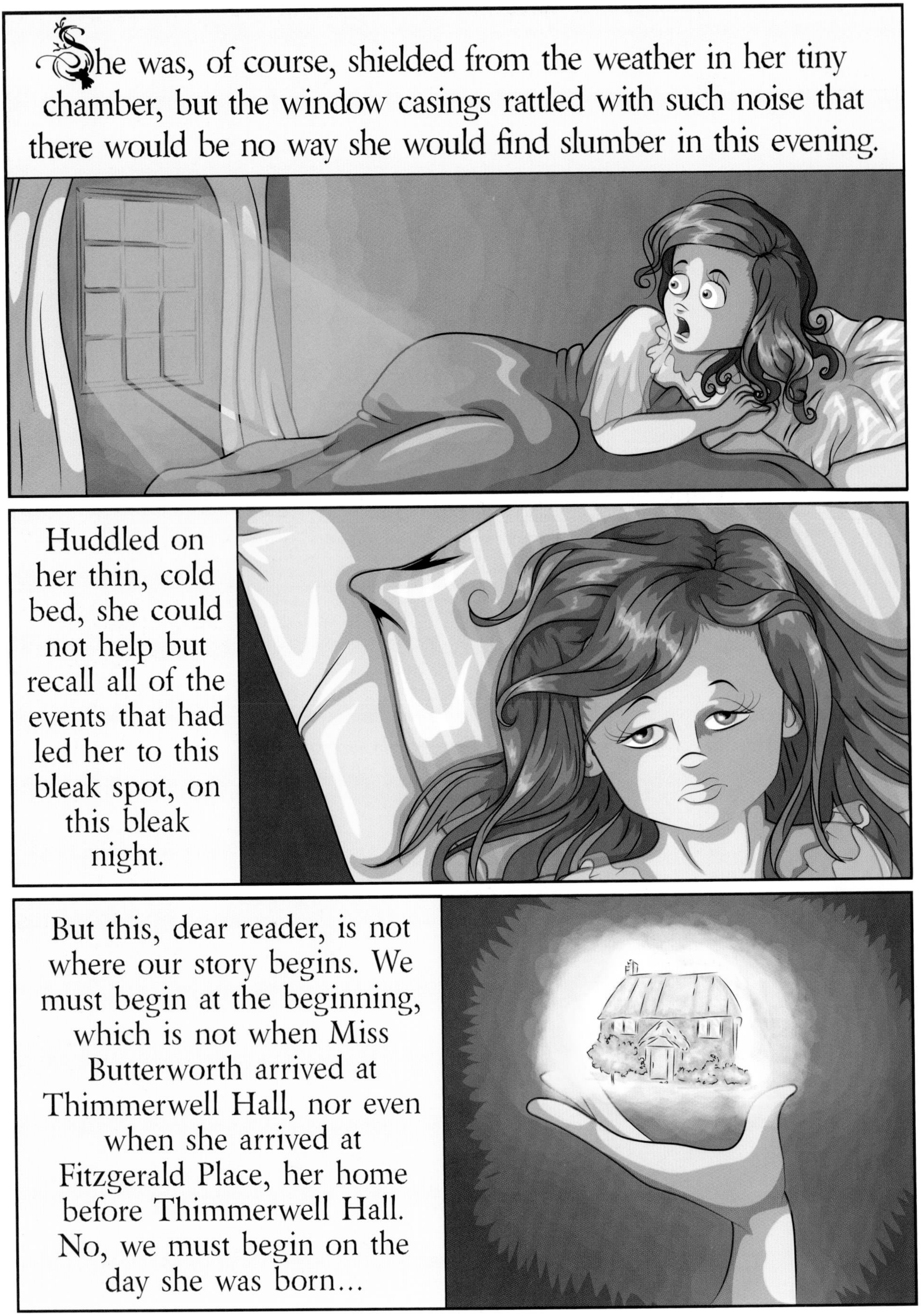
She was, of course, shielded from the weather in her tiny chamber, but the window casings rattled with such noise that there would be no way she would find slumber in this evening.
Huddled on her thin, cold bed, she could not help but recall all of the events that had led her to this bleak spot, on this bleak night.
But this, dear reader, is not where our story begins. We must begin at the beginning, which is not when Miss Butterworth arrived at Thimmerwell Hall, nor even when she arrived at Fitzgerald Place, her home before Thimmerwell Hall. No, we must begin on the day she was born...

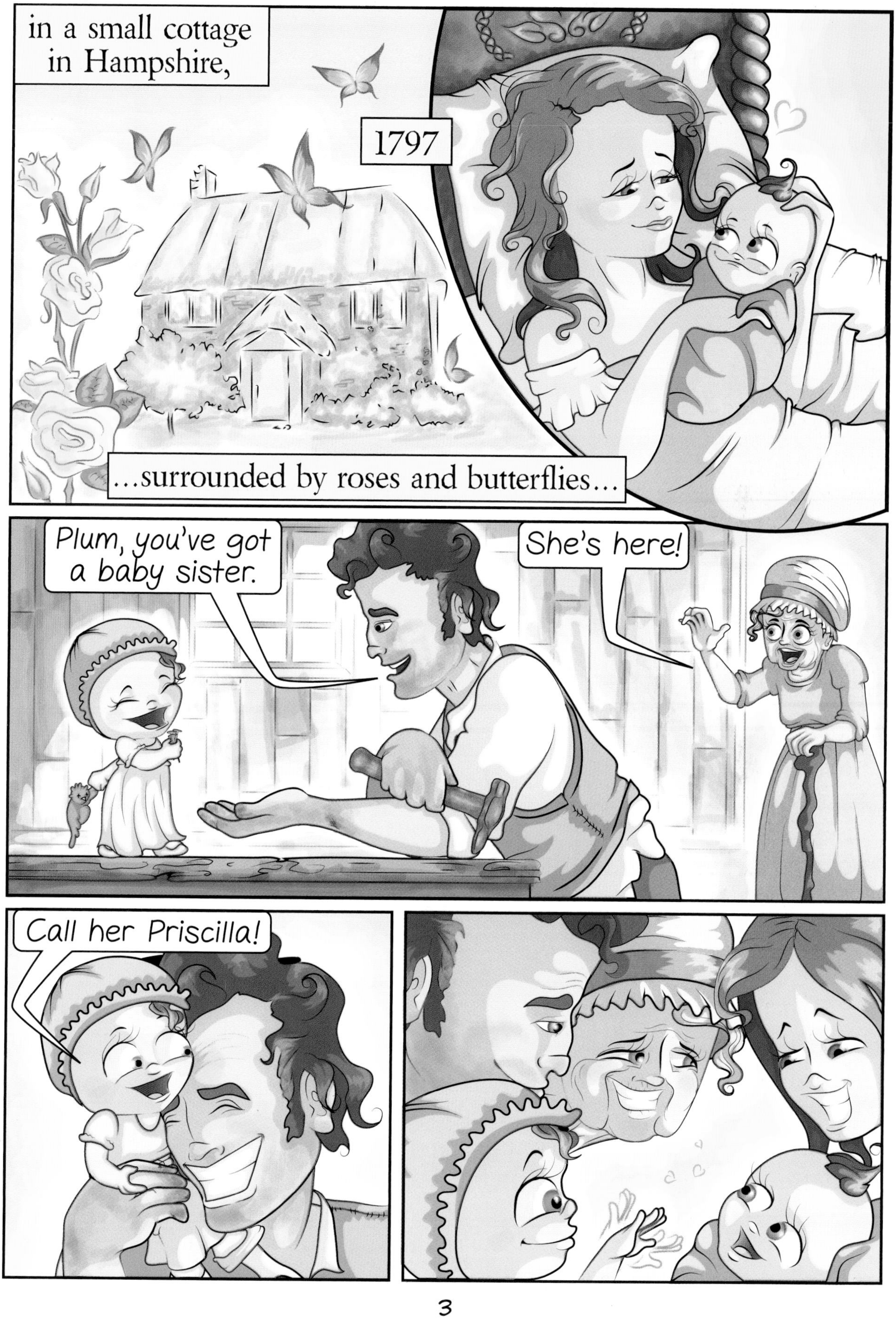
in a small cottage in Hampshire,
1797
...surrounded by roses and butterflies...
Plum, you've got a baby sister.
She's here!
Call her Priscilla!

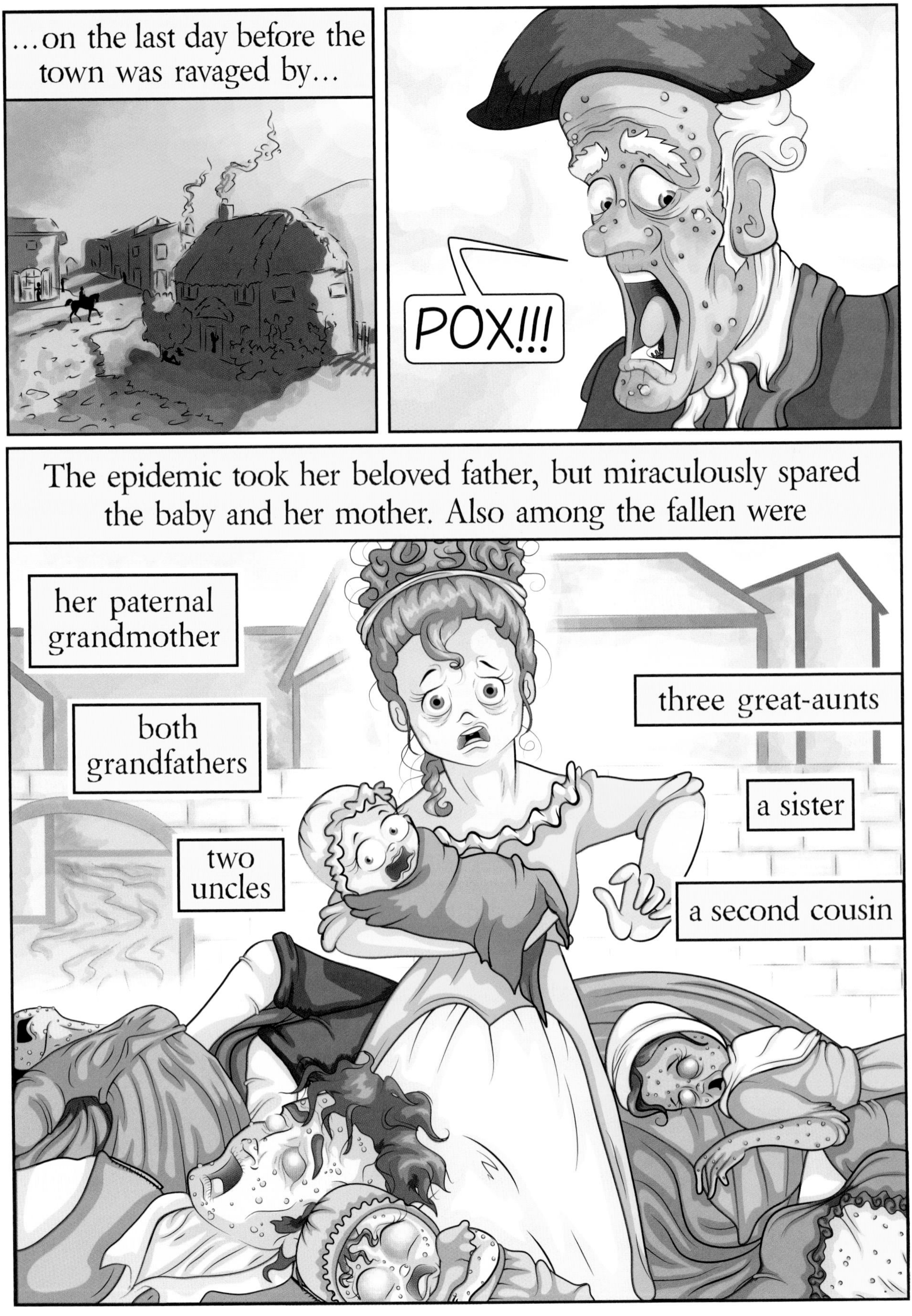

...on the last day before the town was ravaged by...
POX!!!
The epidemic took her beloved father, but miraculously spared the baby and her mother. Also among the fallen were
her paternal grandmother
both grandfathers
two uncles
three great-aunts
a sister
a second cousin

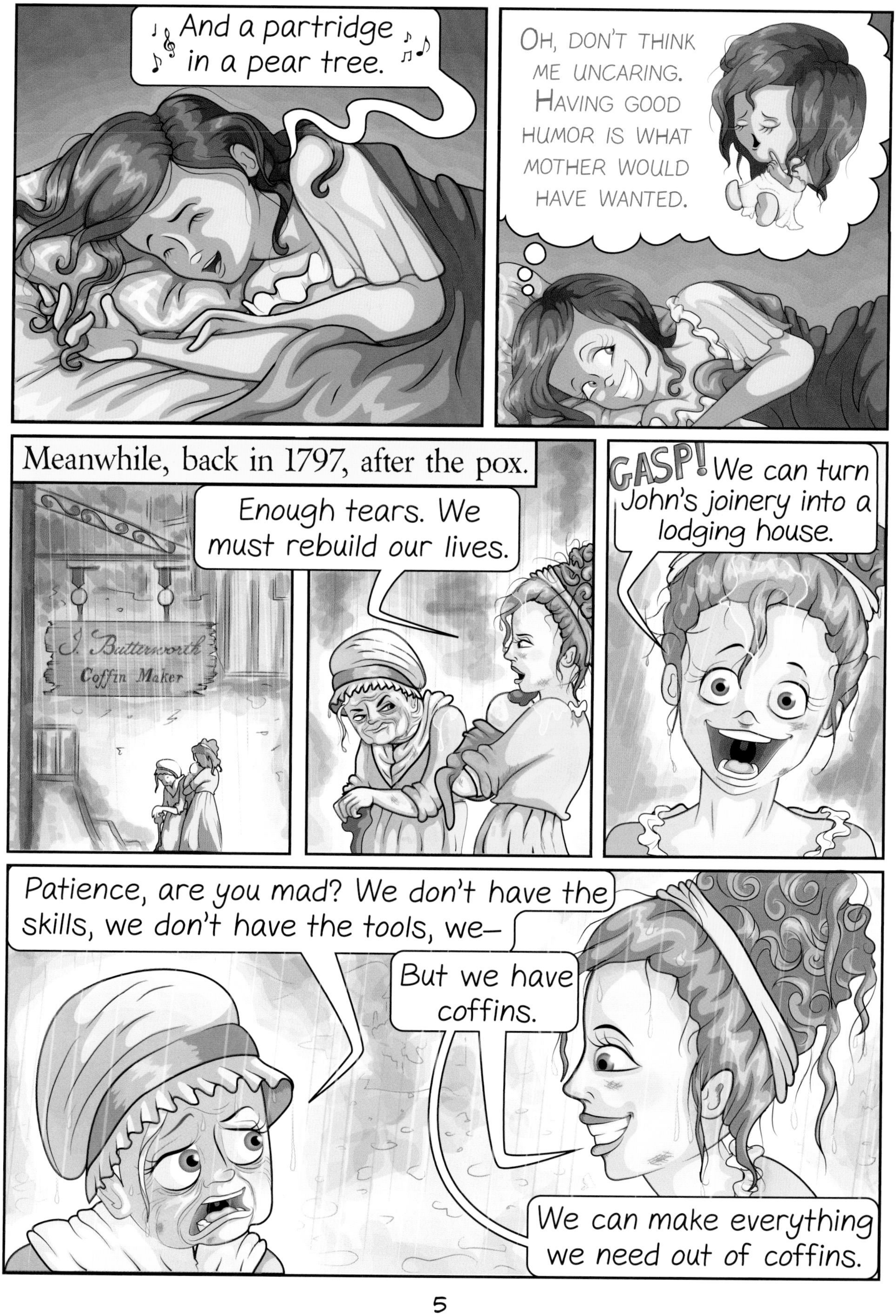
And a partridge in a pear tree.
OH, DON'T THINK ME UNCARING. HAVING GOOD HUMOR IS WHAT MOTHER WOULD HAVE WANTED.
Meanwhile, back in 1797, after the pox.
J. Butterworth Coffin Maker
Enough tears. We must rebuild our lives.
GASP! We can turn John's joinery into a lodging house.
Patience, are you mad? We don't have the skills, we don't have the tools, we–
But we have coffins.
We can make everything we need out of coffins.

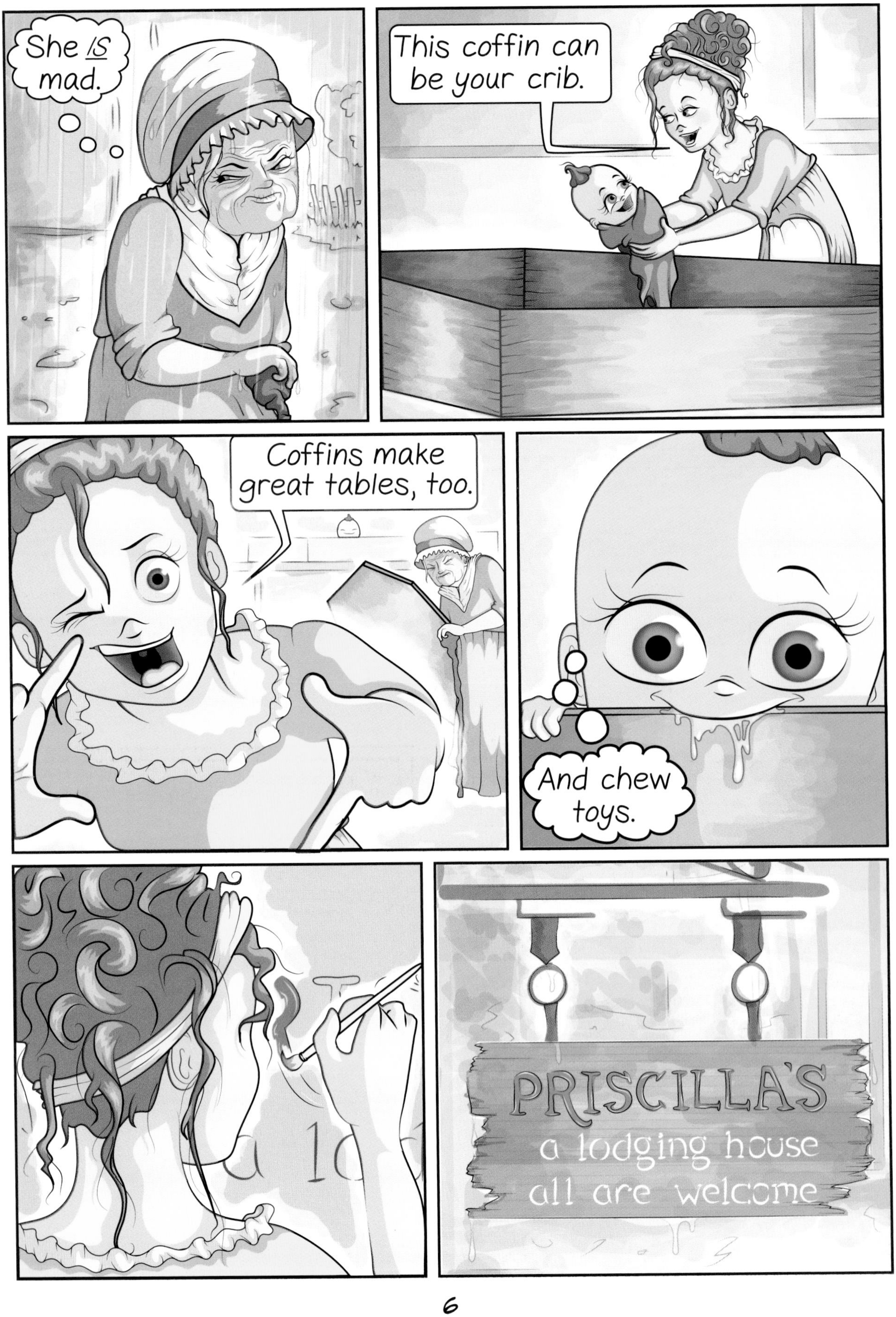
She IS mad.
This coffin can be your crib.
Coffins make great tables, too.
And chew toys.
PRISCILLA'S
a lodging house
all are welcome

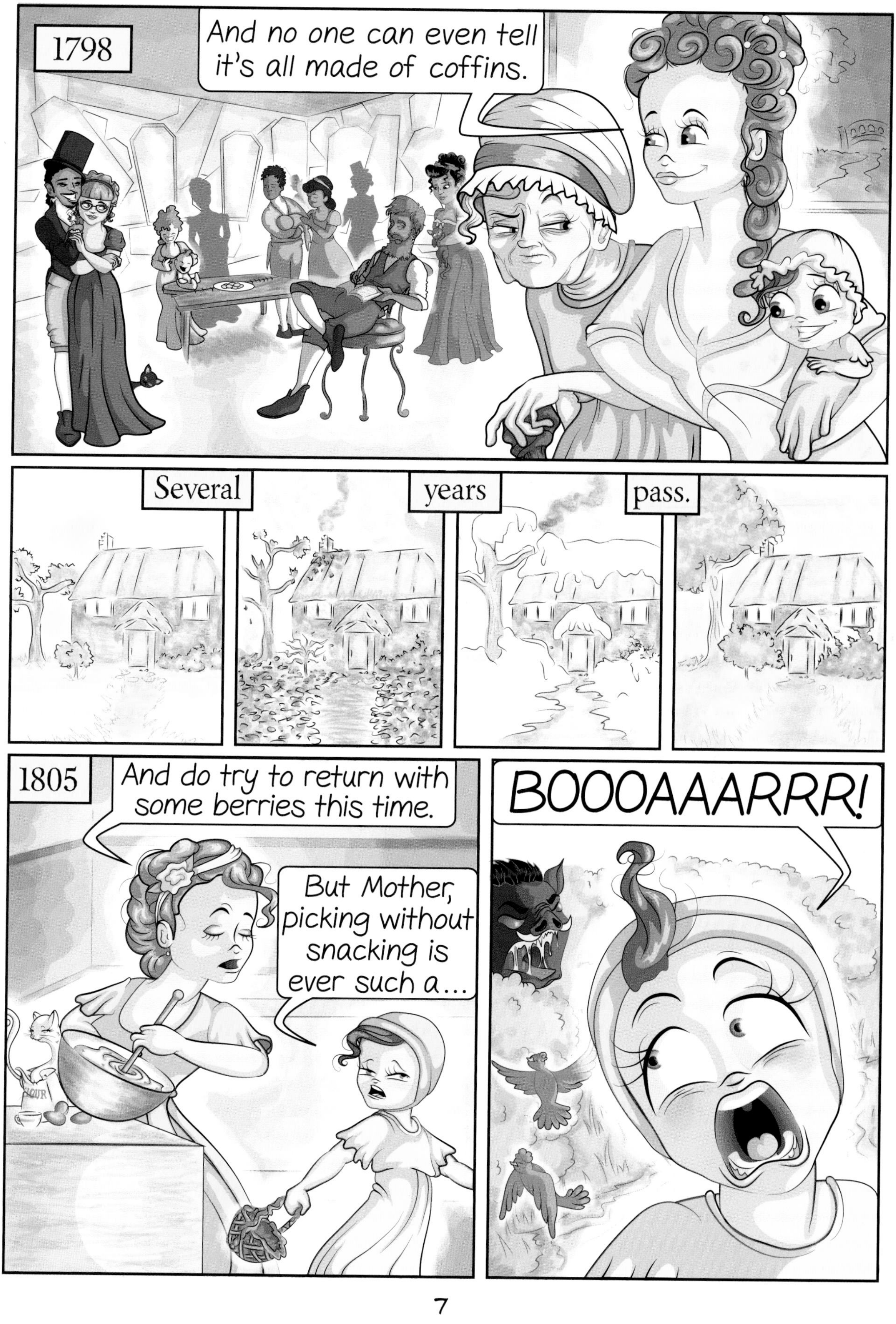
1798
And no one can even tell it's all made of coffins.
Several
years
pass.
1805
And do try to return with some berries this time.
But Mother, picking without snacking is ever such a...
BOOOAAARRRR!

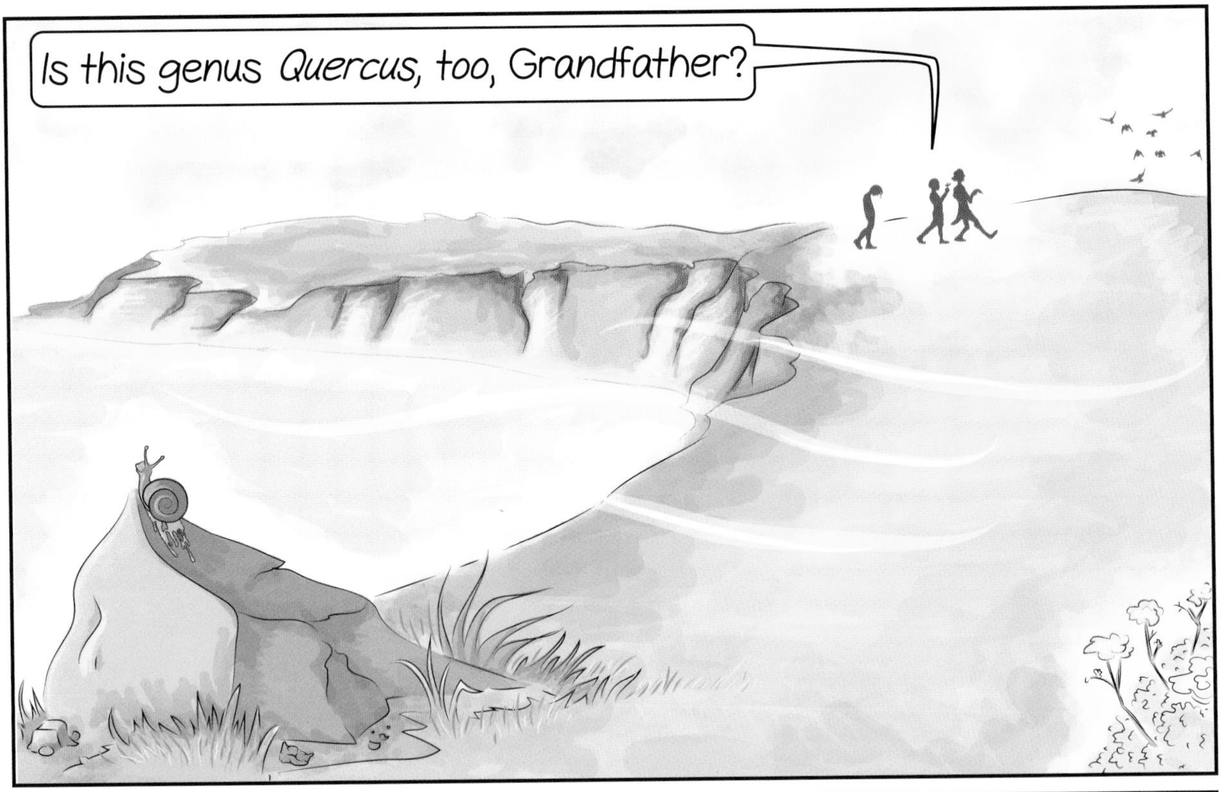
Is this genus *Quercus*, too, Grandfather?

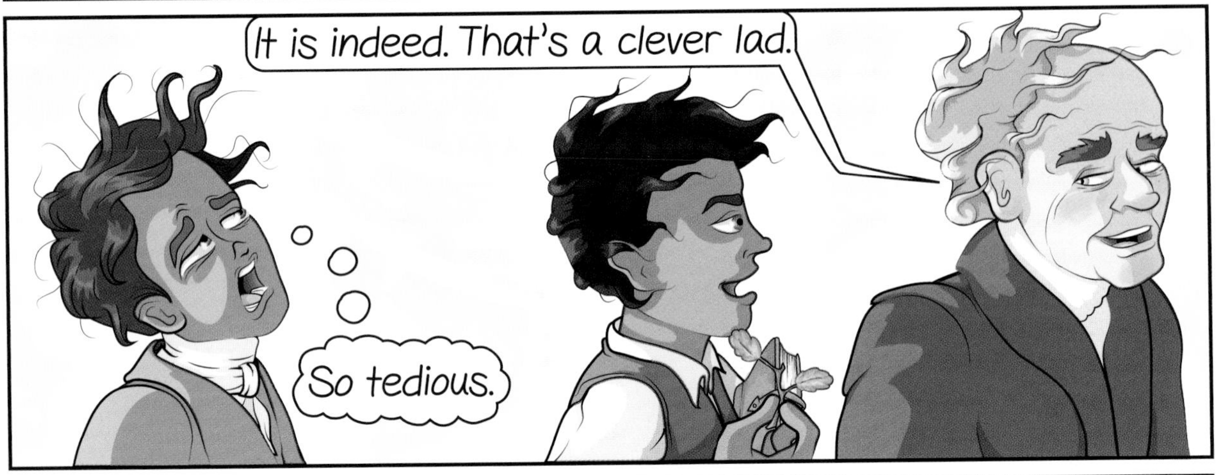
It is indeed. That's a clever lad.
So tedious.

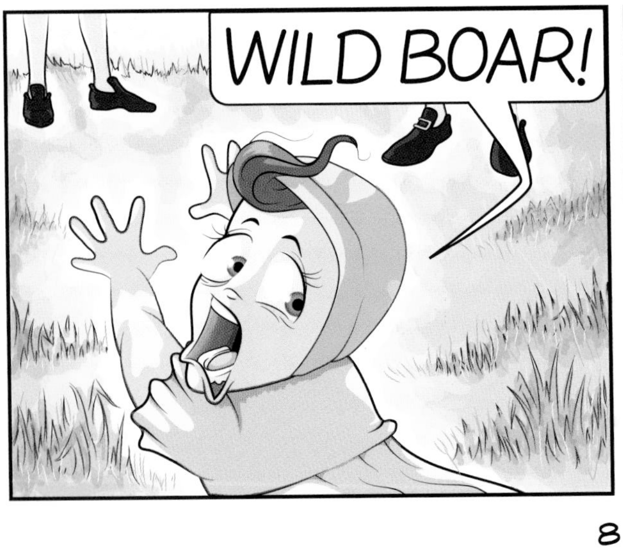
WILD BOAR!

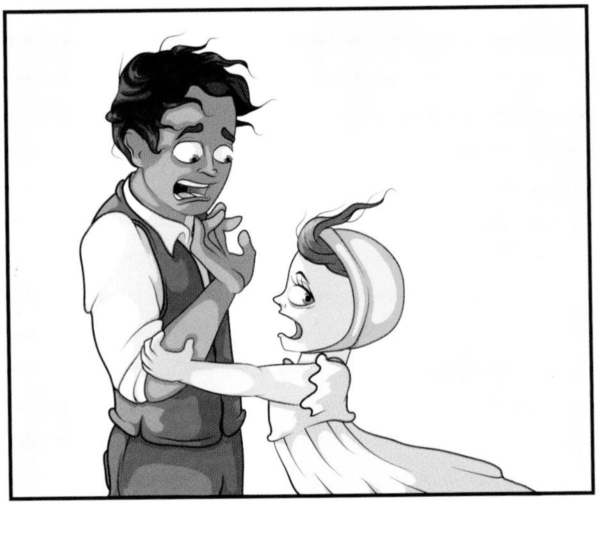

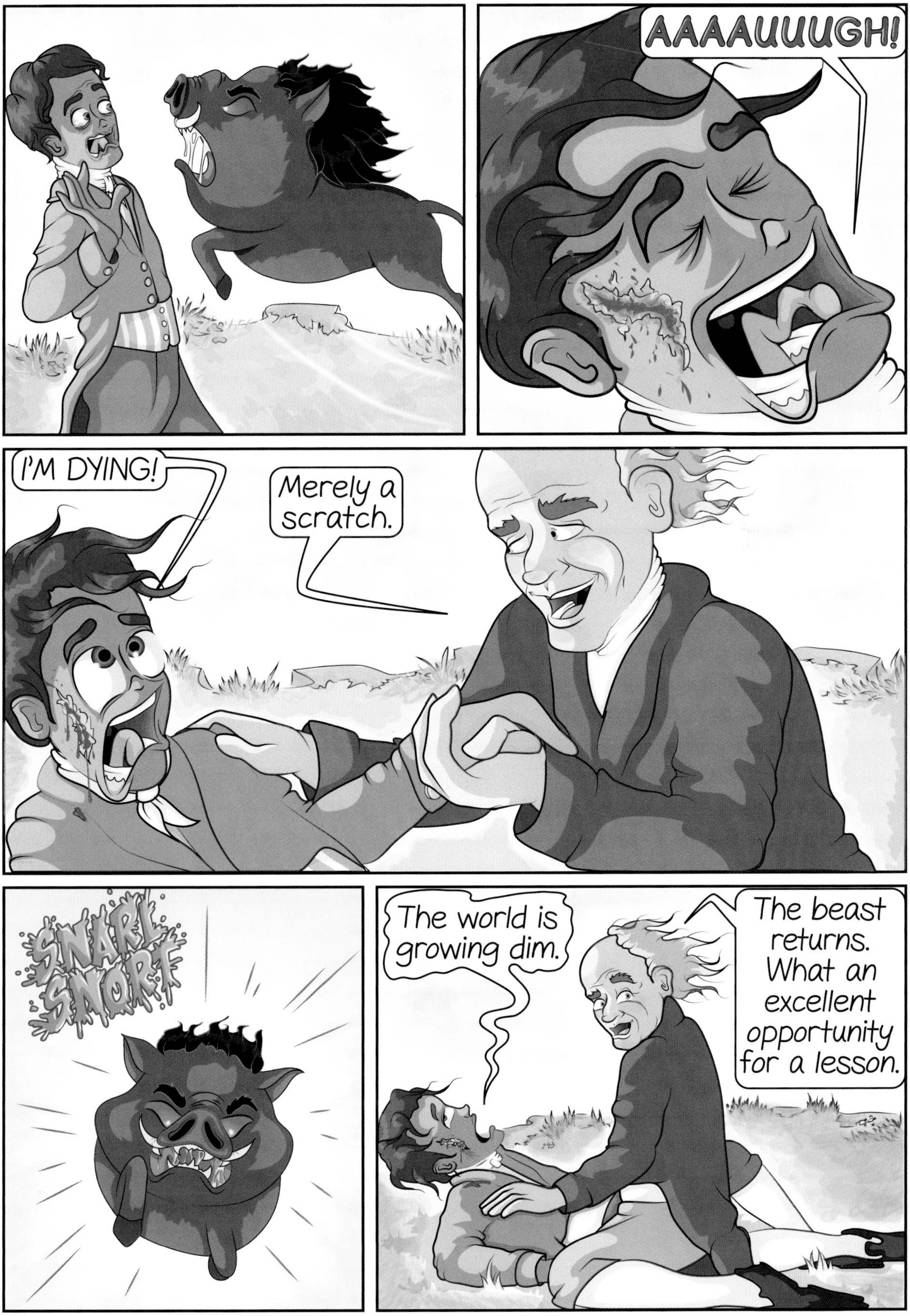
AAAAUUUGH!
I'M DYING!
Merely a scratch.
SNARL SNORT
The world is growing dim.
The beast returns. What an excellent opportunity for a lesson.

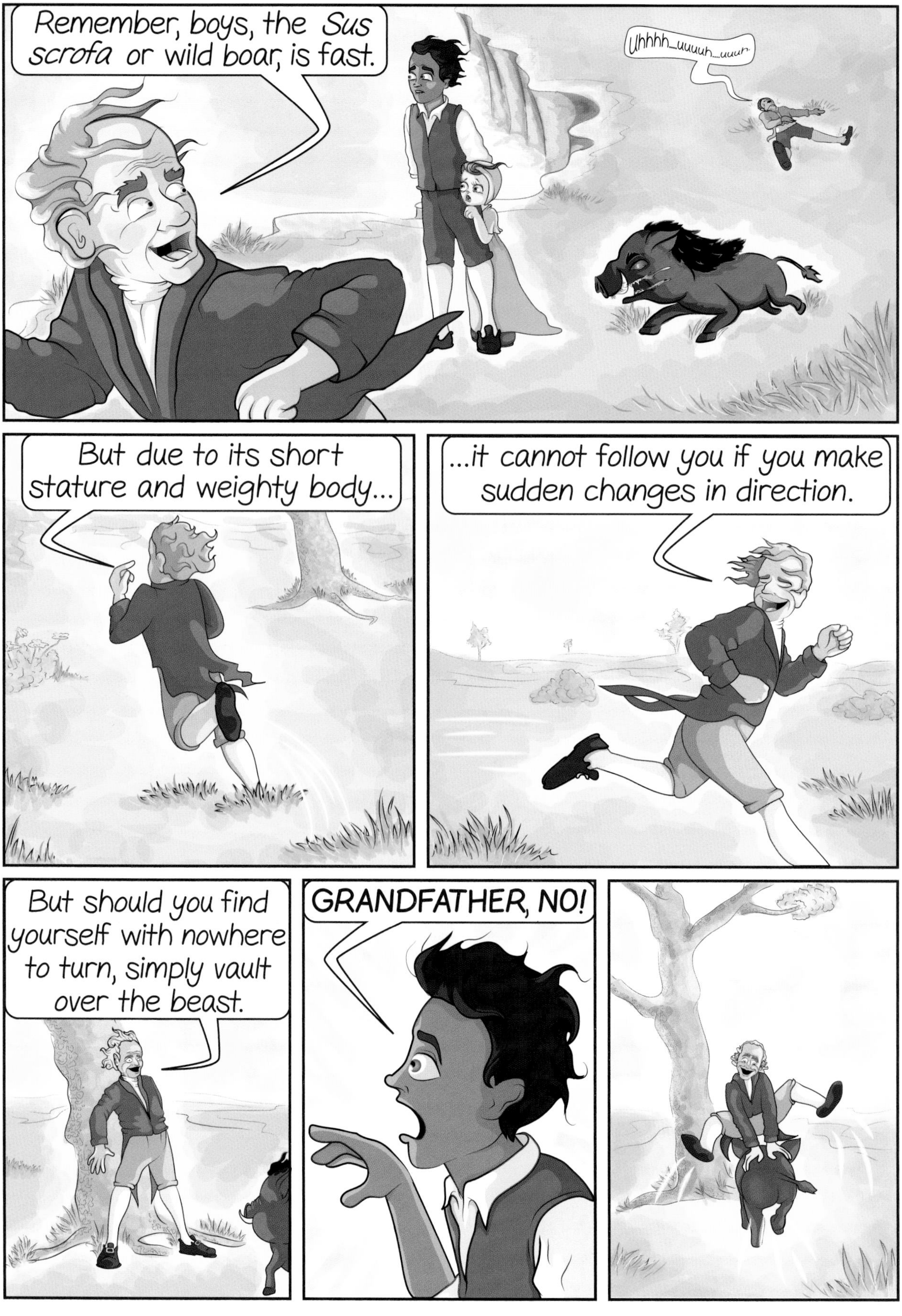
Remember, boys, the *Sus scrofa* or wild boar, is fast.
Uhhhh....uuuuh....uuur.
But due to its short stature and weighty body...
...it cannot follow you if you make sudden changes in direction.
But should you find yourself with nowhere to turn, simply vault over the beast.
GRANDFATHER, NO!

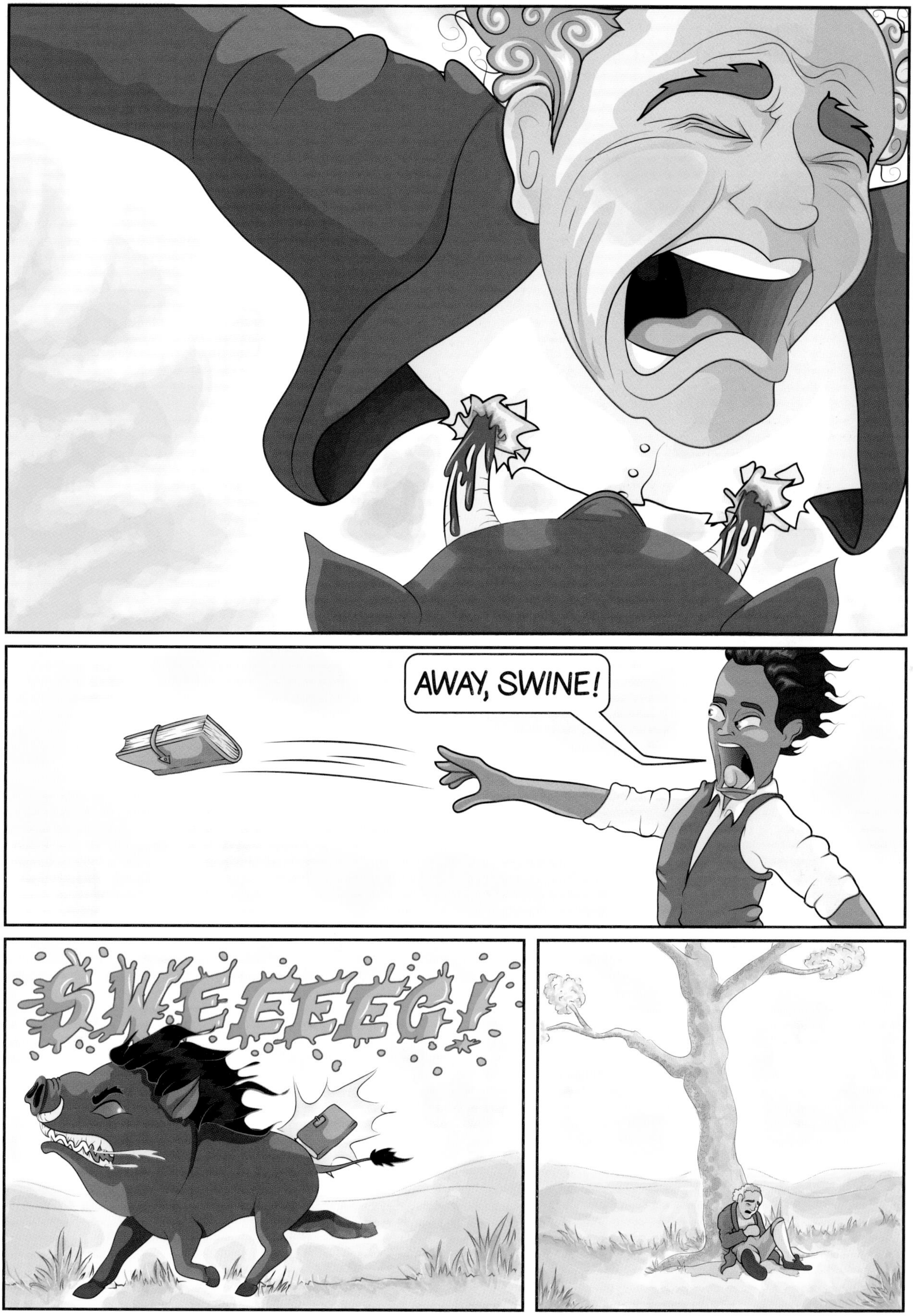
AWAY, SWINE!
SWEEEEG!

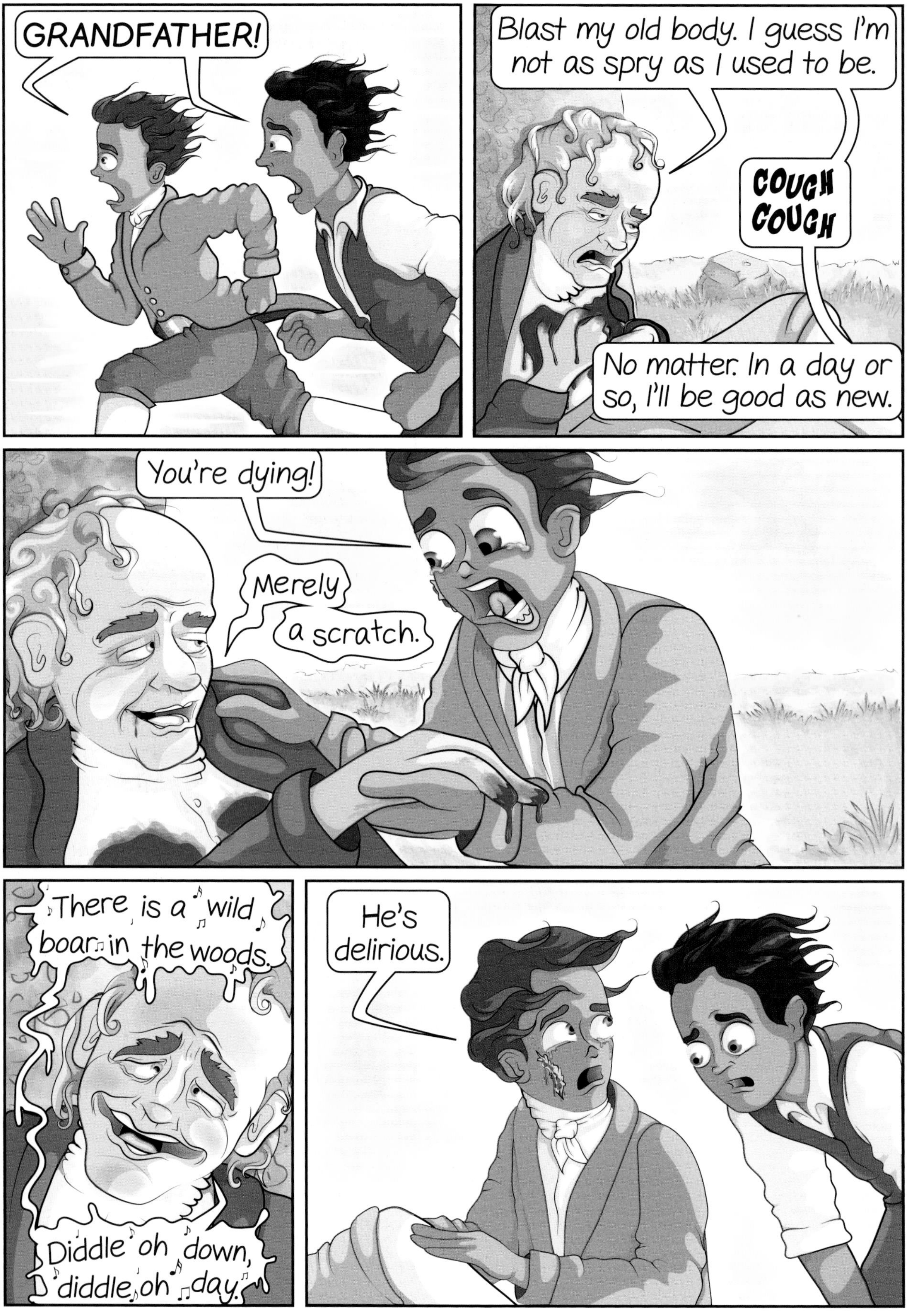
GRANDFATHER!
Blast my old body. I guess I'm not as spry as I used to be.
COUGH COUGH
No matter. In a day or so, I'll be good as new.
You're dying!
Merely
a scratch.
There is a wild boar in the woods.
Diddle oh down, diddle oh day.
He's delirious.

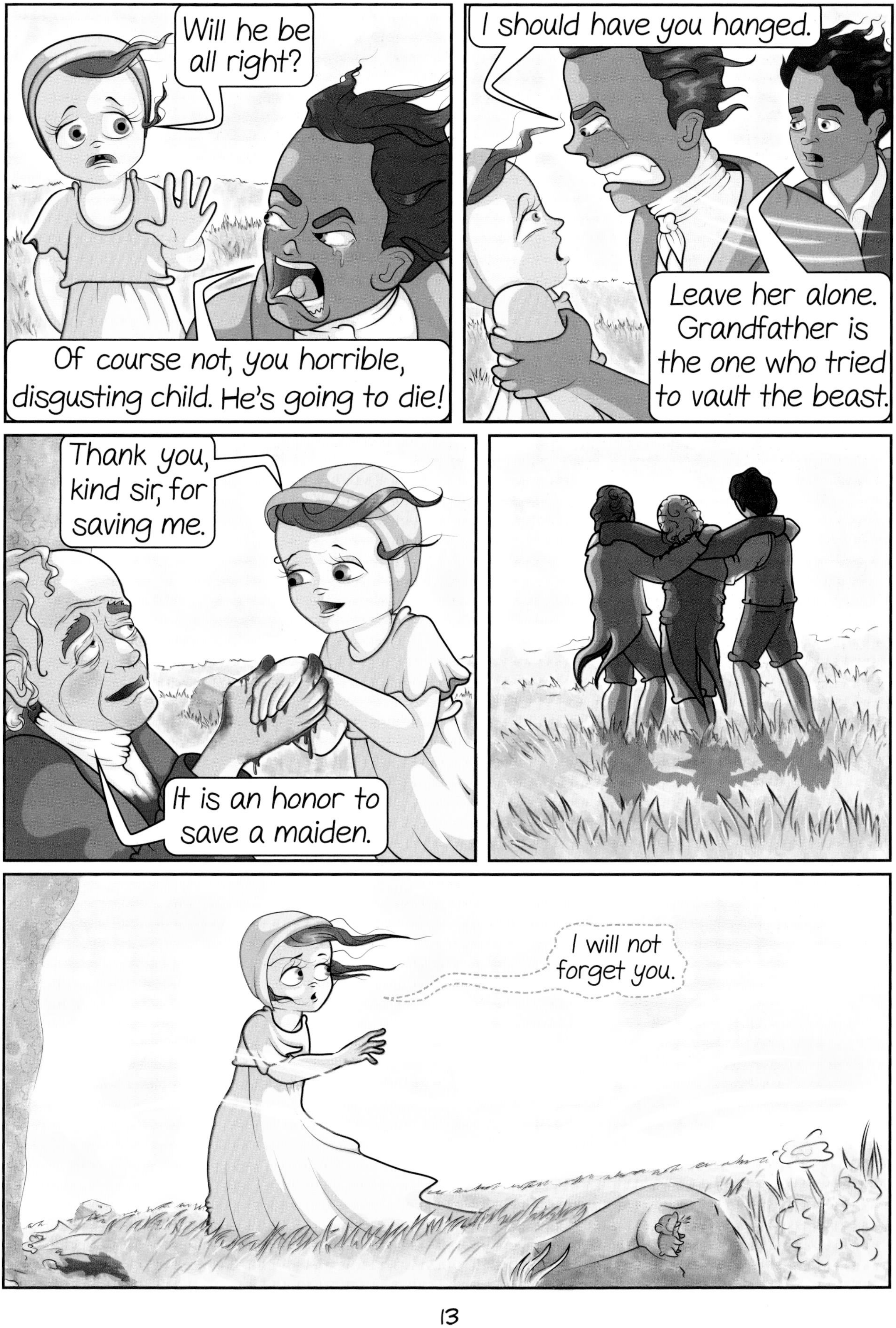
Will he be all right?
Of course not, you horrible, disgusting child. He's going to die!
I should have you hanged.
Leave her alone. Grandfather is the one who tried to vault the beast.
Thank you, kind sir, for saving me.
It is an honor to save a maiden.
I will not forget you.

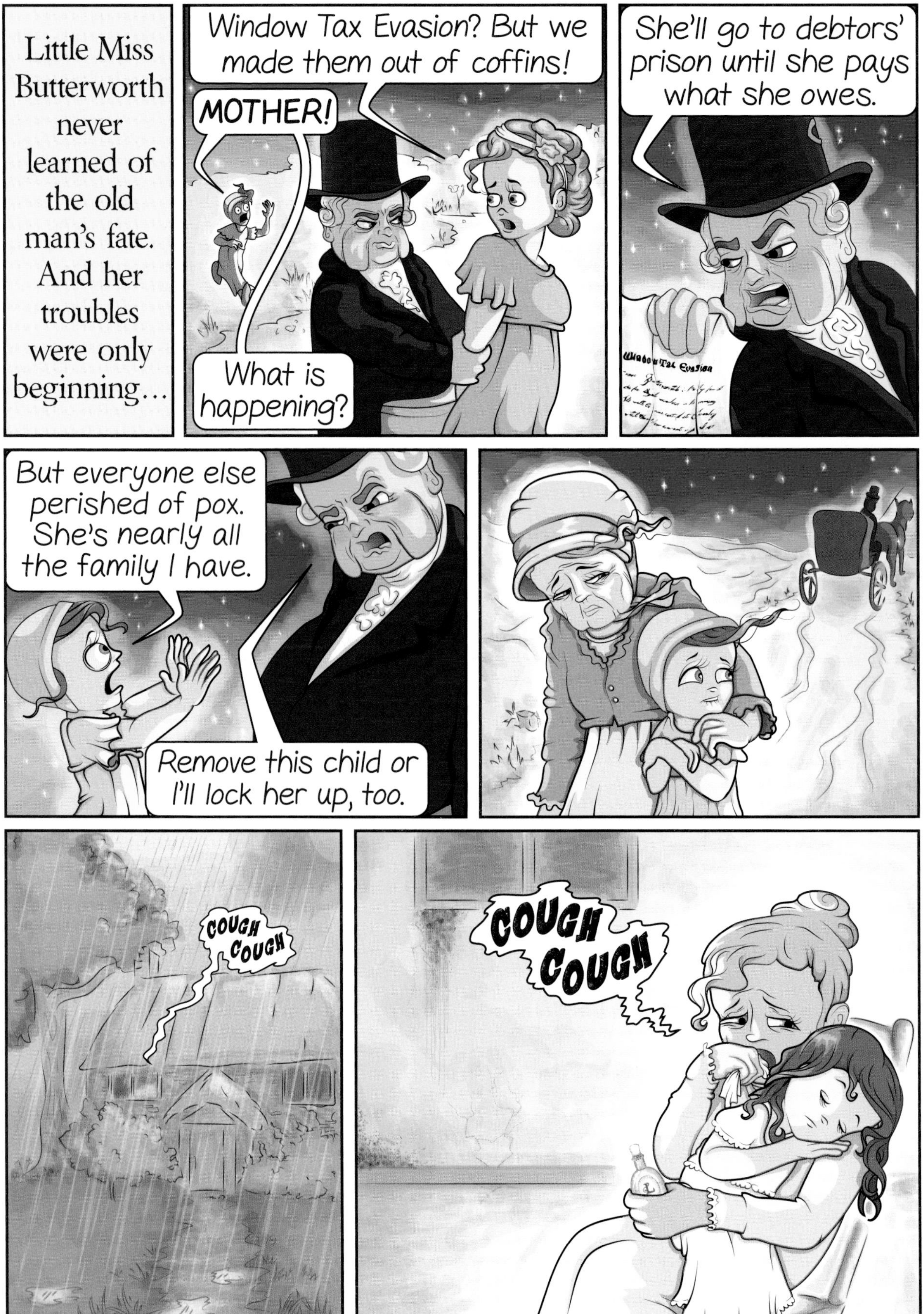
Little Miss Butterworth never learned of the old man's fate. And her troubles were only beginning…
Window Tax Evasion? But we made them out of coffins!
MOTHER!
What is happening?
She'll go to debtors' prison until she pays what she owes.
Window Tax Evasion
But everyone else perished of pox. She's nearly all the family I have.
Remove this child or I'll lock her up, too.
COUGH COUGH
COUGH COUGH

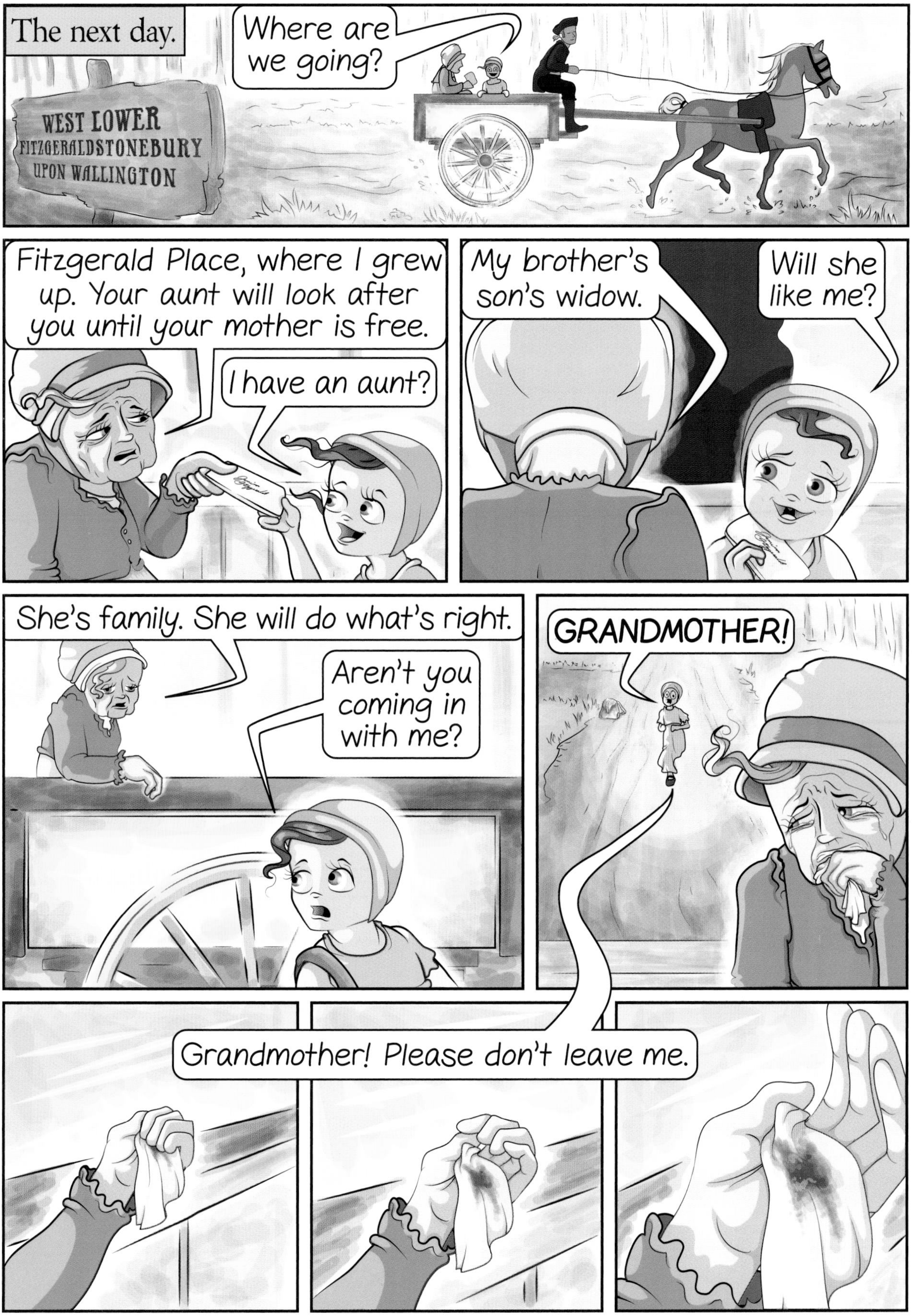

The next day.
WEST LOWER
FITZGERALDSTONEBURY
UPON WALLINGTON
Where are we going?
Fitzgerald Place, where I grew up. Your aunt will look after you until your mother is free.
I have an aunt?
My brother's son's widow.
Will she like me?
She's family. She will do what's right.
Aren't you coming in with me?
GRANDMOTHER!
Grandmother! Please don't leave me.

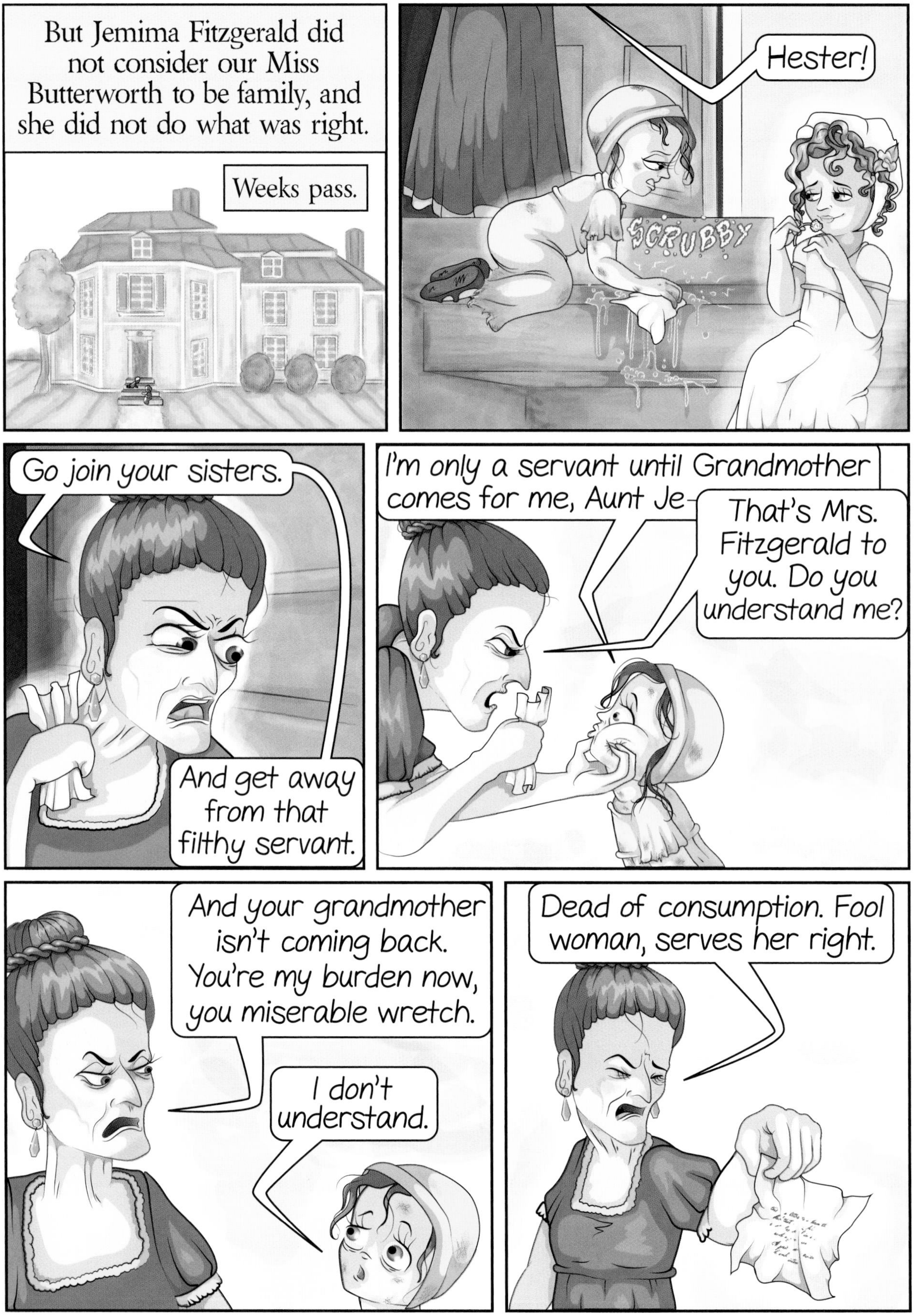
But Jemima Fitzgerald did not consider our Miss Butterworth to be family, and she did not do what was right.
Weeks pass.
Hester!
SCRUBBY
Go join your sisters.
And get away from that filthy servant.
I'm only a servant until Grandmother comes for me, Aunt Je-
That's Mrs. Fitzgerald to you. Do you understand me?
And your grandmother isn't coming back. You're my burden now, you miserable wretch.
I don't understand.
Dead of consumption. Fool woman, serves her right.

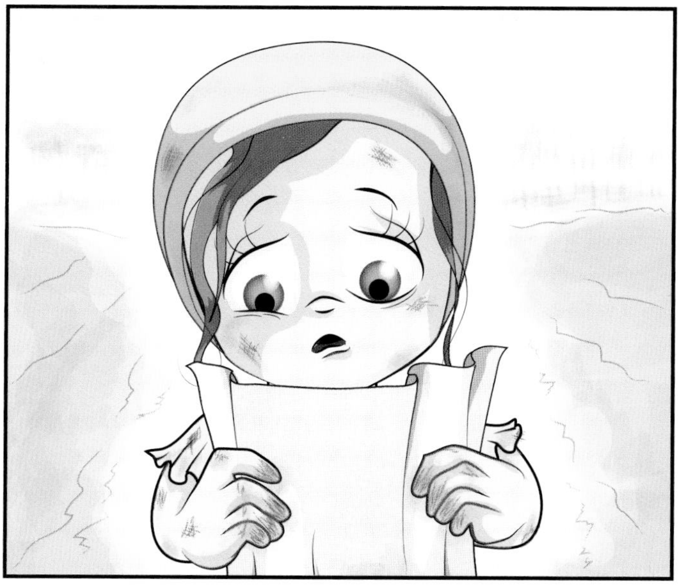

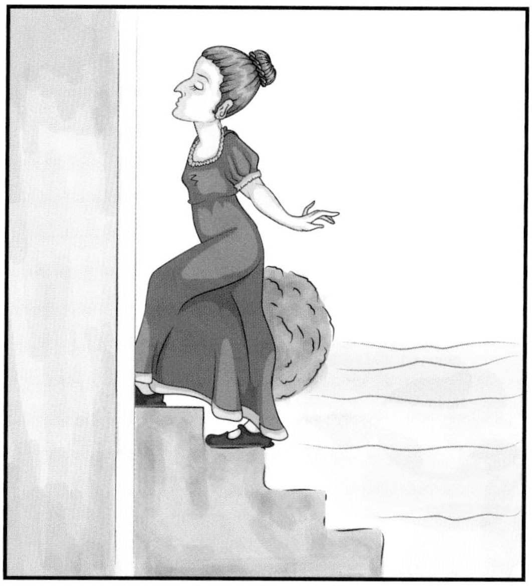

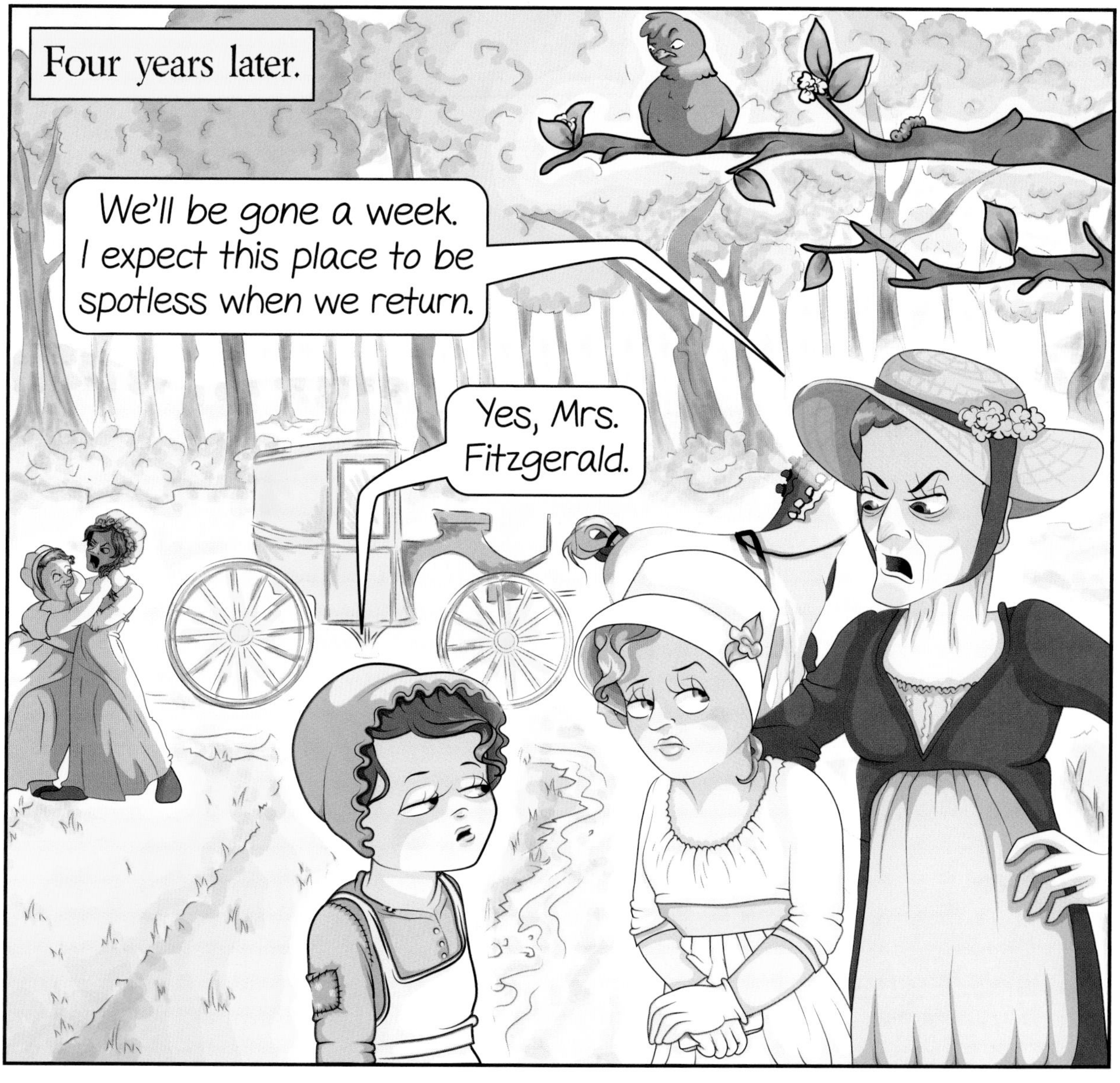
Four years later.
We'll be gone a week. I expect this place to be spotless when we return.
Yes, Mrs. Fitzgerald.

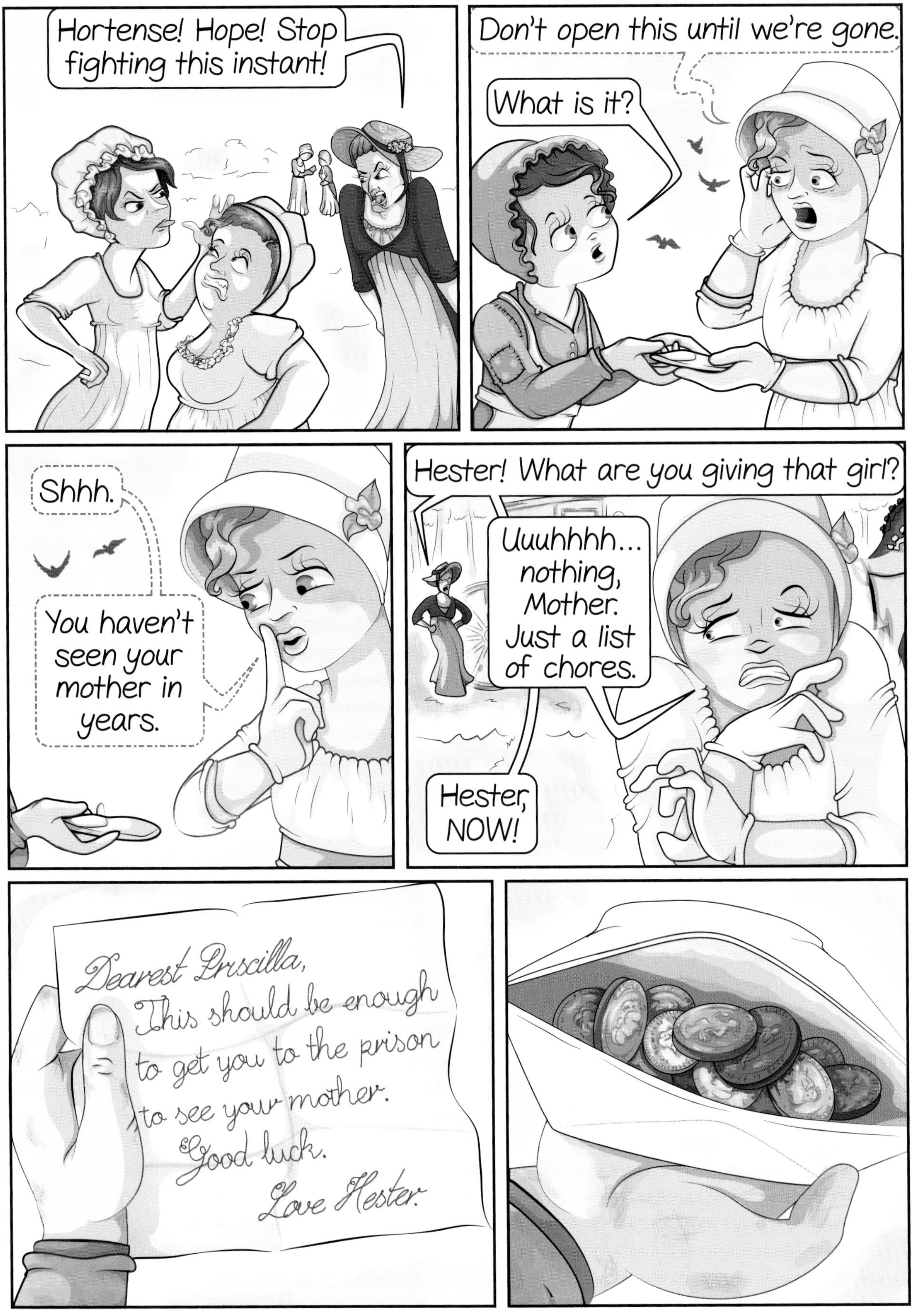
Hortense! Hope! Stop fighting this instant!
Don't open this until we're gone.
What is it?
Shhh.
You haven't seen your mother in years.
Hester! What are you giving that girl?
Uuuhhhh... nothing, Mother. Just a list of chores.
Hester, NOW!
Dearest Priscilla,
This should be enough to get you to the prison to see your mother.
Good luck.
Love Hester

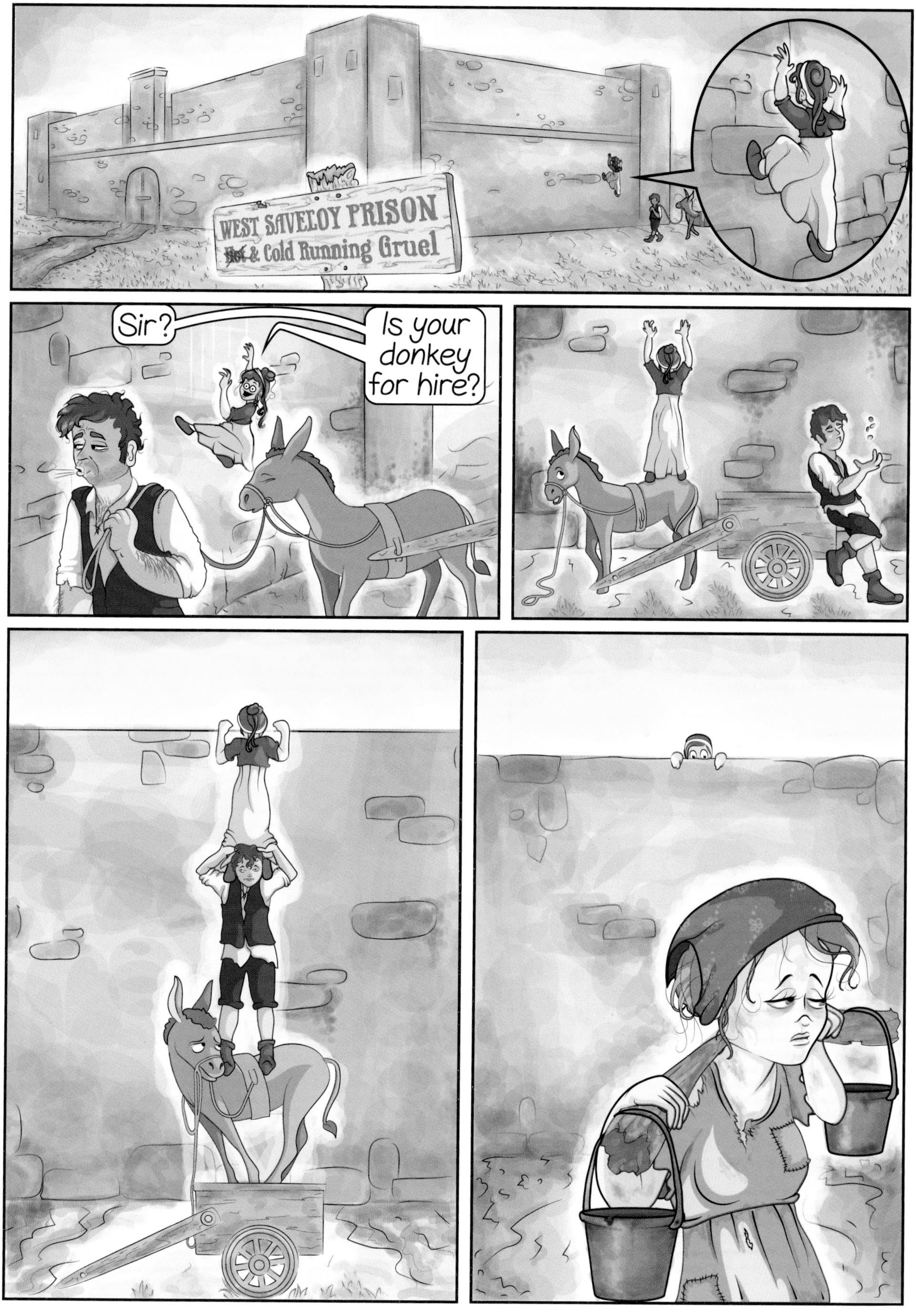
WEST SAVELOY PRISON
Hot & Cold Running Gruel
Sir?
Is your donkey for hire?

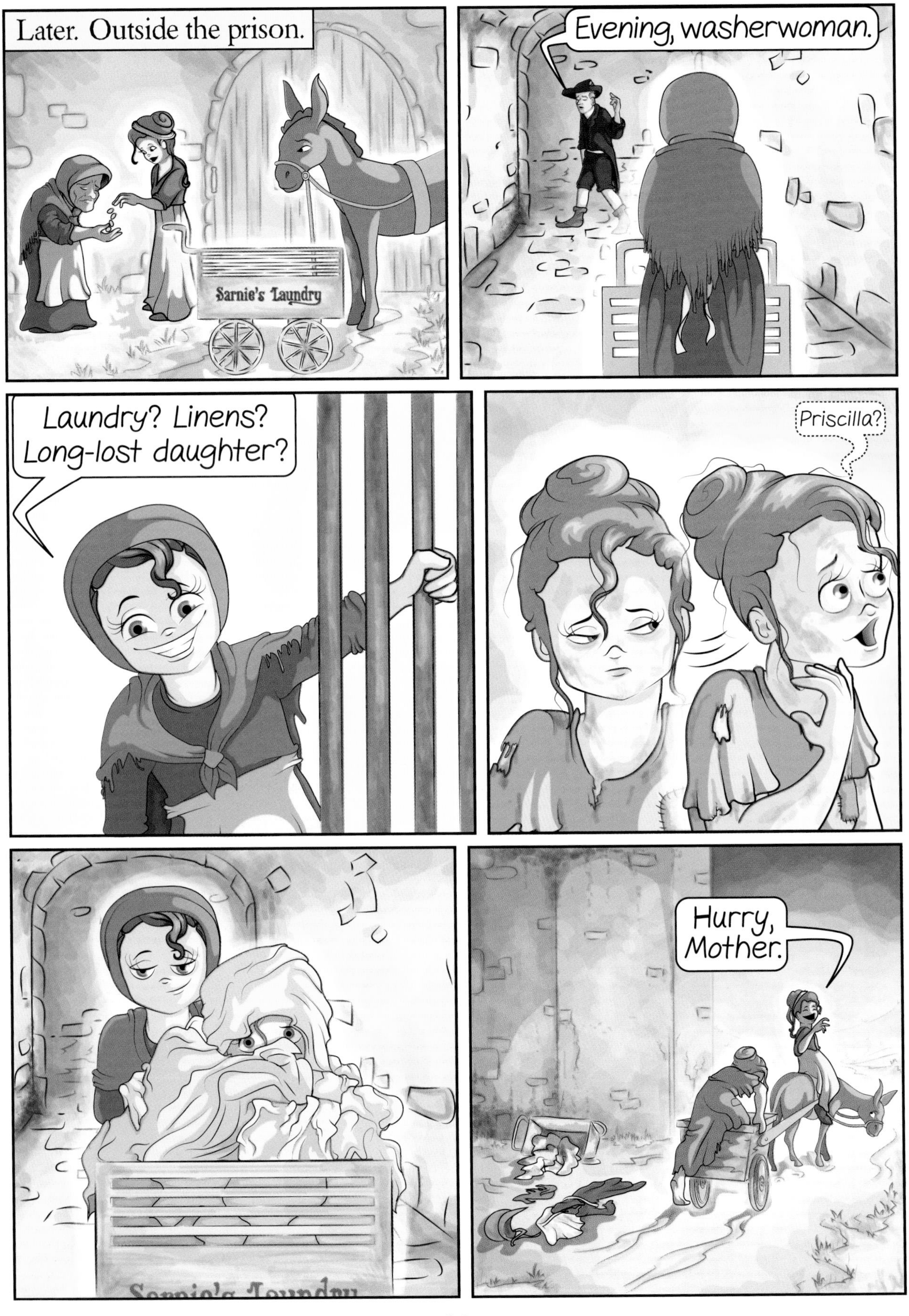

Later. Outside the prison.
Sarnie's Laundry
Evening, washerwoman.
Laundry? Linens? Long-lost daughter?
Priscilla?
Hurry, Mother.

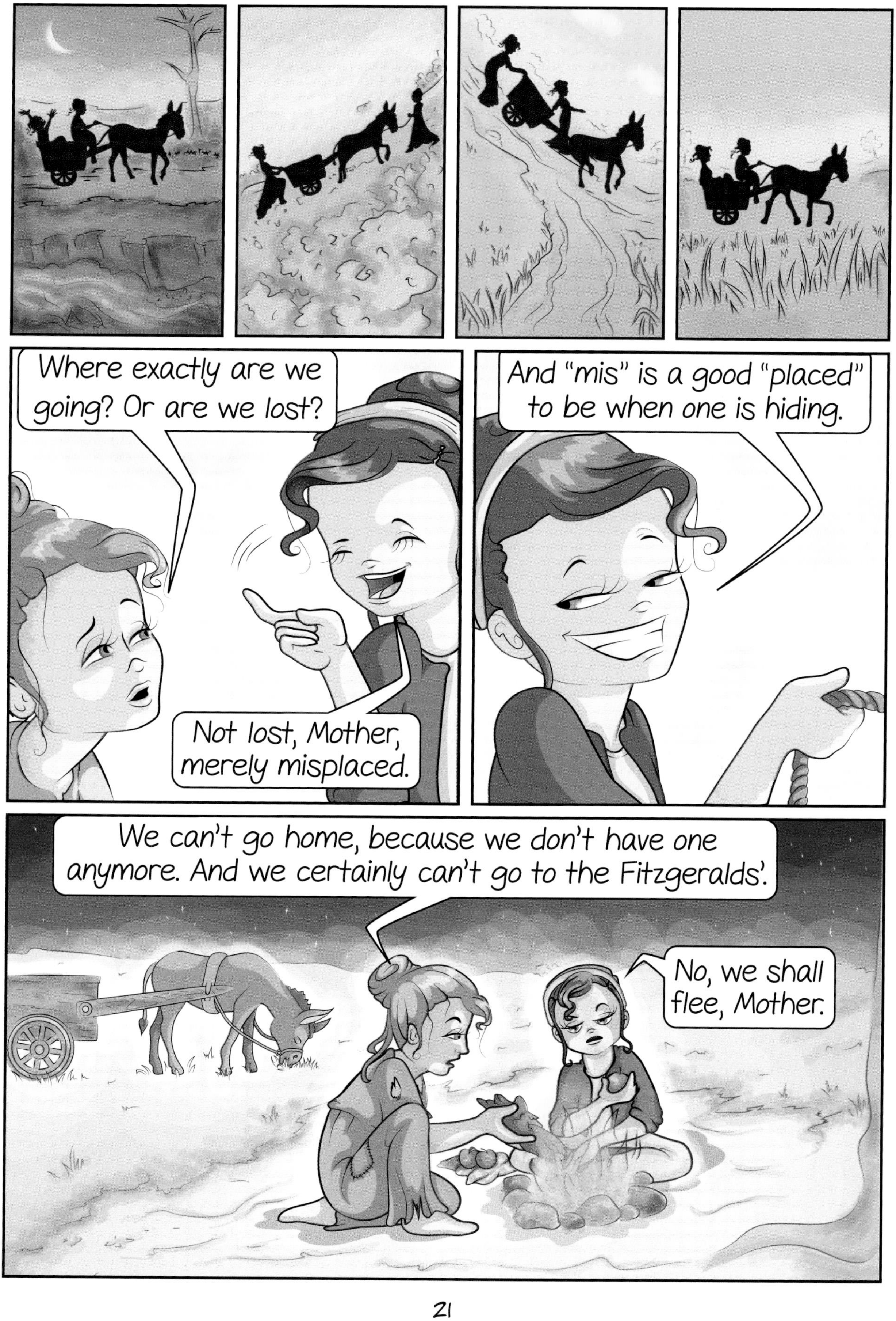
Where exactly are we going? Or are we lost?
Not lost, Mother, merely misplaced.
And "mis" is a good "placed" to be when one is hiding.
We can't go home, because we don't have one anymore. And we certainly can't go to the Fitzgeralds'.
No, we shall flee, Mother.

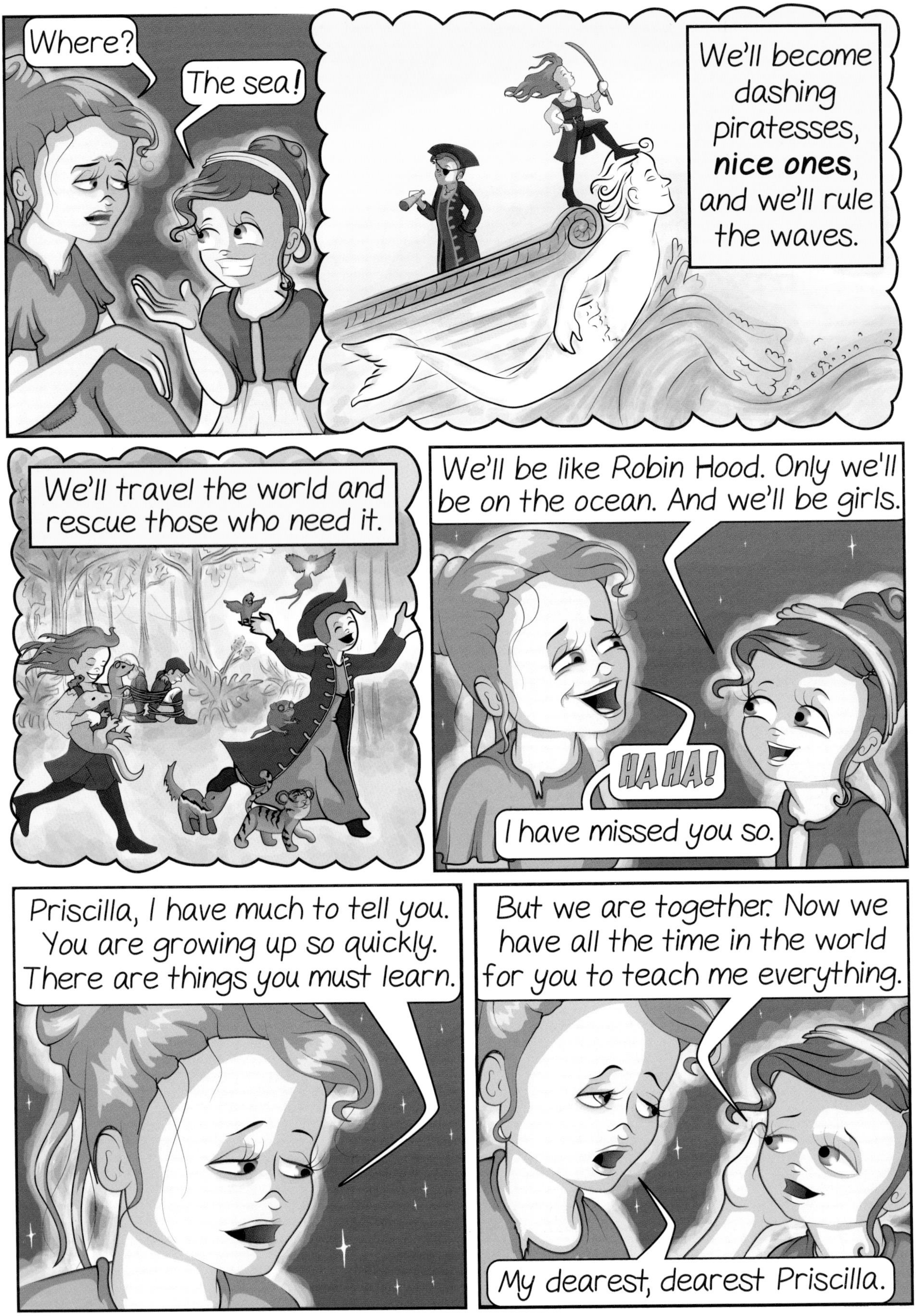
Where?
The sea!
We'll become dashing piratesses, **nice ones**, and we'll rule the waves.
We'll travel the world and rescue those who need it.
We'll be like Robin Hood. Only we'll be on the ocean. And we'll be girls.
HA HA!
I have missed you so.
Priscilla, I have much to tell you. You are growing up so quickly. There are things you must learn.
But we are together. Now we have all the time in the world for you to teach me everything.
My dearest, dearest Priscilla.

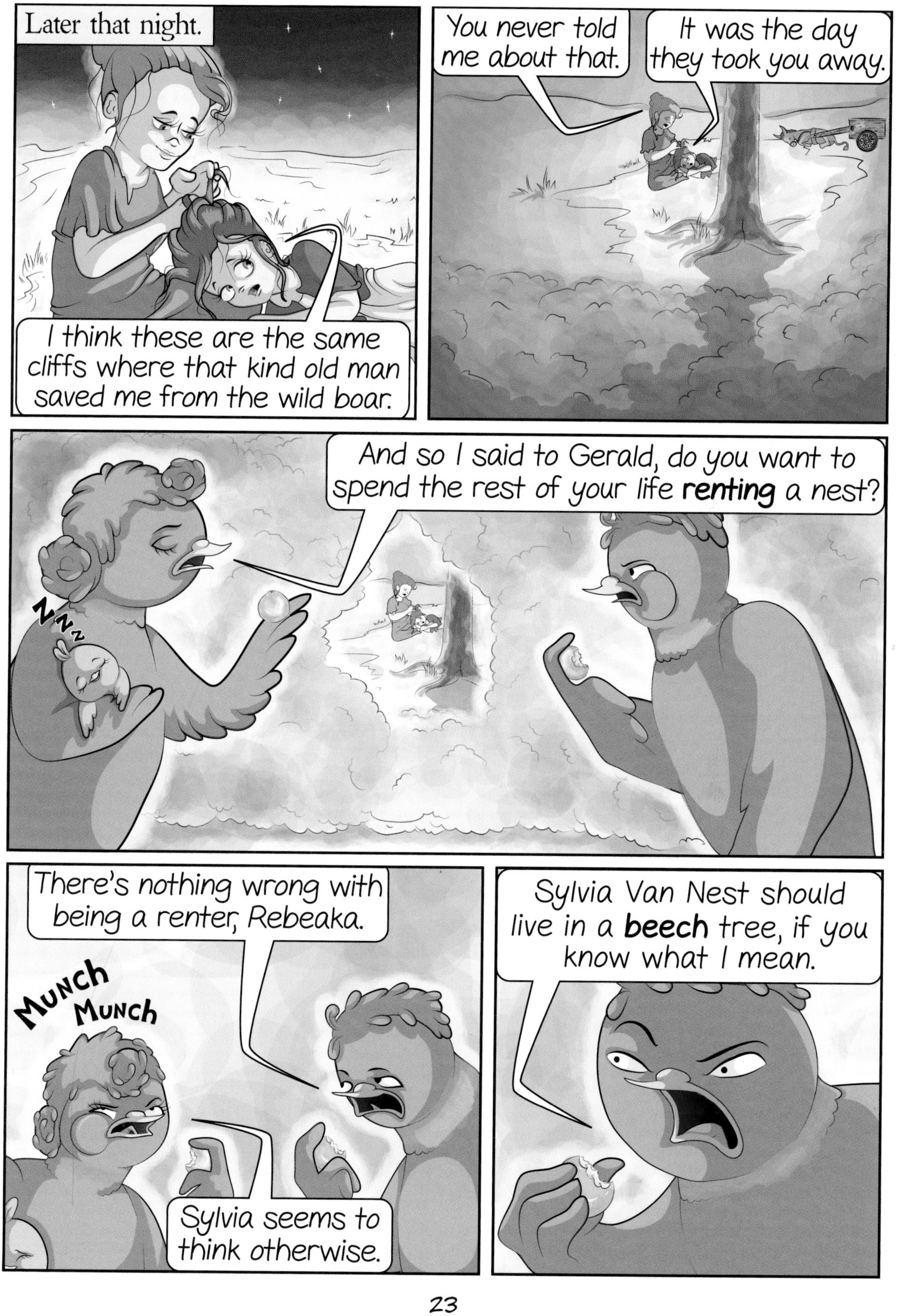

Later that night.
I think these are the same cliffs where that kind old man saved me from the wild boar.
You never told me about that.
It was the day they took you away.
And so I said to Gerald, do you want to spend the rest of your life **renting** a nest?
ZZZ
There's nothing wrong with being a renter, Rebeaka.
MUNCH MUNCH
Sylvia seems to think otherwise.
Sylvia Van Nest should live in a **beech** tree, if you know what I mean.

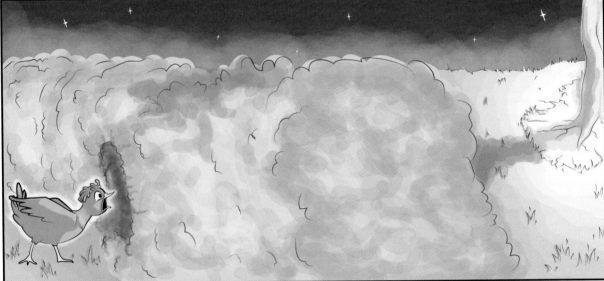

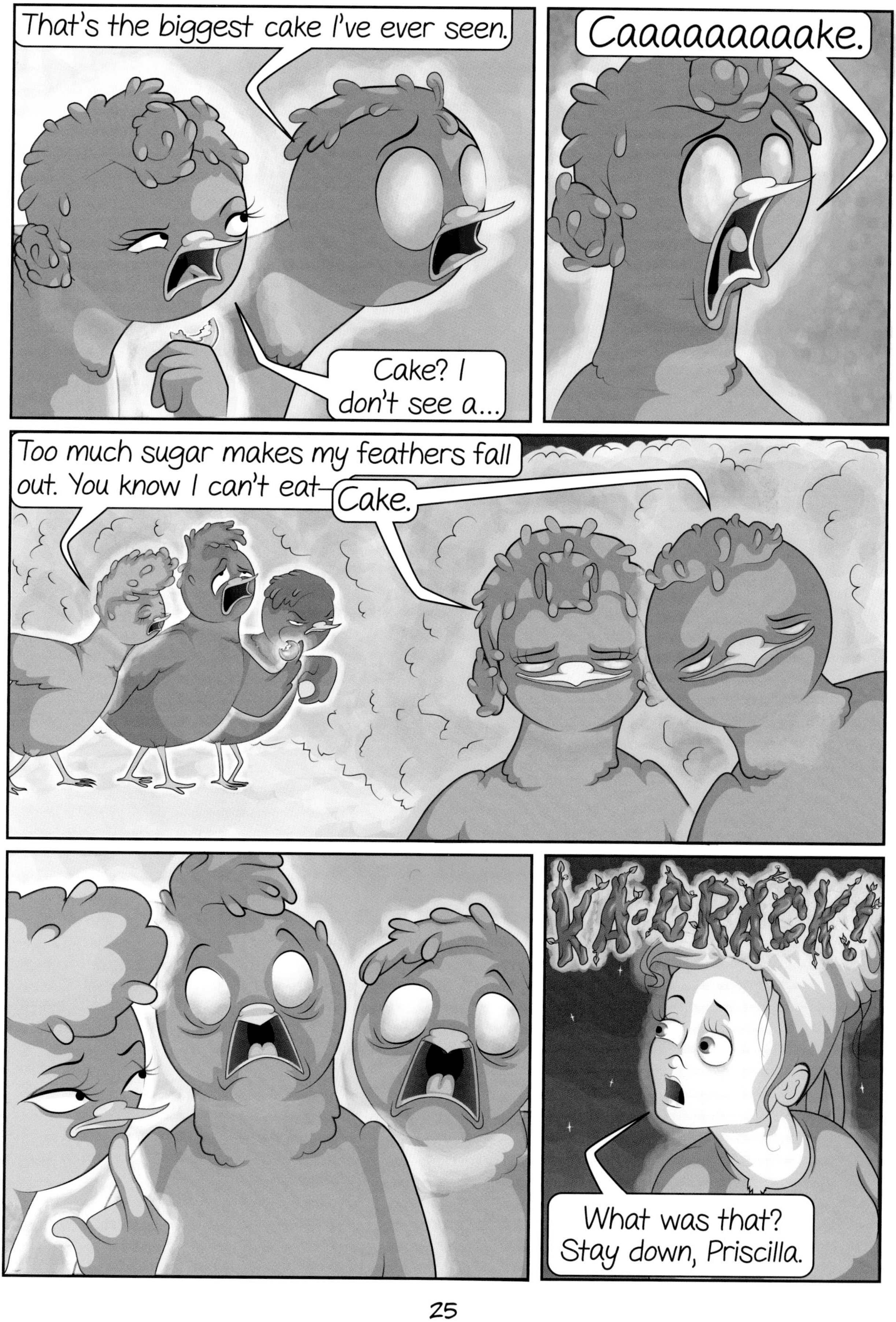

That's the biggest cake I've ever seen.
Cake? I don't see a...
Caaaaaaaaake.
Too much sugar makes my feathers fall out. You know I can't eat—
Cake.
KA-CRACK!
What was that? Stay down, Priscilla.

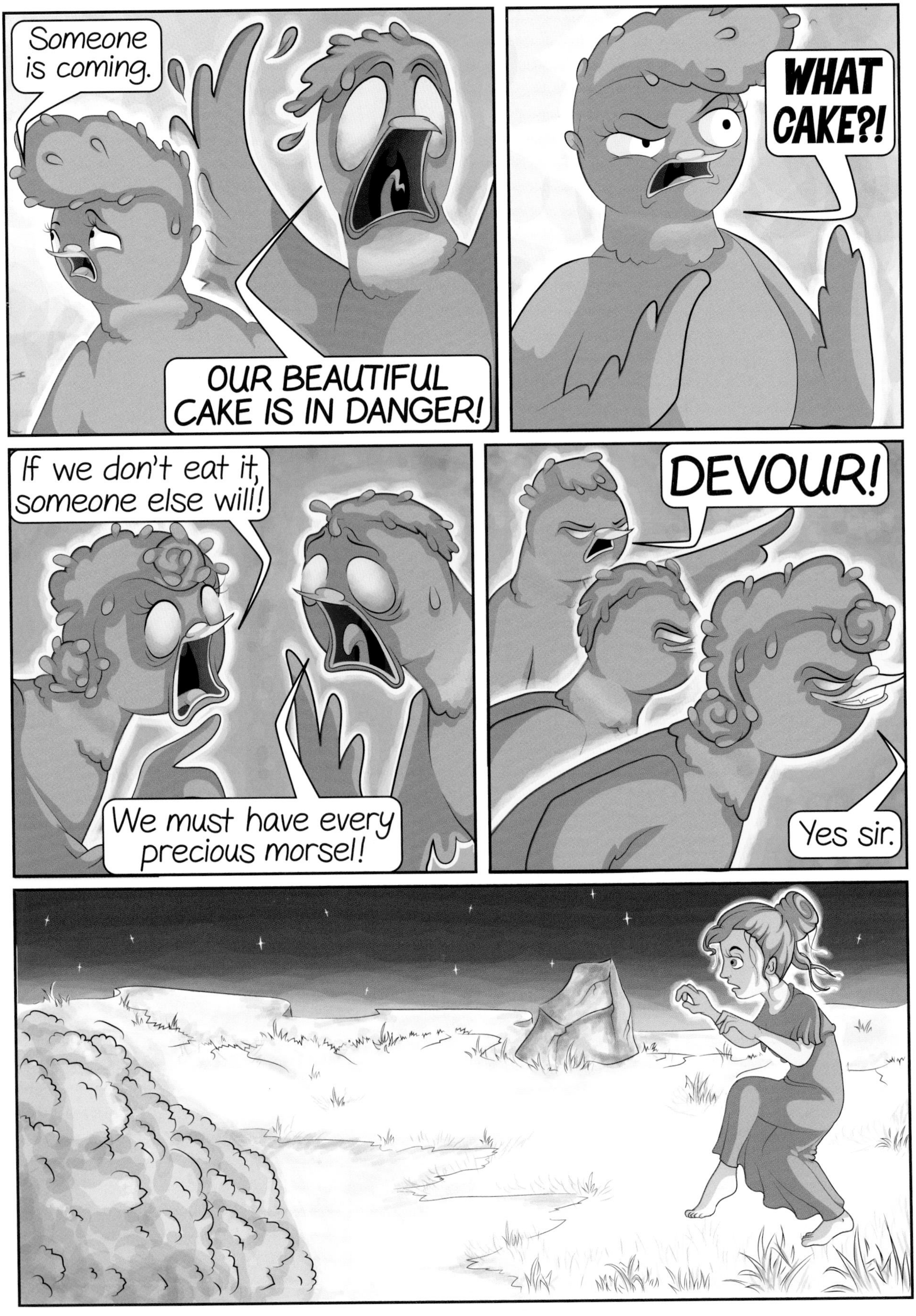
Someone is coming.
OUR BEAUTIFUL CAKE IS IN DANGER!
WHAT CAKE?!
If we don't eat it, someone else will!
We must have every precious morsel!
DEVOUR!
Yes sir.

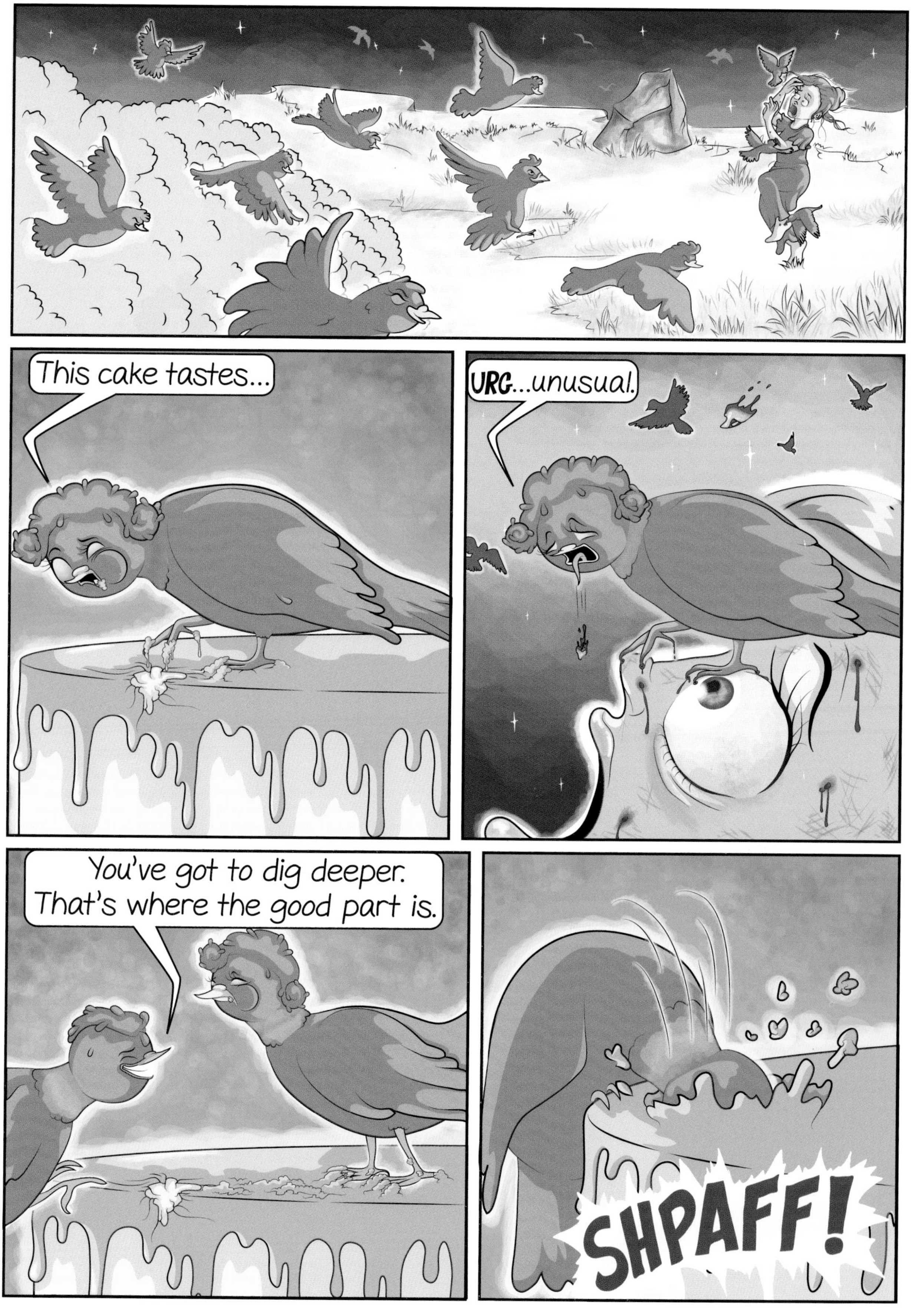
This cake tastes...
URG...unusual.
You've got to dig deeper. That's where the good part is.
SHPAFF!

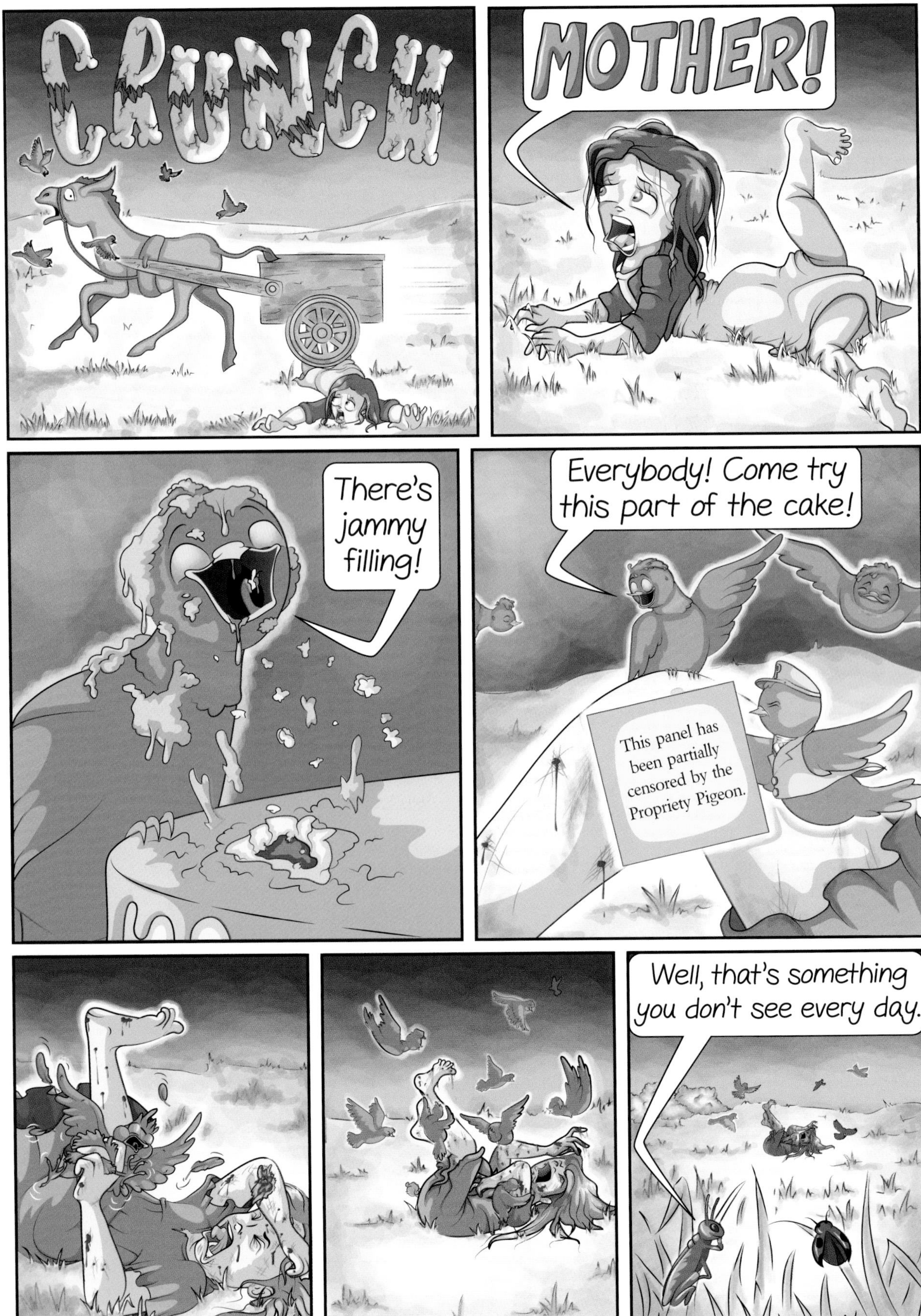
CRUNCH
MOTHER!
There's jammy filling!
Everybody! Come try this part of the cake!
This panel has been partially censored by the Propriety Pigeon.
Well, that's something you don't see every day.

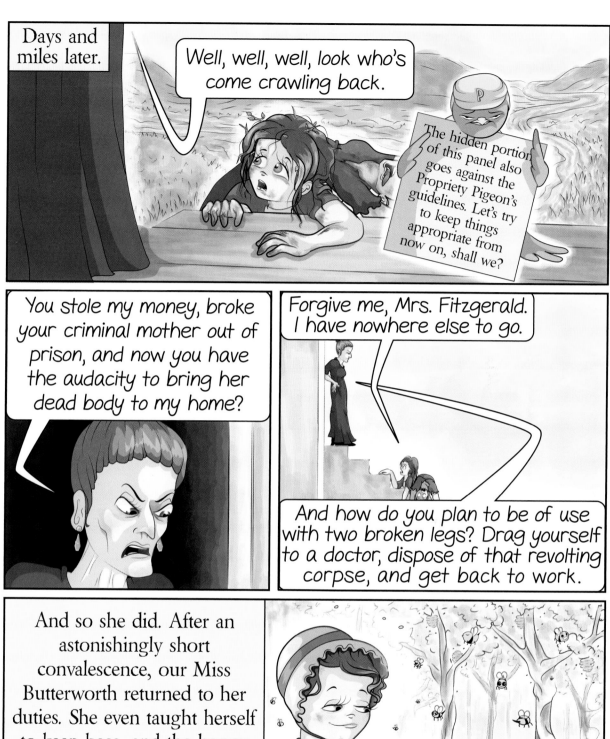

Days and miles later.

Well, well, well, look who's come crawling back.

The hidden portion of this panel also goes against the Propriety Pigeon's guidelines. Let's try to keep things appropriate from now on, shall we?

You stole my money, broke your criminal mother out of prison, and now you have the audacity to bring her dead body to my home?

Forgive me, Mrs. Fitzgerald. I have nowhere else to go.

And how do you plan to be of use with two broken legs? Drag yourself to a doctor, dispose of that revolting corpse, and get back to work.

And so she did. After an astonishingly short convalescence, our Miss Butterworth returned to her duties. She even taught herself to keep bees, and the honey brought the Fitzgeralds more than enough income to earn her keep. Her life wasn't easy, but it was secure and unchanging, until...

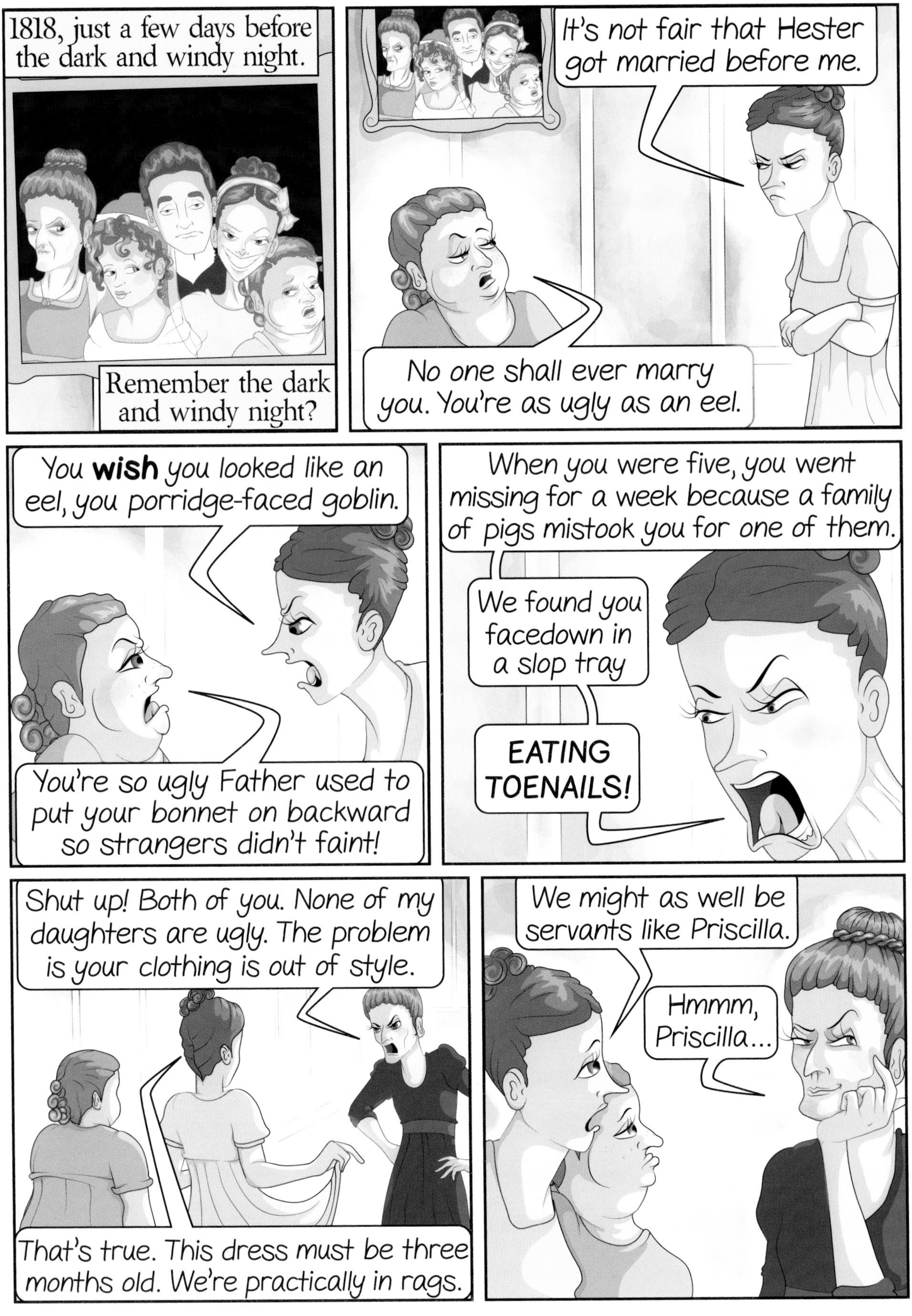
1818, just a few days before the dark and windy night.
Remember the dark and windy night?
It's not fair that Hester got married before me.
No one shall ever marry you. You're as ugly as an eel.
You **wish** you looked like an eel, you porridge-faced goblin.
You're so ugly Father used to put your bonnet on backward so strangers didn't faint!
When you were five, you went missing for a week because a family of pigs mistook you for one of them.
We found you facedown in a slop tray
EATING TOENAILS!
Shut up! Both of you. None of my daughters are ugly. The problem is your clothing is out of style.
That's true. This dress must be three months old. We're practically in rags.
We might as well be servants like Priscilla.
Hmmm, Priscilla...

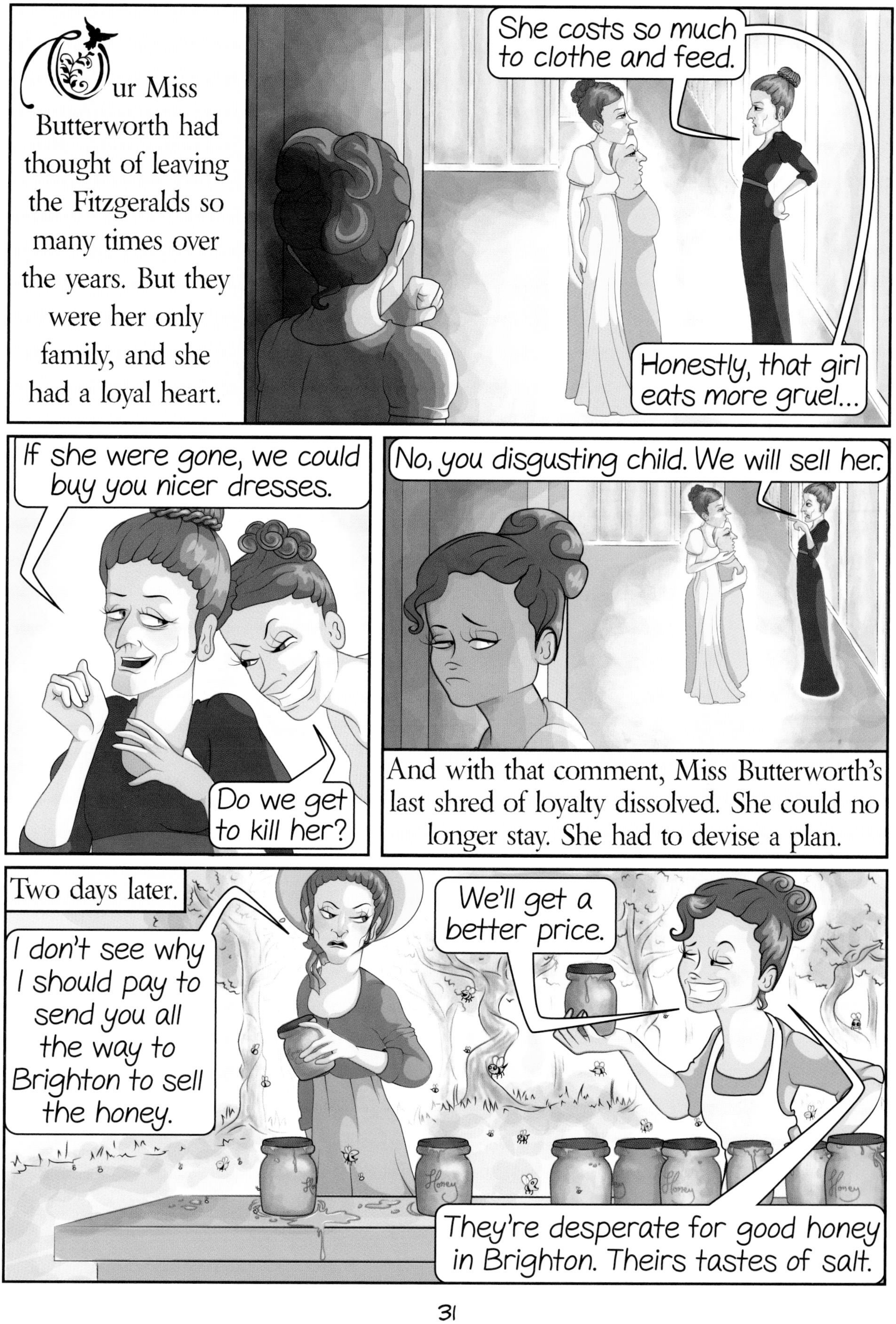
Our Miss Butterworth had thought of leaving the Fitzgeralds so many times over the years. But they were her only family, and she had a loyal heart.
She costs so much to clothe and feed.
Honestly, that girl eats more gruel...
If she were gone, we could buy you nicer dresses.
Do we get to kill her?
No, you disgusting child. We will sell her.
And with that comment, Miss Butterworth's last shred of loyalty dissolved. She could no longer stay. She had to devise a plan.
Two days later.
I don't see why I should pay to send you all the way to Brighton to sell the honey.
We'll get a better price.
They're desperate for good honey in Brighton. Theirs tastes of salt.
Honey
Honey
Honey

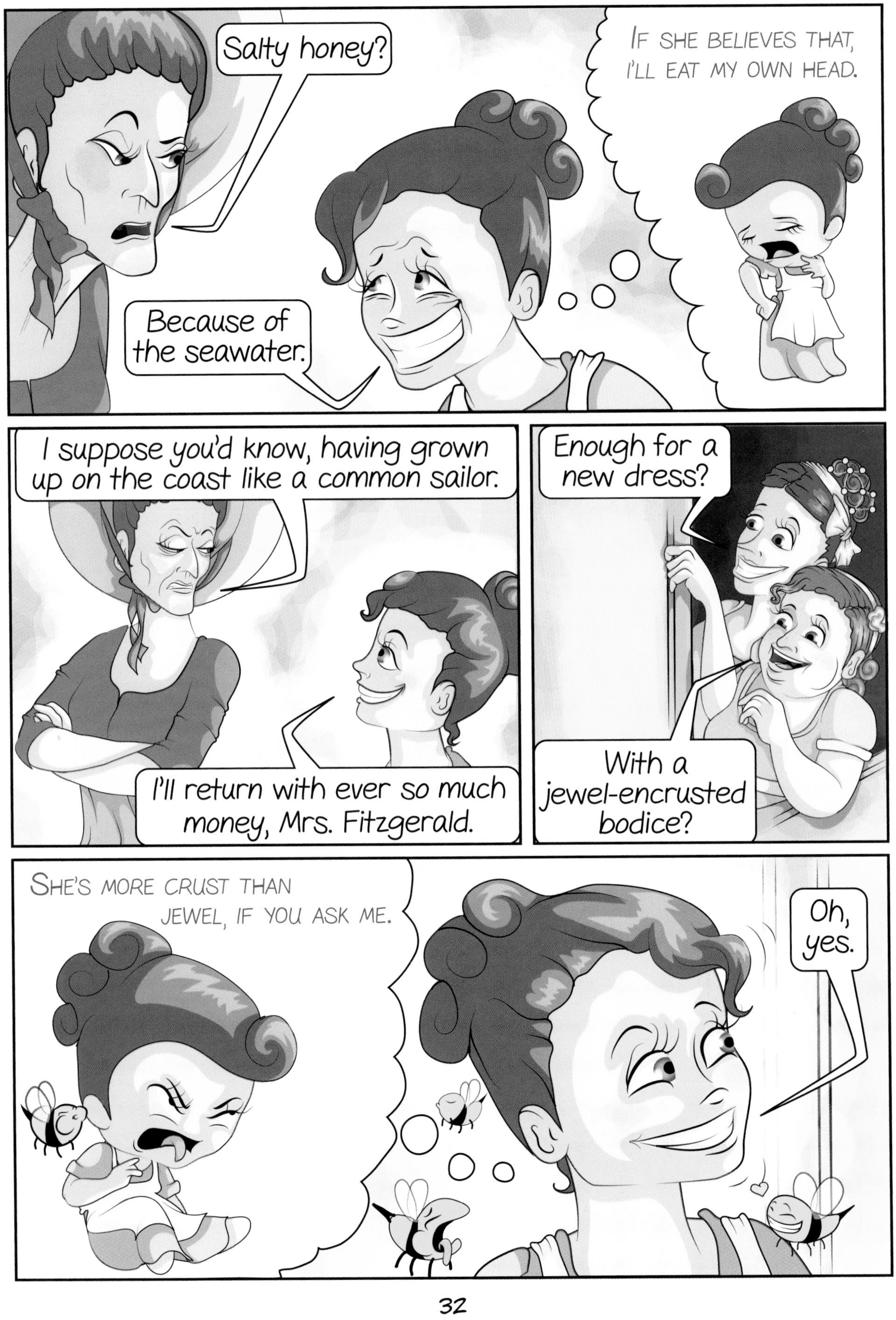
Salty honey?
Because of the seawater.
IF SHE BELIEVES THAT, I'LL EAT MY OWN HEAD.
I suppose you'd know, having grown up on the coast like a common sailor.
I'll return with ever so much money, Mrs. Fitzgerald.
Enough for a new dress?
With a jewel-encrusted bodice?
SHE'S MORE CRUST THAN JEWEL, IF YOU ASK ME.
Oh, yes.

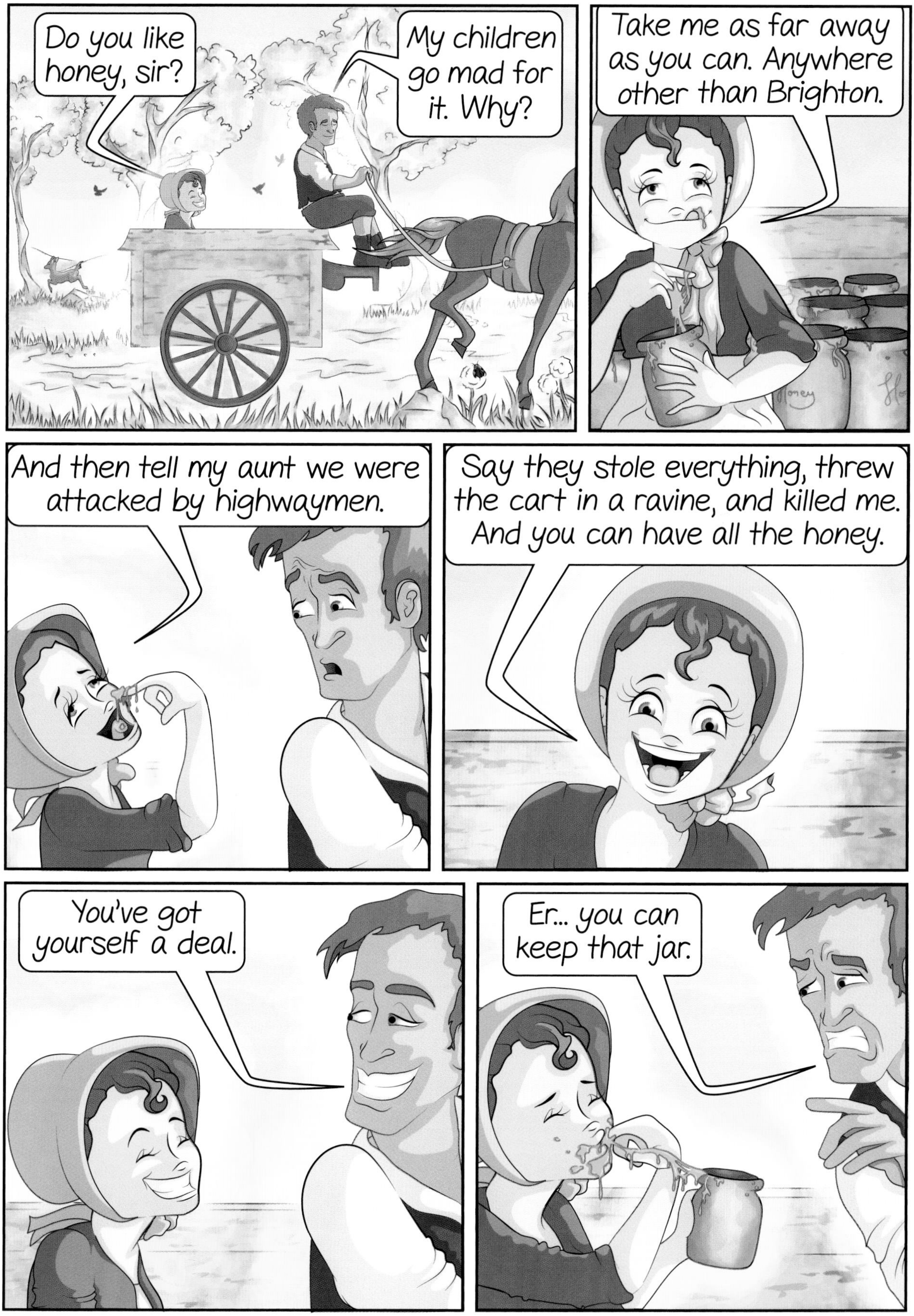
Do you like honey, sir?
My children go mad for it. Why?
Take me as far away as you can. Anywhere other than Brighton.
And then tell my aunt we were attacked by highwaymen.
Say they stole everything, threw the cart in a ravine, and killed me. And you can have all the honey.
You've got yourself a deal.
Er... you can keep that jar.

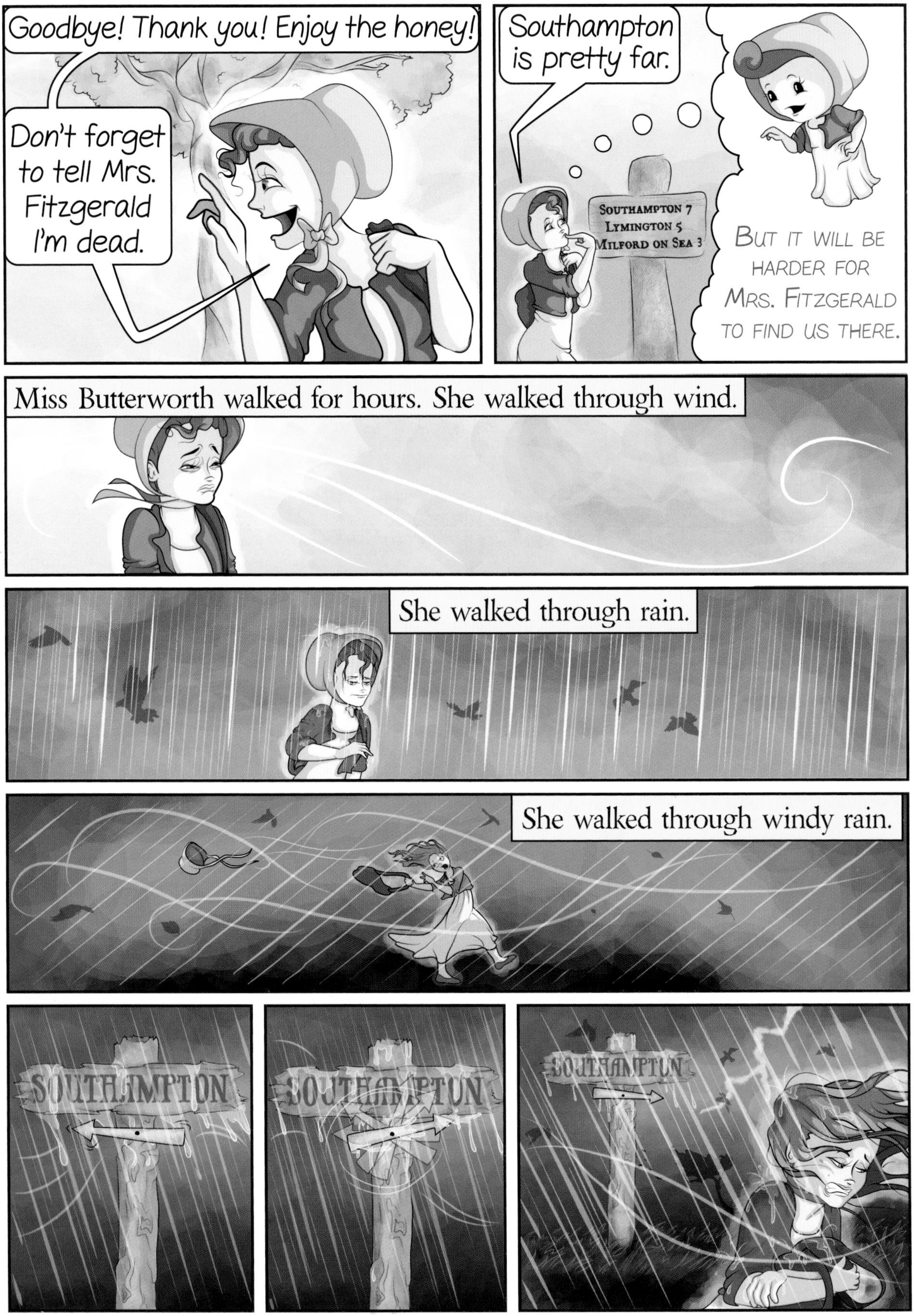
Goodbye! Thank you! Enjoy the honey!
Don't forget to tell Mrs. Fitzgerald I'm dead.
Southampton is pretty far.
SOUTHAMPTON 7
LYMINGTON 5
MILFORD ON SEA 3
BUT IT WILL BE HARDER FOR MRS. FITZGERALD TO FIND US THERE.
Miss Butterworth walked for hours. She walked through wind.
She walked through rain.
She walked through windy rain.
SOUTHAMPTON
SOUTHAMPTON
SOUTHAMPTON

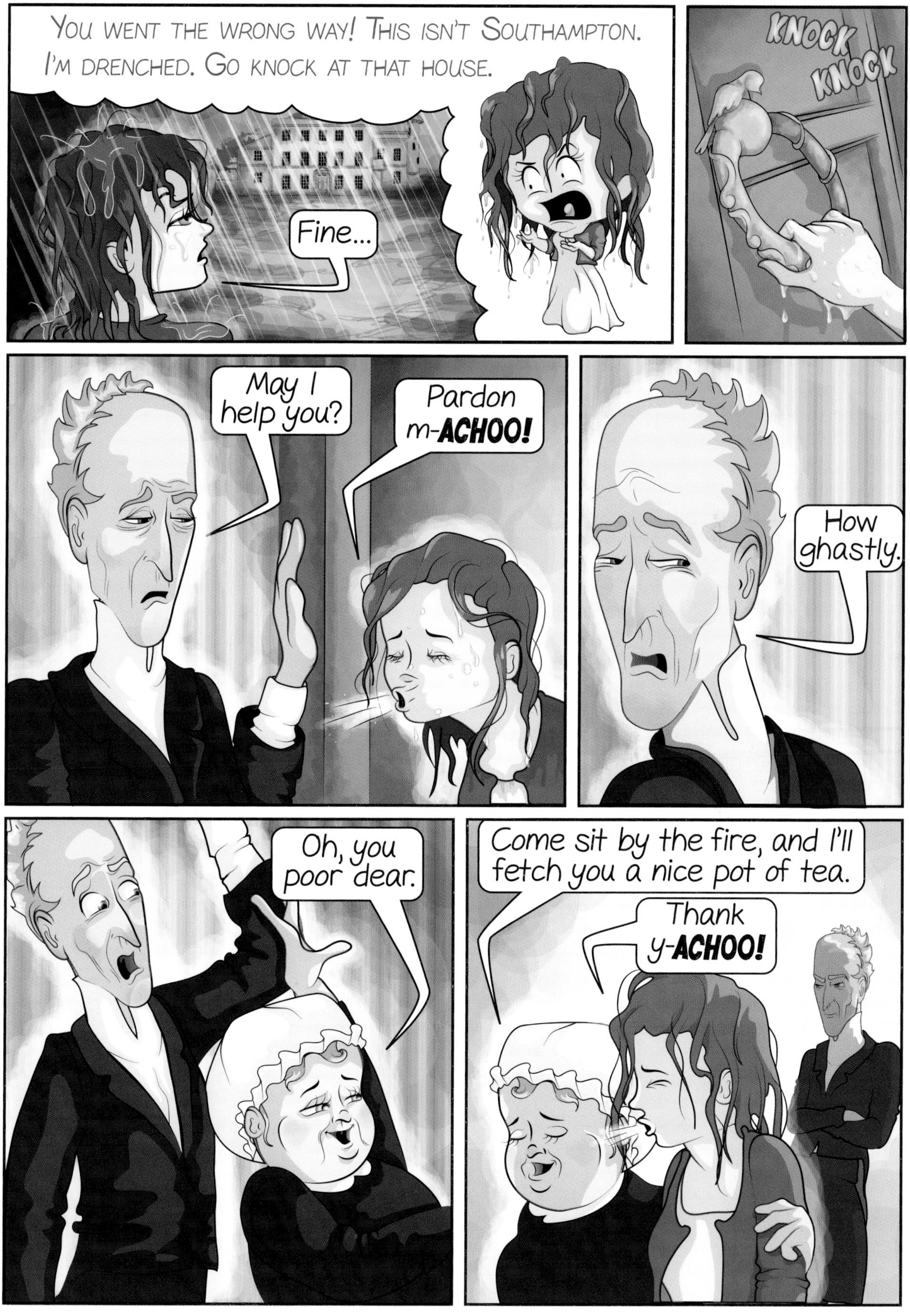
YOU WENT THE WRONG WAY! THIS ISN'T SOUTHAMPTON. I'M DRENCHED. GO KNOCK AT THAT HOUSE.
Fine...
KNOCK KNOCK
May I help you?
Pardon m-ACHOO!
How ghastly.
Oh, you poor dear.
Come sit by the fire, and I'll fetch you a nice pot of tea.
Thank y-ACHOO!

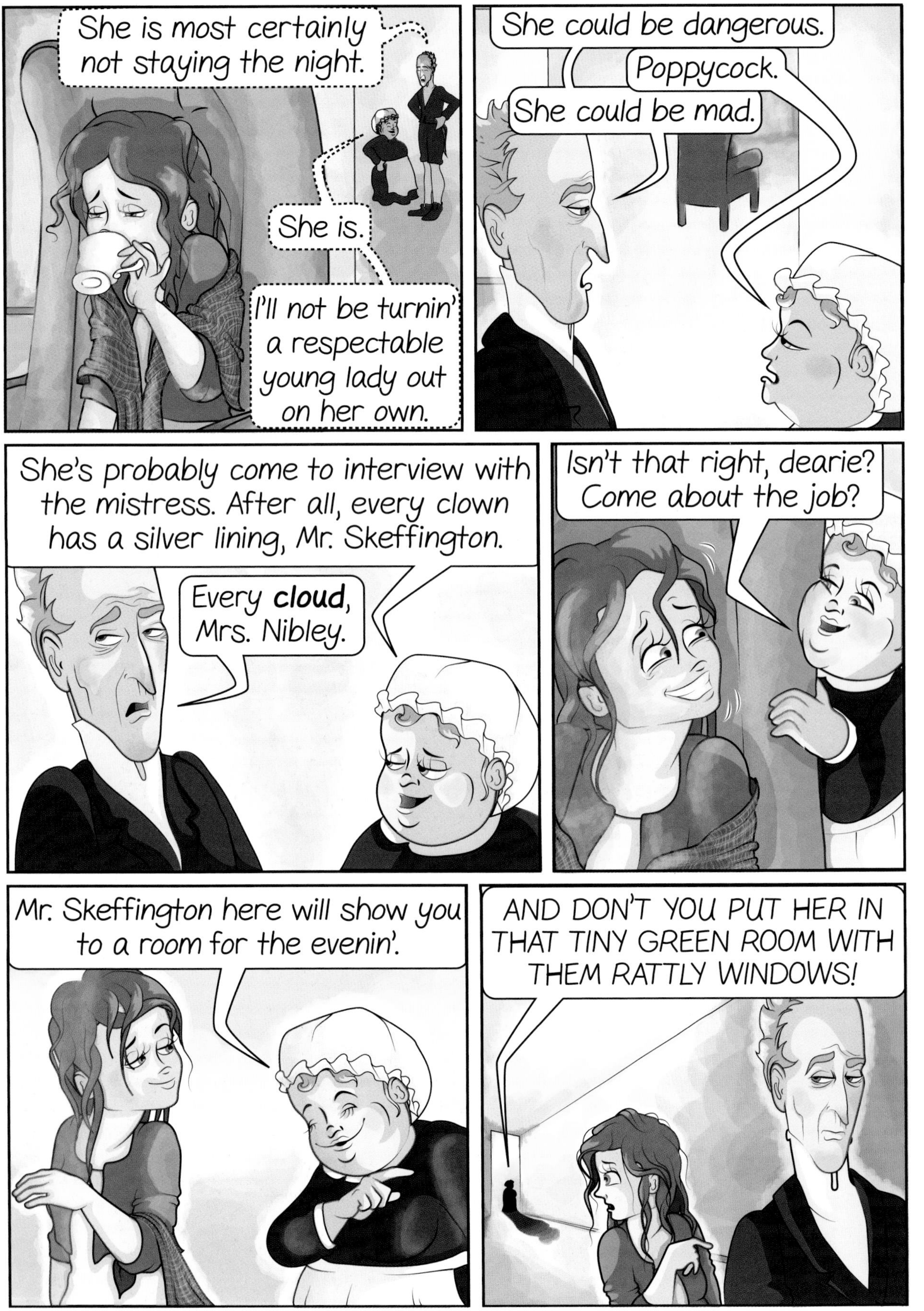
She is most certainly not staying the night.
She is.
I'll not be turnin' a respectable young lady out on her own.
She could be dangerous.
Poppycock.
She could be mad.
She's probably come to interview with the mistress. After all, every clown has a silver lining, Mr. Skeffington.
Every **cloud**, Mrs. Nibley.
Isn't that right, dearie? Come about the job?
Mr. Skeffington here will show you to a room for the evenin'.
AND DON'T YOU PUT HER IN THAT TINY GREEN ROOM WITH THEM RATTLY WINDOWS!

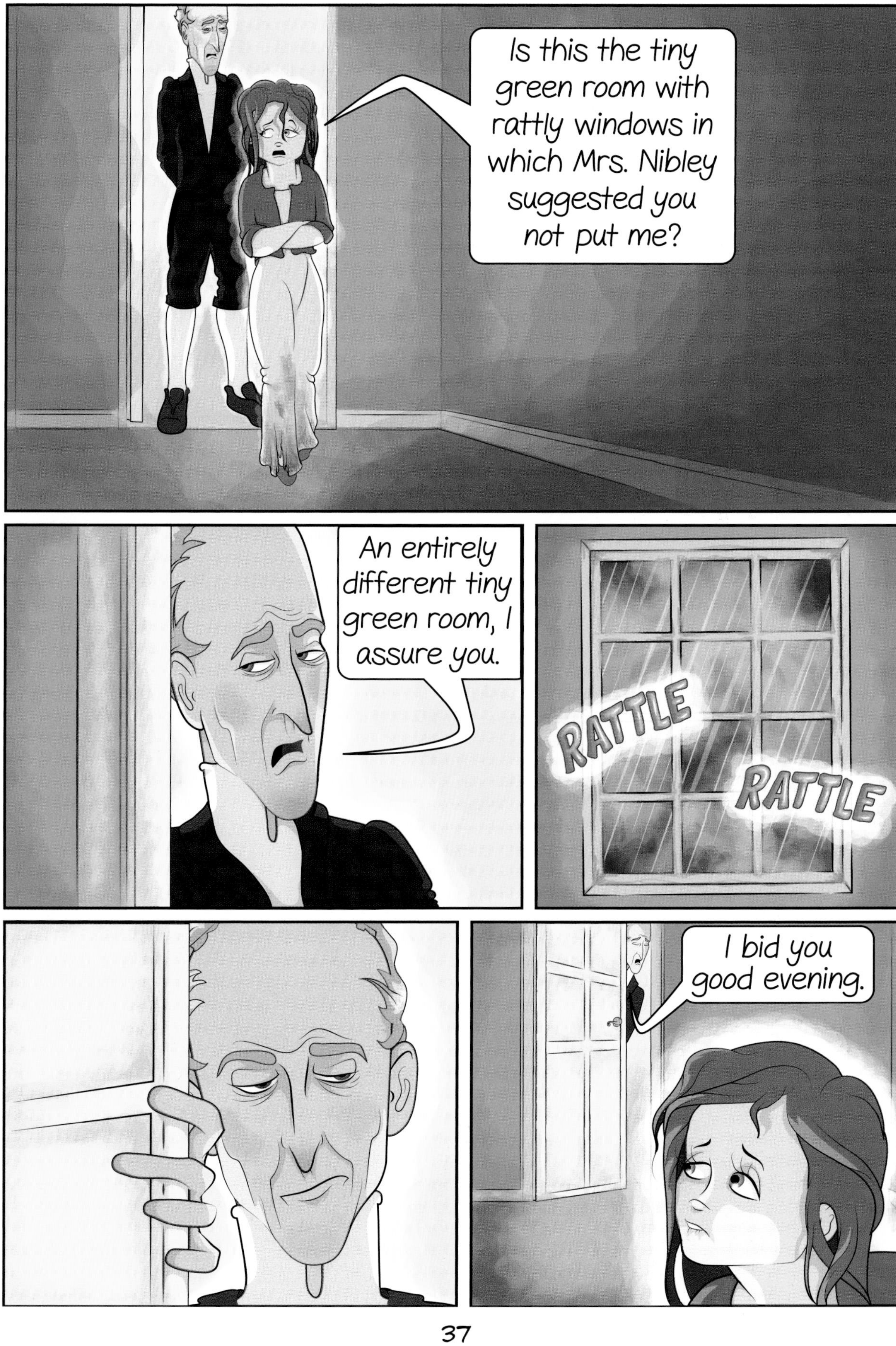
Is this the tiny green room with rattly windows in which Mrs. Nibley suggested you not put me?
An entirely different tiny green room, I assure you.
RATTLE
RATTLE
I bid you good evening.

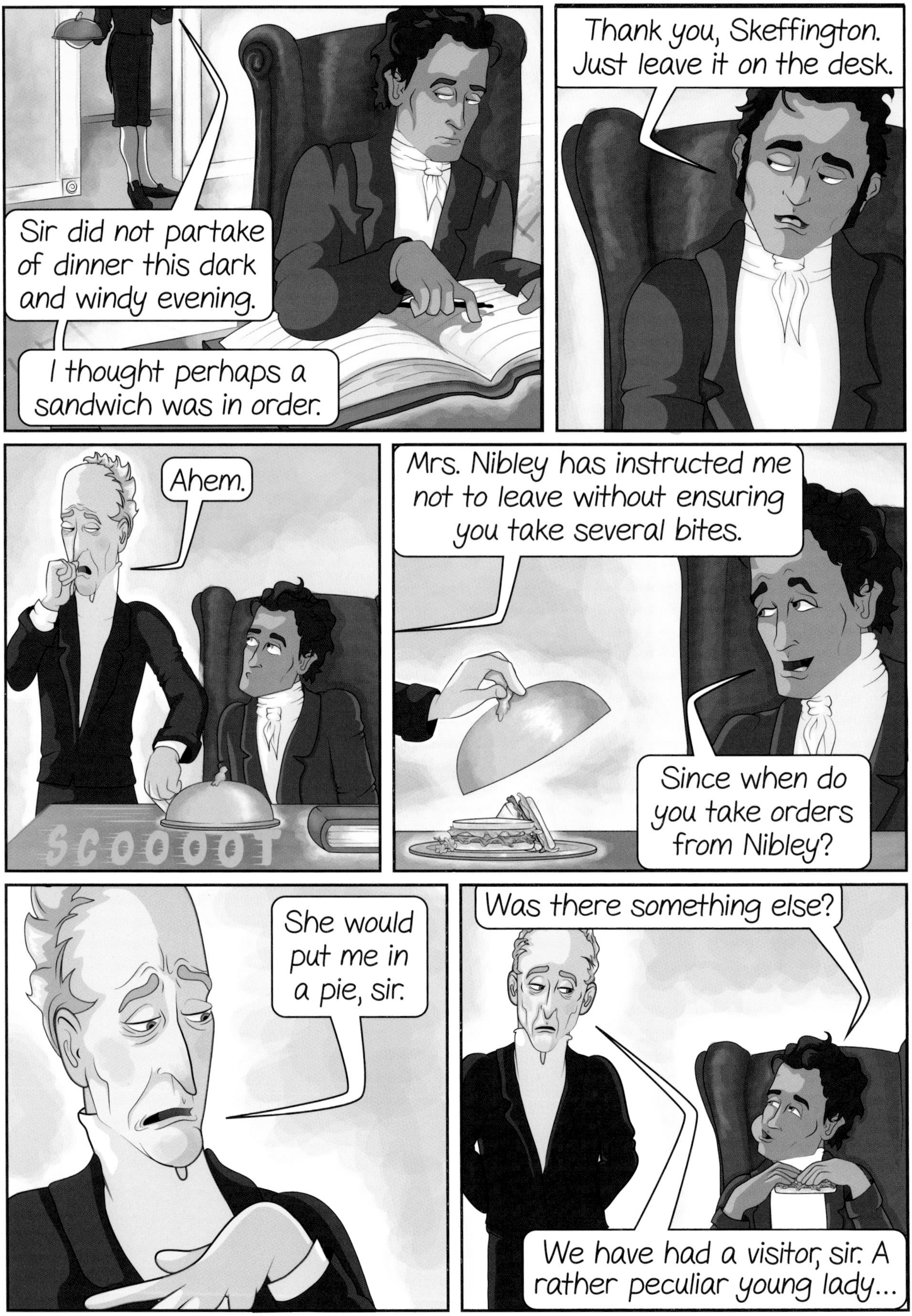
Sir did not partake of dinner this dark and windy evening.
I thought perhaps a sandwich was in order.
Thank you, Skeffington. Just leave it on the desk.
Ahem.
SCOOOOT
Mrs. Nibley has instructed me not to leave without ensuring you take several bites.
Since when do you take orders from Nibley?
She would put me in a pie, sir.
Was there something else?
We have had a visitor, sir. A rather peculiar young lady...

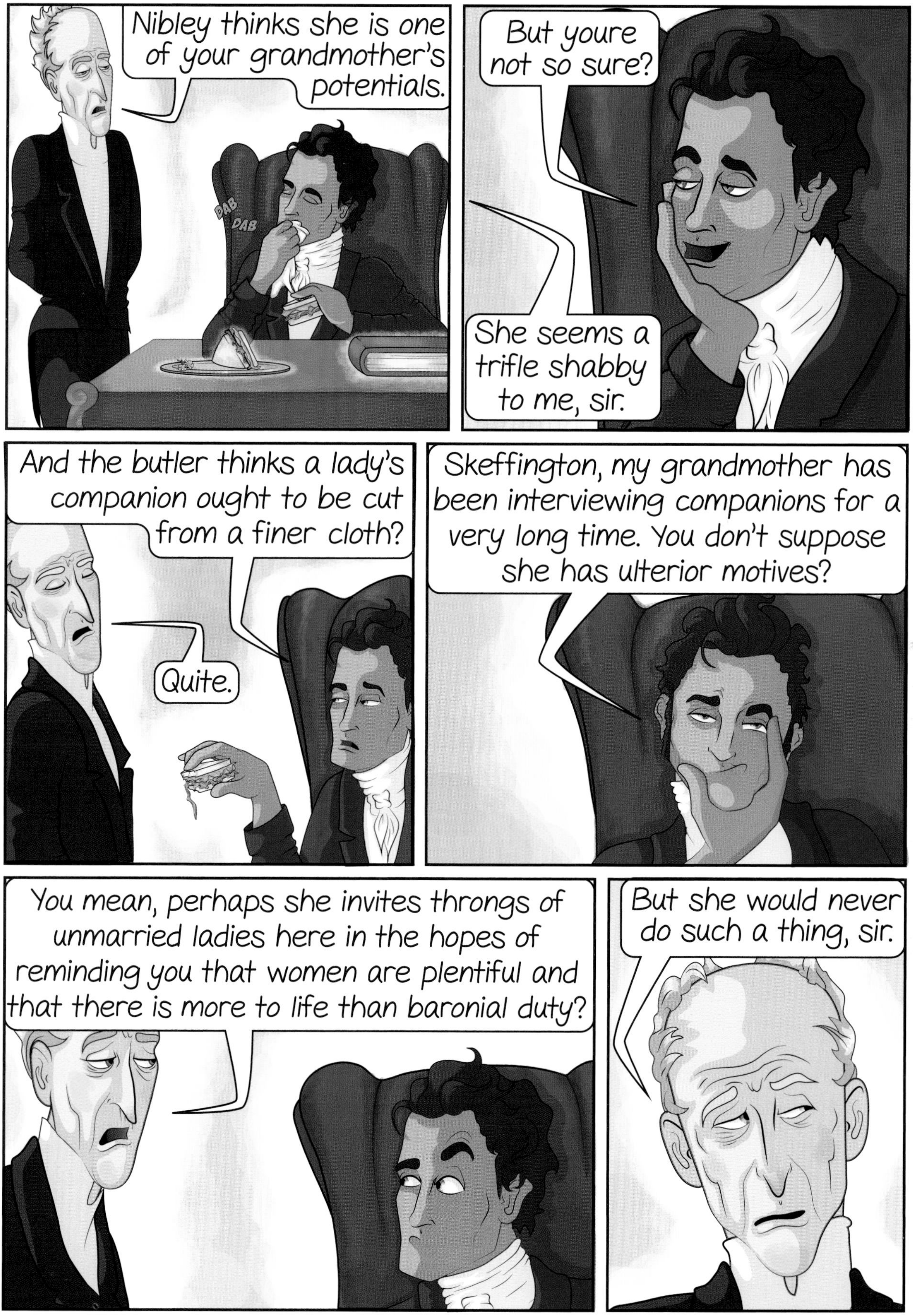
Nibley thinks she is one of your grandmother's potentials.
DAB
DAB
But youre not so sure?
She seems a trifle shabby to me, sir.
And the butler thinks a lady's companion ought to be cut from a finer cloth?
Quite.
Skeffington, my grandmother has been interviewing companions for a very long time. You don't suppose she has ulterior motives?
You mean, perhaps she invites throngs of unmarried ladies here in the hopes of reminding you that women are plentiful and that there is more to life than baronial duty?
But she would never do such a thing, sir.

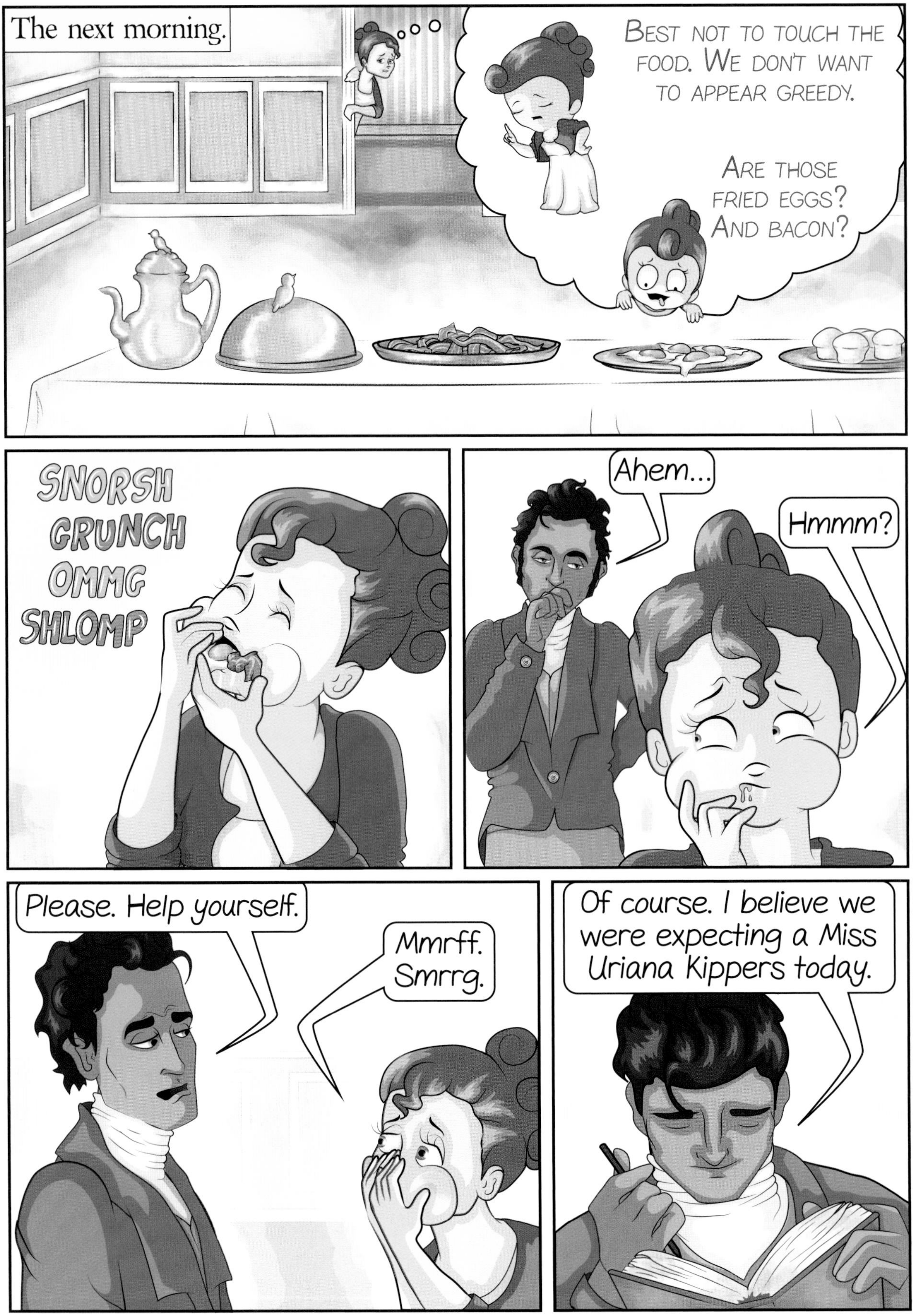
The next morning.
BEST NOT TO TOUCH THE FOOD. WE DON'T WANT TO APPEAR GREEDY.
ARE THOSE FRIED EGGS? AND BACON?
SNORSH
GRUNCH
OMMG
SHLOMP
Ahem...
Hmmm?
Please. Help yourself.
Mmrff. Smrrg.
Of course. I believe we were expecting a Miss Uriana Kippers today.

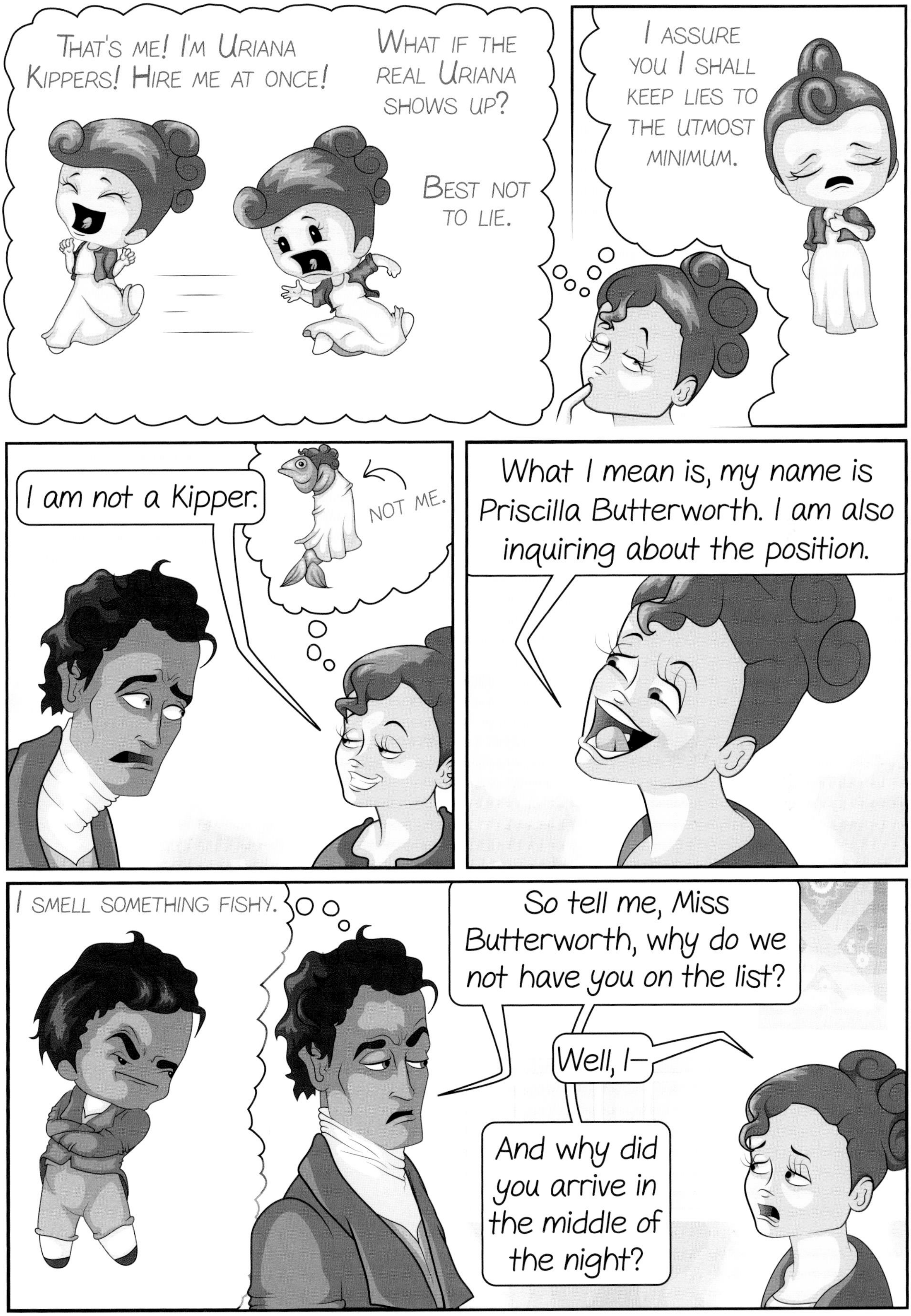
THAT'S ME! I'M URIANA KIPPERS! HIRE ME AT ONCE!
WHAT IF THE REAL URIANA SHOWS UP?
BEST NOT TO LIE.
I ASSURE YOU I SHALL KEEP LIES TO THE UTMOST MINIMUM.
I am not a Kipper.
NOT ME.
What I mean is, my name is Priscilla Butterworth. I am also inquiring about the position.
I SMELL SOMETHING FISHY.
So tell me, Miss Butterworth, why do we not have you on the list?
Well, I–
And why did you arrive in the middle of the night?

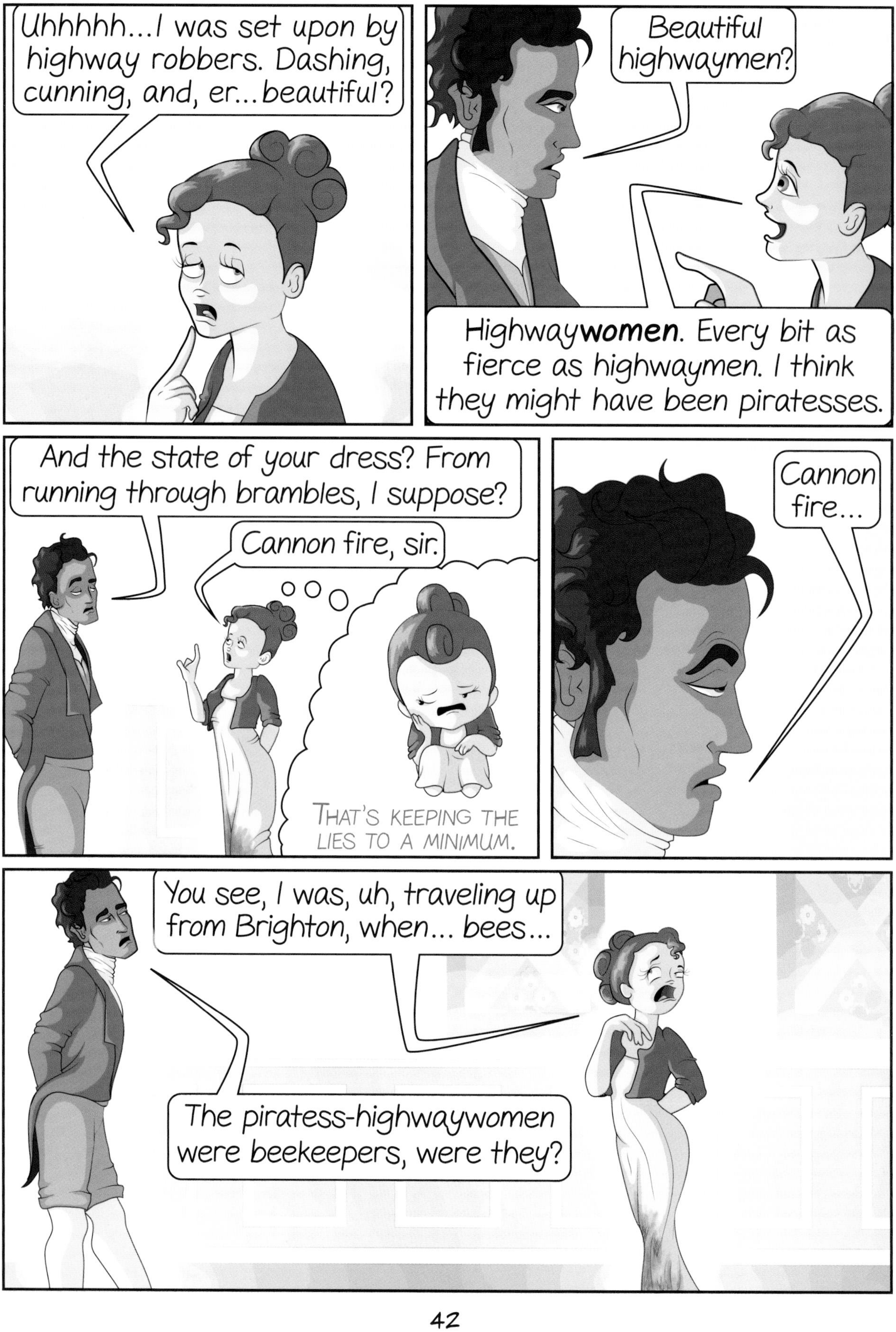

Uhhhhh...I was set upon by highway robbers. Dashing, cunning, and, er...beautiful?
Beautiful highwaymen?
Highway**women**. Every bit as fierce as highwaymen. I think they might have been piratesses.
And the state of your dress? From running through brambles, I suppose?
Cannon fire, sir.
THAT'S KEEPING THE LIES TO A MINIMUM.
Cannon fire...
You see, I was, uh, traveling up from Brighton, when... bees...
The piratess-highwaywomen were beekeepers, were they?

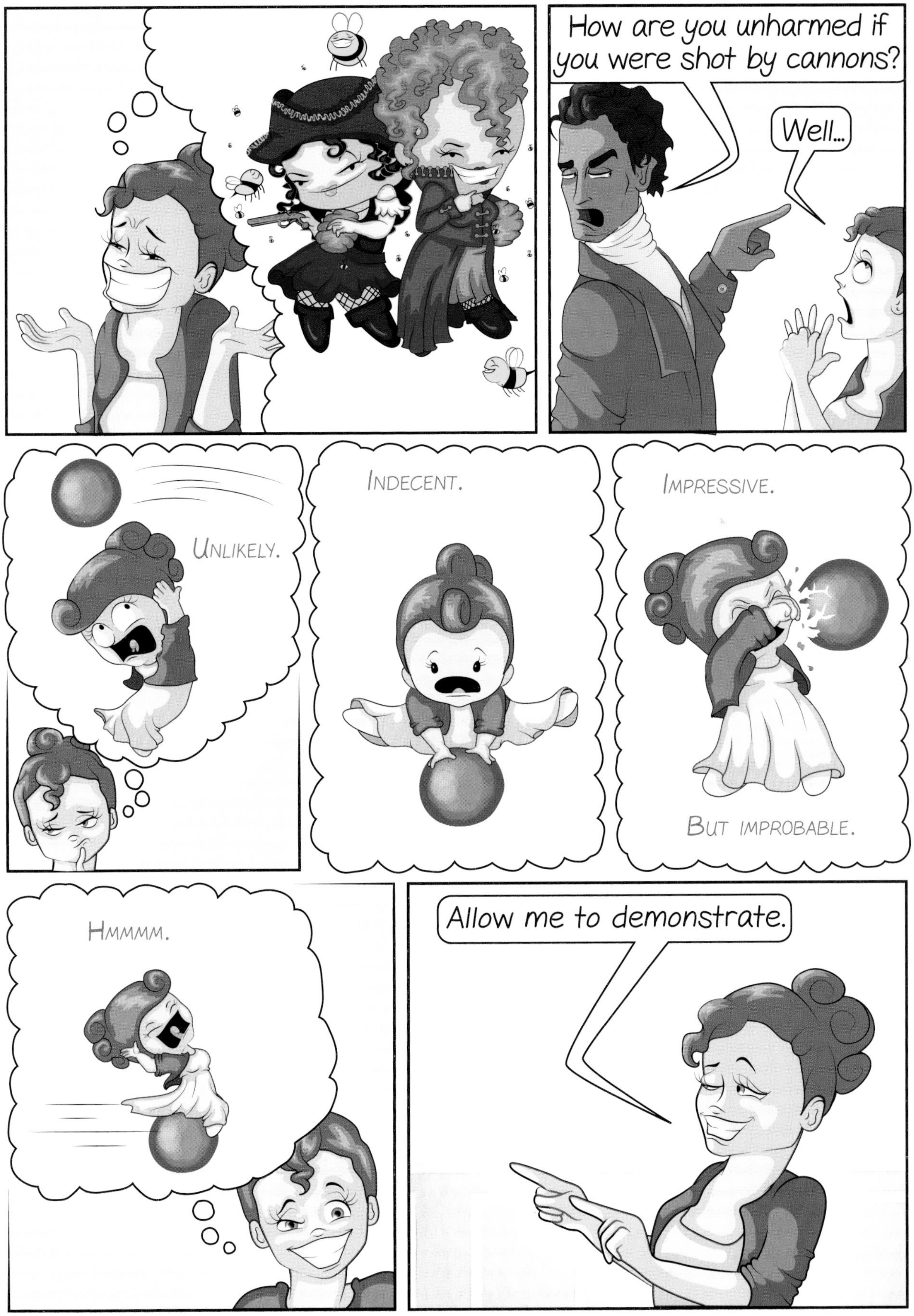
How are you unharmed if you were shot by cannons?
Well...
UNLIKELY.
INDECENT.
IMPRESSIVE.
BUT IMPROBABLE.
HMMMM.
Allow me to demonstrate.

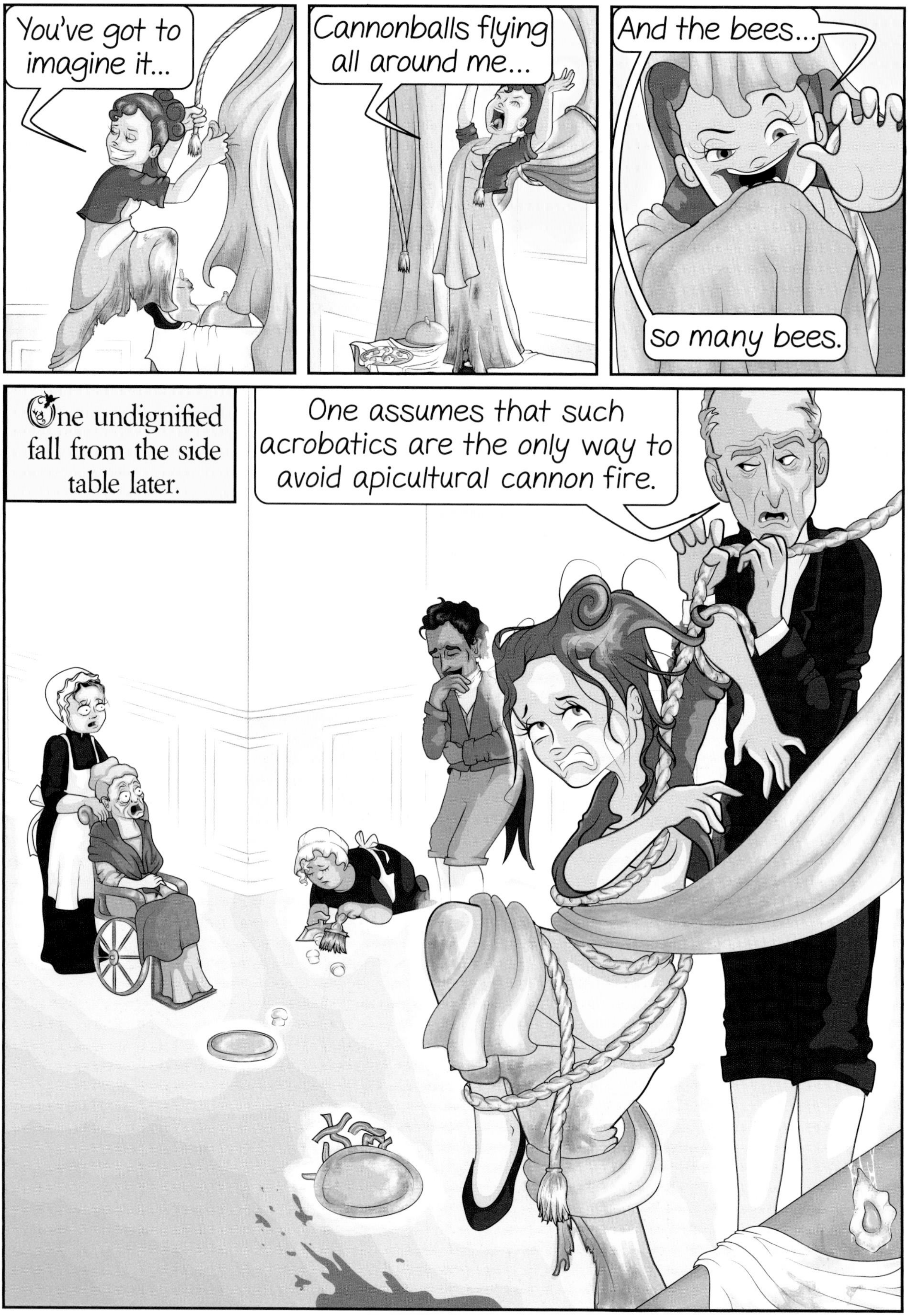
You've got to imagine it...
Cannonballs flying all around me...
And the bees...
so many bees.
One undignified fall from the side table later.
One assumes that such acrobatics are the only way to avoid apicultural cannon fire.

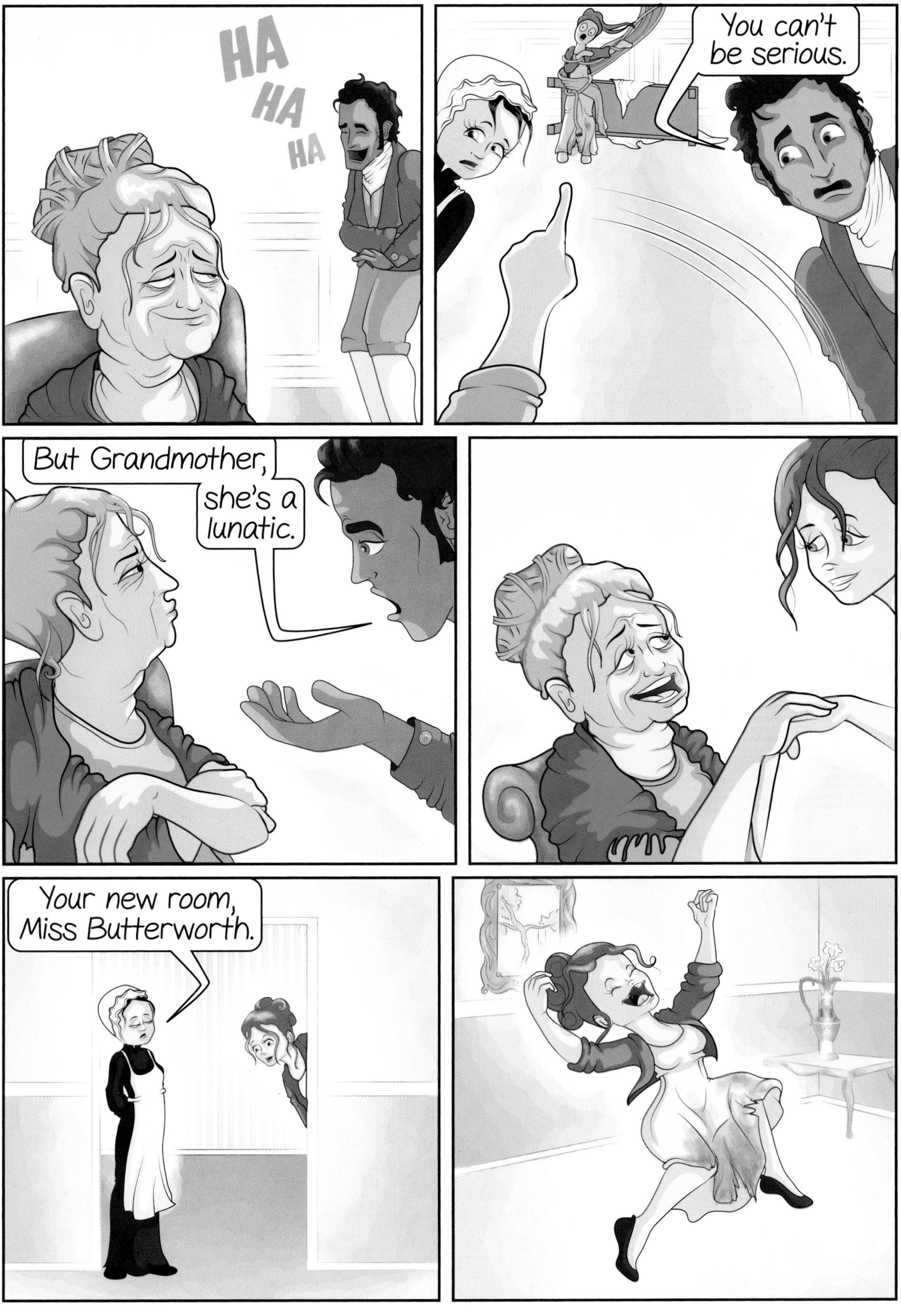
HA
HA
HA
You can't be serious.
But Grandmother,
she's a lunatic.
Your new room, Miss Butterworth.

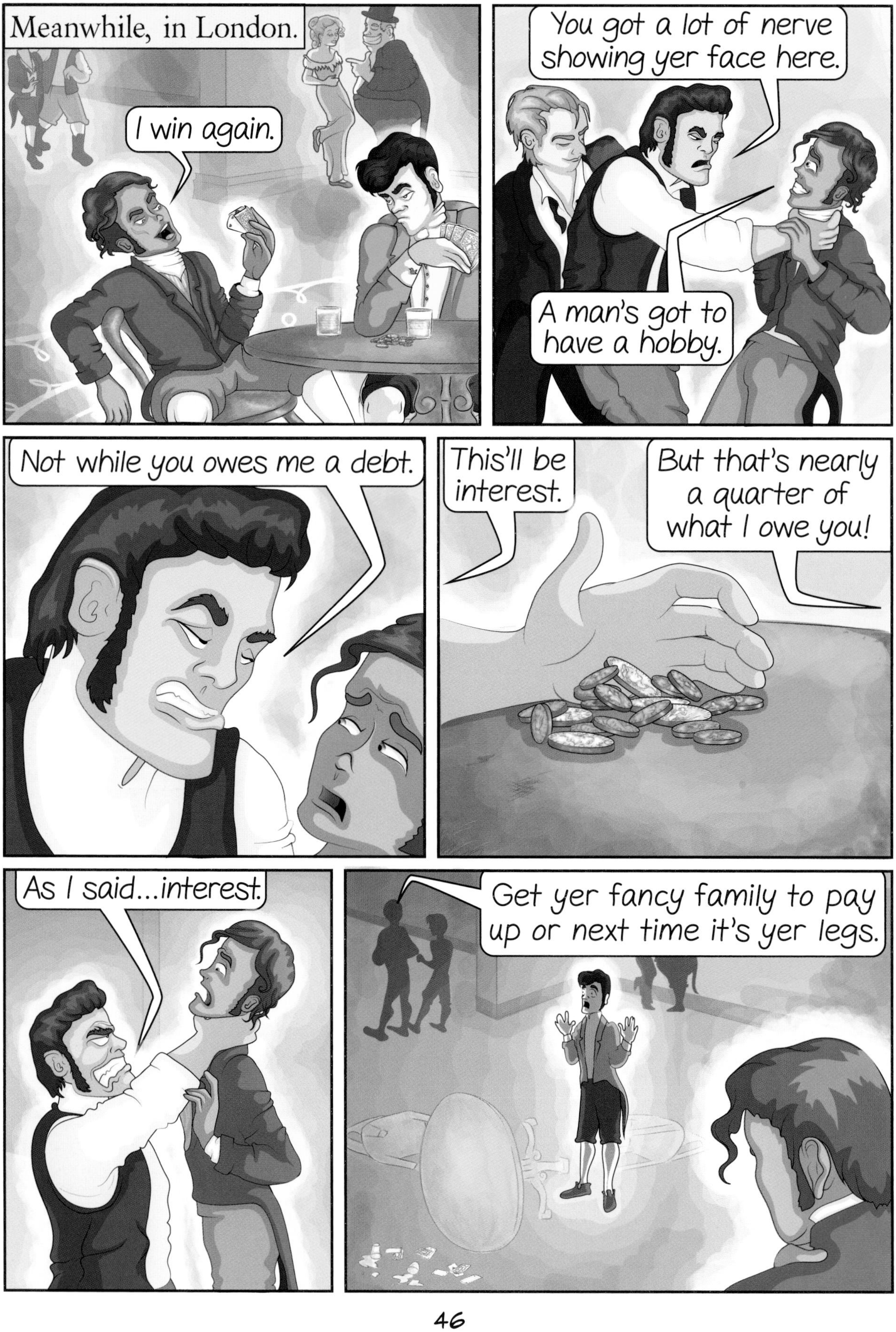

Meanwhile, in London.
I win again.
You got a lot of nerve showing yer face here.
A man's got to have a hobby.
Not while you owes me a debt.
This'll be interest.
But that's nearly a quarter of what I owe you!
As I said...interest.
Get yer fancy family to pay up or next time it's yer legs.

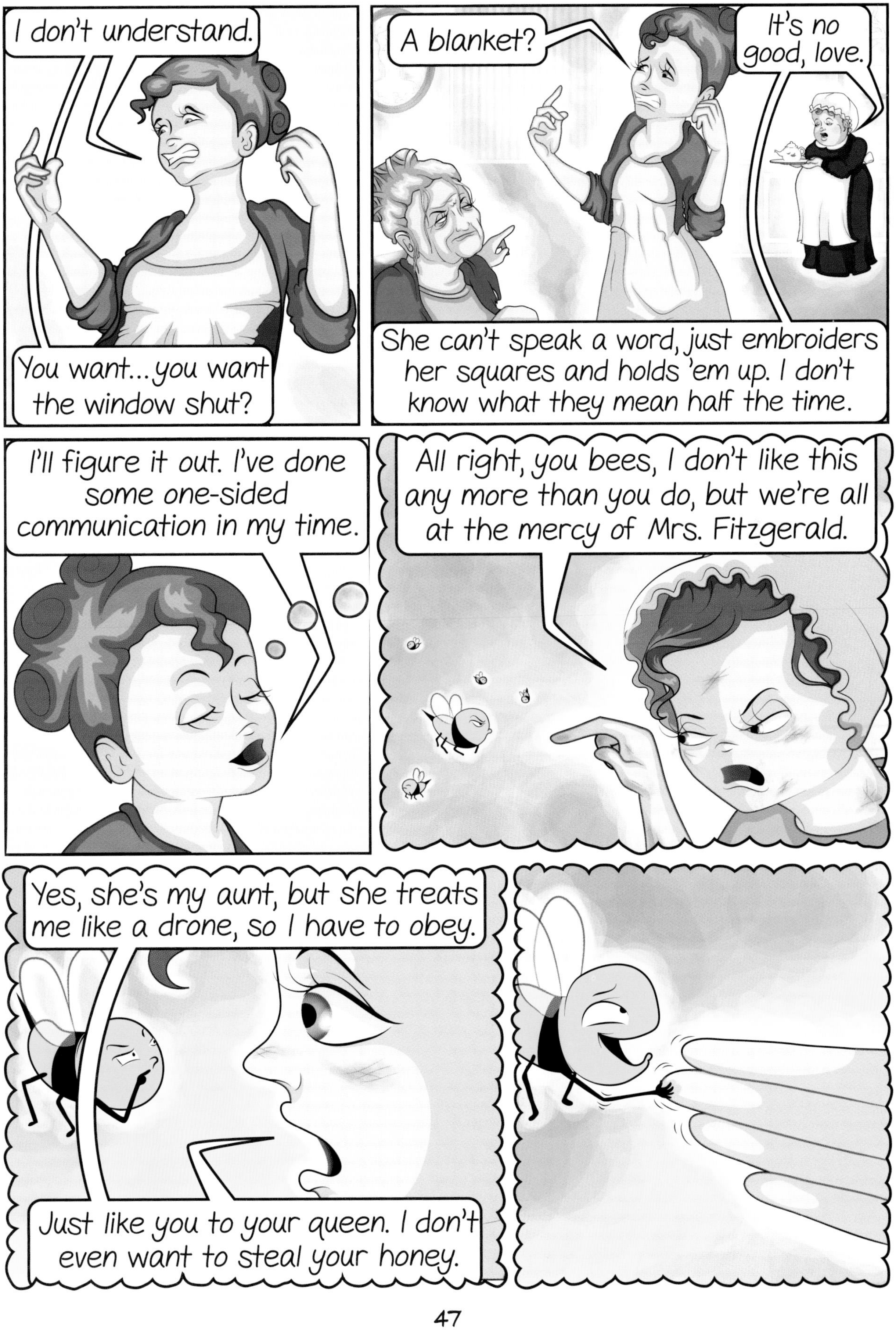

I don't understand.
You want...you want the window shut?
A blanket?
It's no good, love.
She can't speak a word, just embroiders her squares and holds 'em up. I don't know what they mean half the time.
I'll figure it out. I've done some one-sided communication in my time.
All right, you bees, I don't like this any more than you do, but we're all at the mercy of Mrs. Fitzgerald.
Yes, she's my aunt, but she treats me like a drone, so I have to obey.
Just like you to your queen. I don't even want to steal your honey.

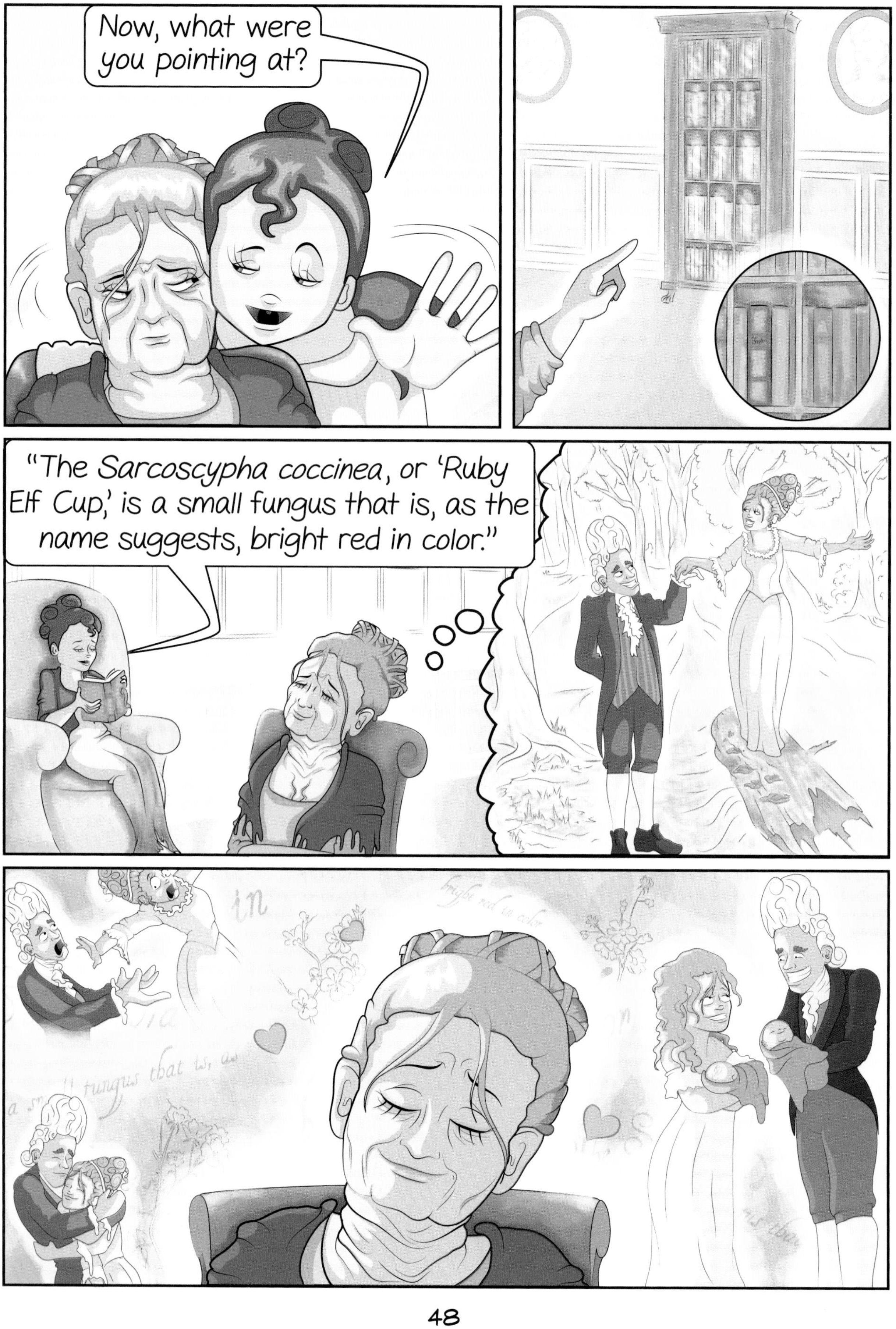
Now, what were you pointing at?
"The *Sarcoscypha coccinea*, or 'Ruby Elf Cup,' is a small fungus that is, as the name suggests, bright red in color."

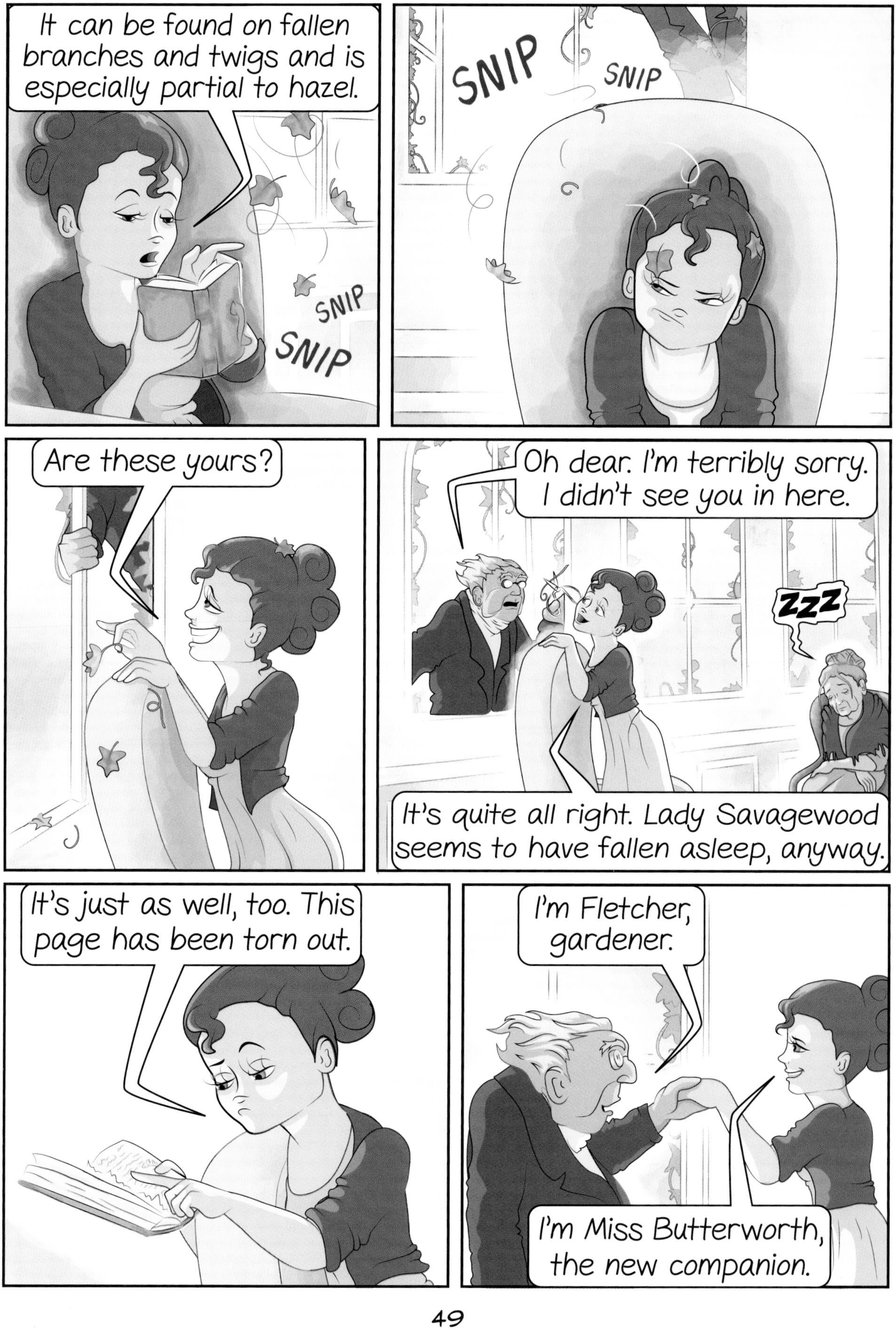

It can be found on fallen branches and twigs and is especially partial to hazel.
SNIP
SNIP
SNIP
SNIP
Are these yours?
Oh dear. I'm terribly sorry. I didn't see you in here.
ZZZ
It's quite all right. Lady Savagewood seems to have fallen asleep, anyway.
It's just as well, too. This page has been torn out.
I'm Fletcher, gardener.
I'm Miss Butterworth, the new companion.

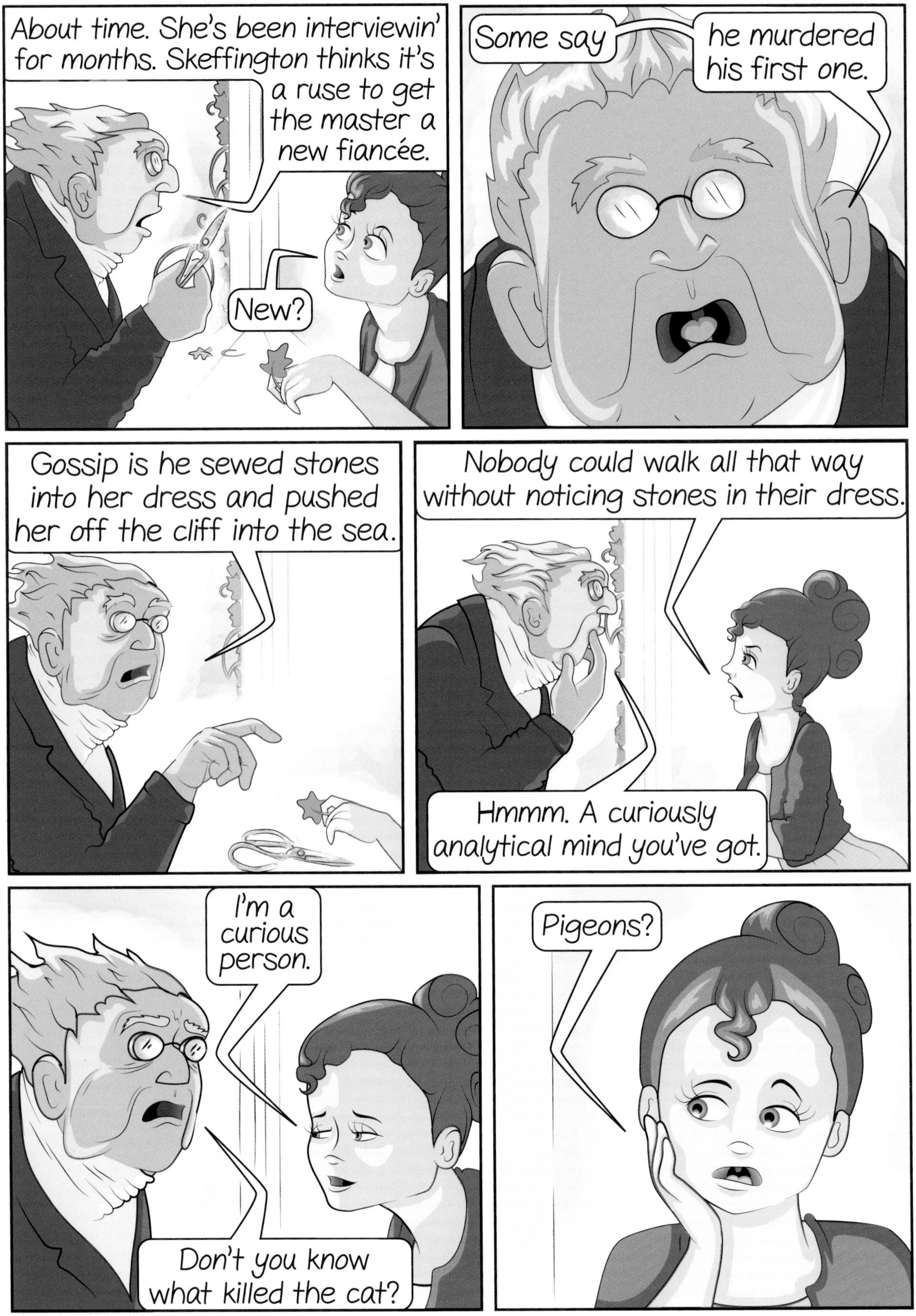
About time. She's been interviewin' for months. Skeffington thinks it's a ruse to get the master a new fiancée.
New?
Some say
he murdered his first one.
Gossip is he sewed stones into her dress and pushed her off the cliff into the sea.
Nobody could walk all that way without noticing stones in their dress.
Hmmm. A curiously analytical mind you've got.
I'm a curious person.
Don't you know what killed the cat?
Pigeons?

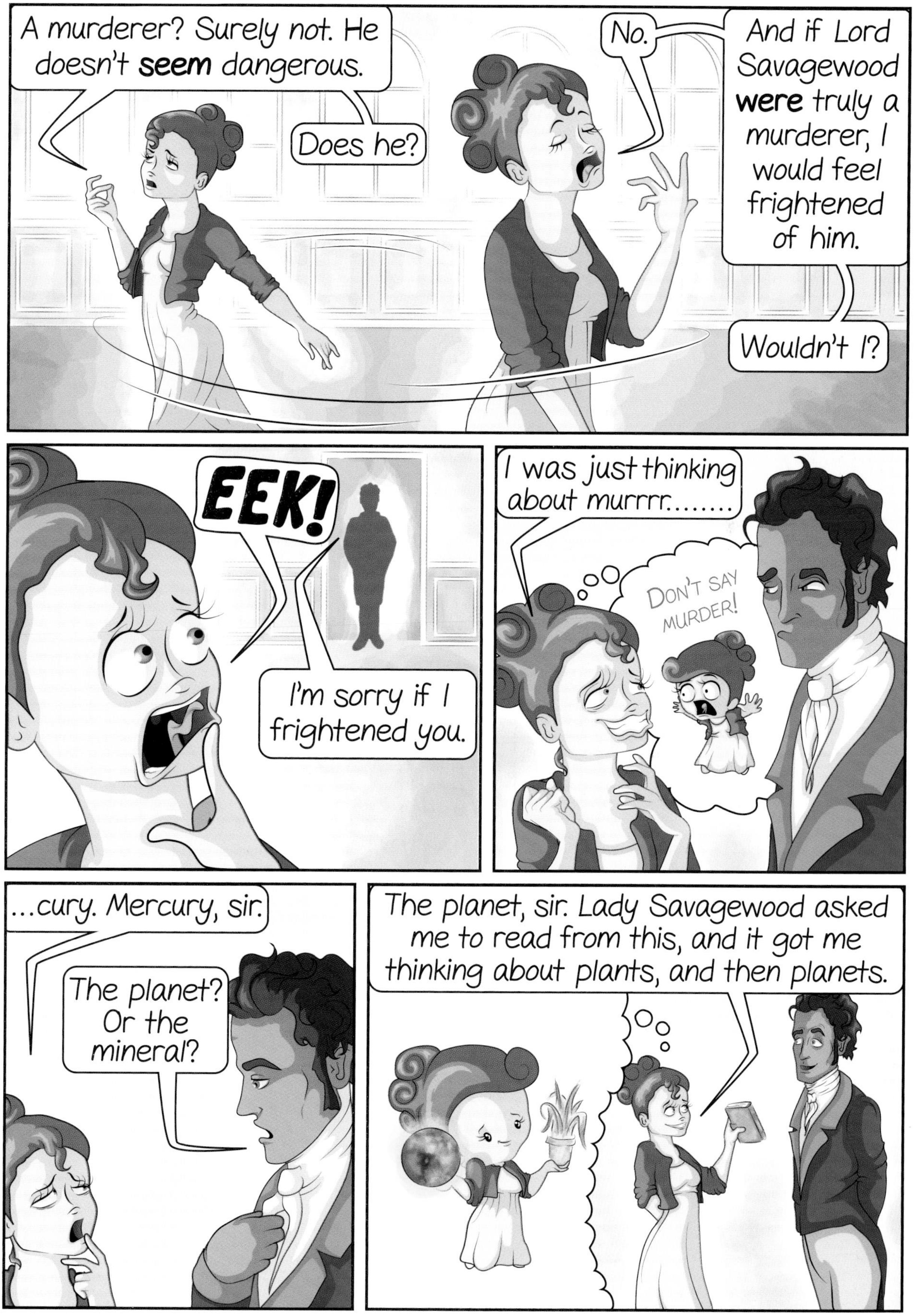
A murderer? Surely not. He doesn't **seem** dangerous.
Does he?
No.
And if Lord Savagewood **were** truly a murderer, I would feel frightened of him.
Wouldn't I?
EEK!
I'm sorry if I frightened you.
I was just thinking about murrrr........
DON'T SAY MURDER!
...cury. Mercury, sir.
The planet? Or the mineral?
The planet, sir. Lady Savagewood asked me to read from this, and it got me thinking about plants, and then planets.

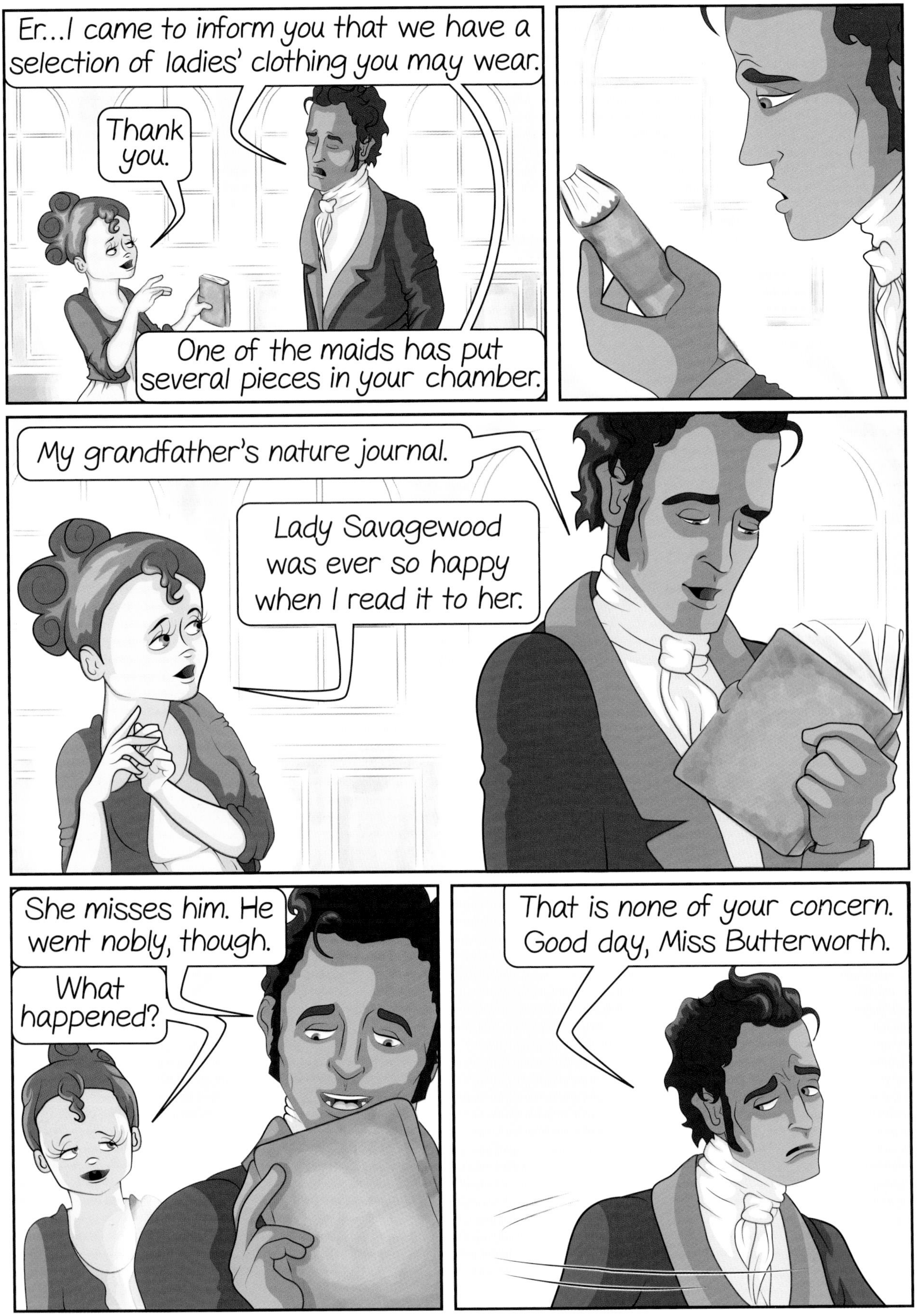
Er...I came to inform you that we have a selection of ladies' clothing you may wear.
Thank you.
One of the maids has put several pieces in your chamber.
My grandfather's nature journal.
Lady Savagewood was ever so happy when I read it to her.
She misses him. He went nobly, though.
What happened?
That is none of your concern. Good day, Miss Butterworth.

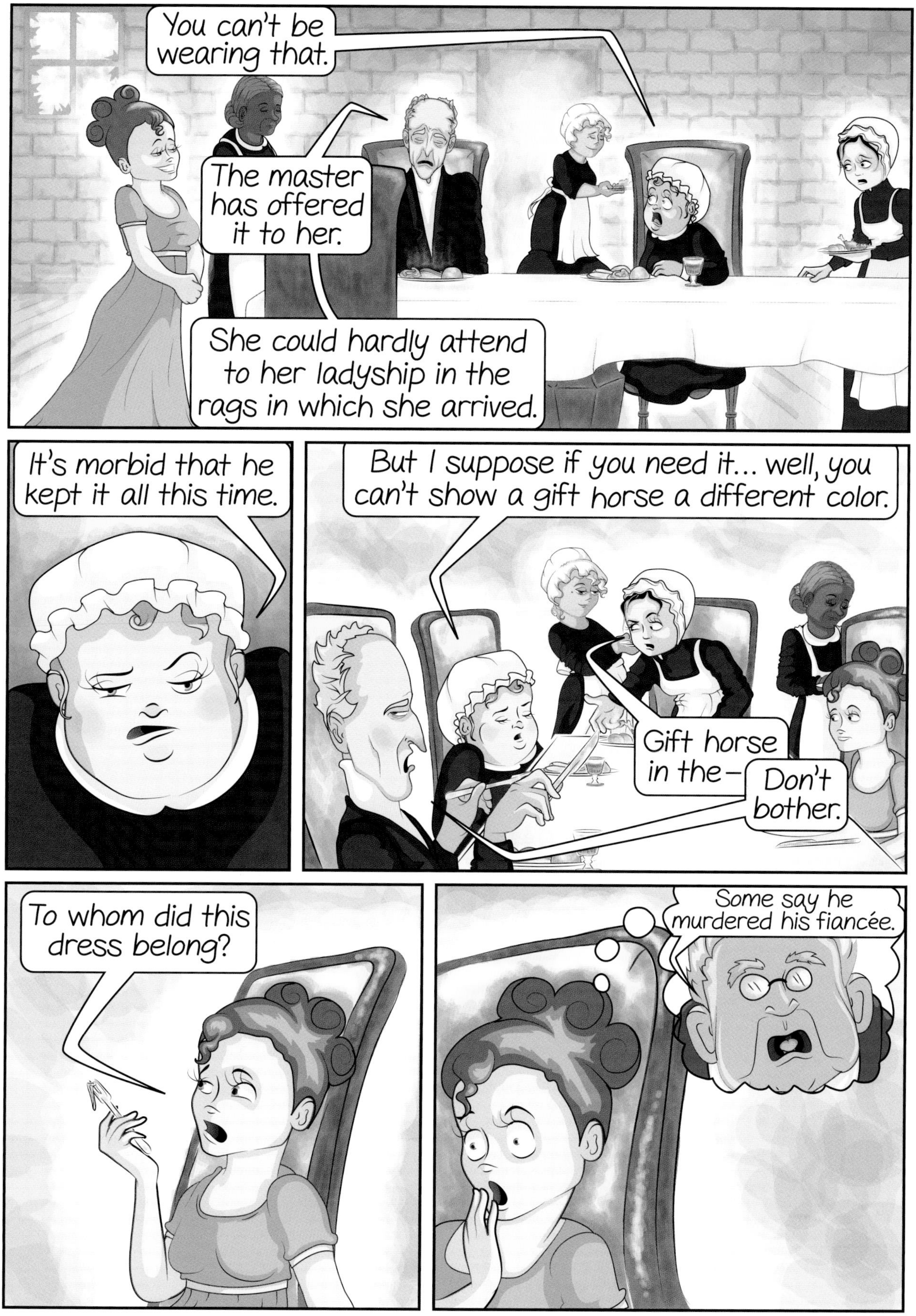
You can't be wearing that.
The master has offered it to her.
She could hardly attend to her ladyship in the rags in which she arrived.
It's morbid that he kept it all this time.
But I suppose if you need it... well, you can't show a gift horse a different color.
Gift horse in the–
Don't bother.
To whom did this dress belong?
Some say he murdered his fiancée.

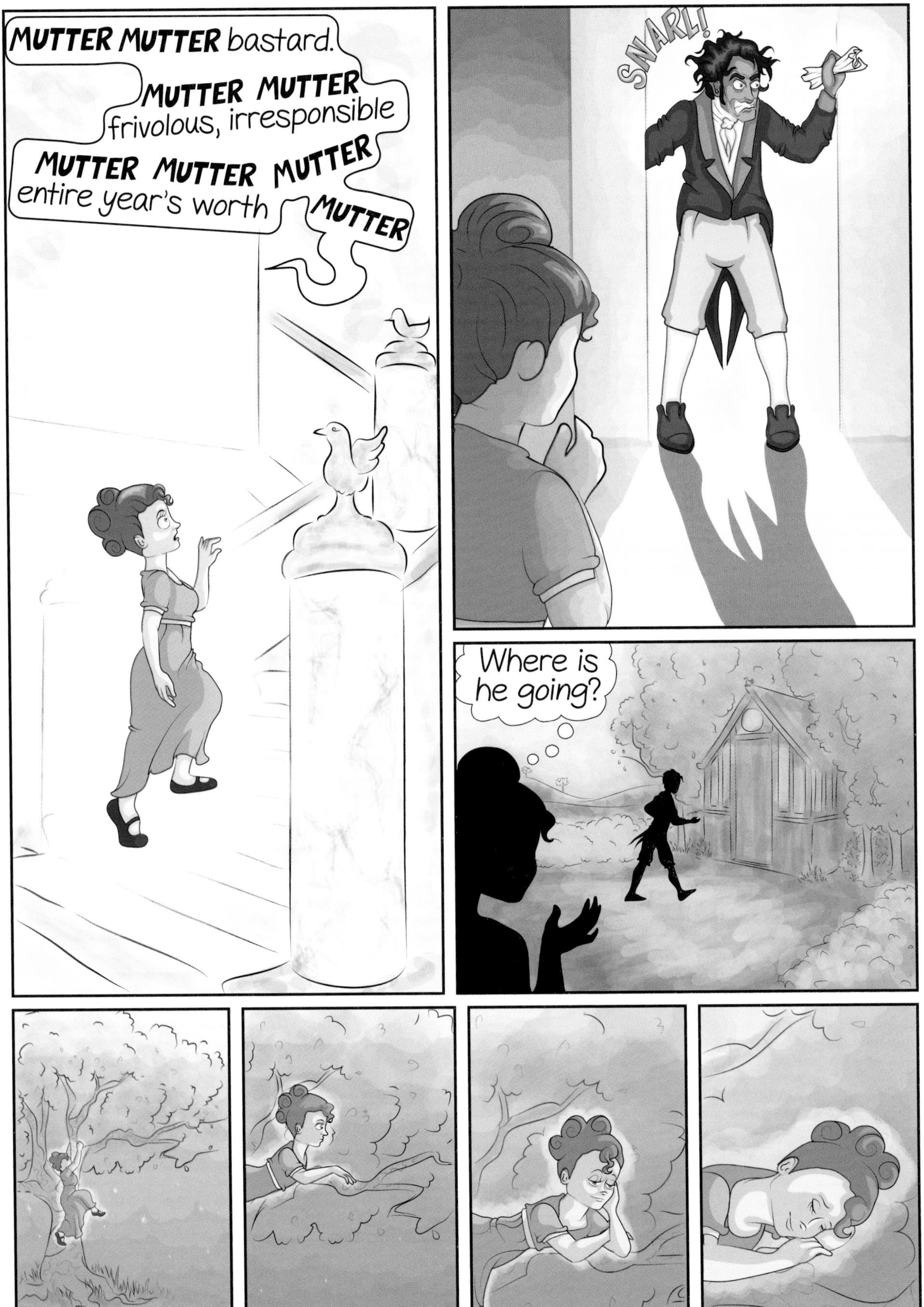
MUTTER MUTTER bastard.
MUTTER MUTTER frivolous, irresponsible
MUTTER MUTTER MUTTER entire year's worth
MUTTER
SNARL!
Where is he going?

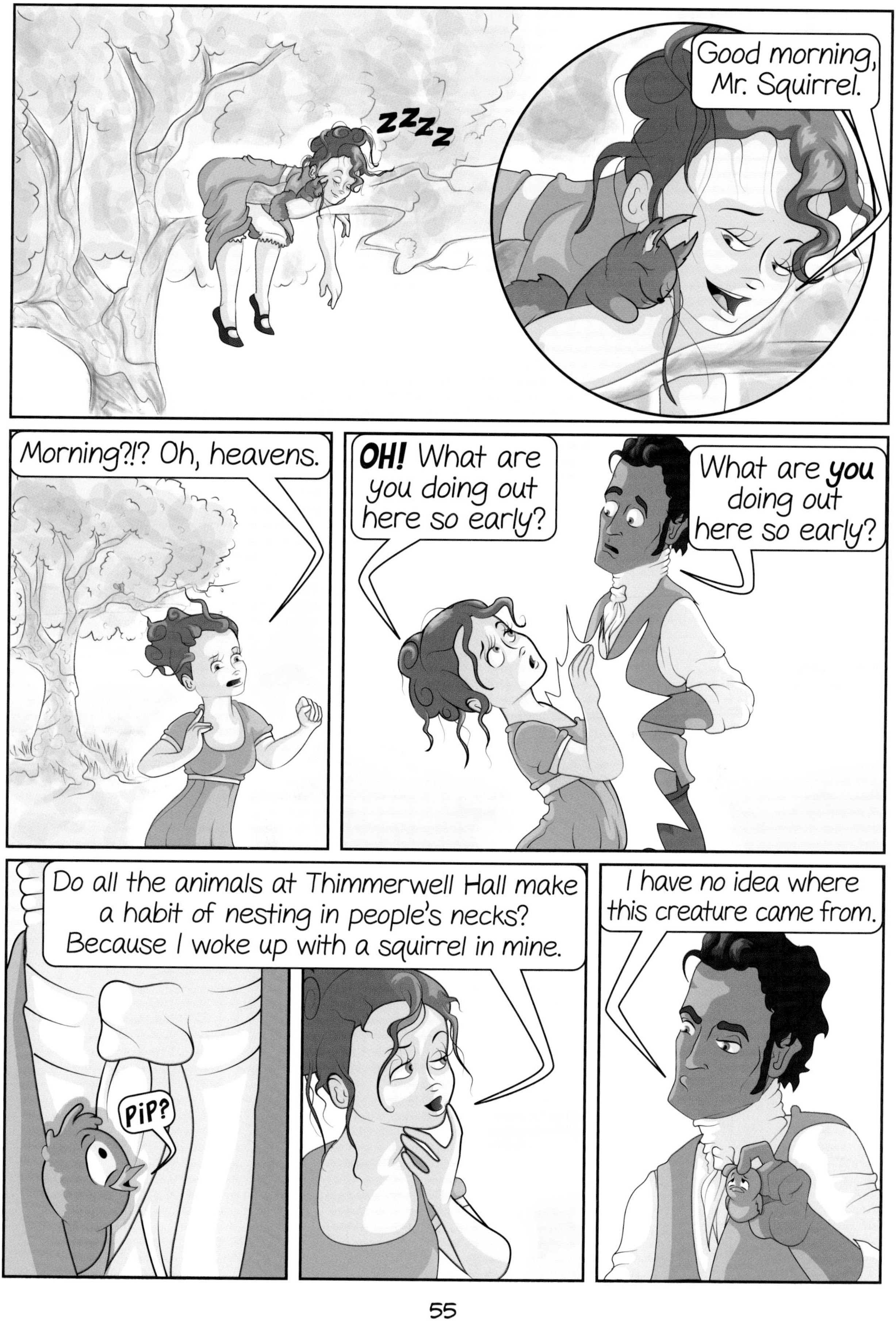

ZZZZ
Good morning, Mr. Squirrel.
Morning?!? Oh, heavens.
OH! What are you doing out here so early?
What are you doing out here so early?
Do all the animals at Thimmerwell Hall make a habit of nesting in people's necks? Because I woke up with a squirrel in mine.
PIP?
I have no idea where this creature came from.

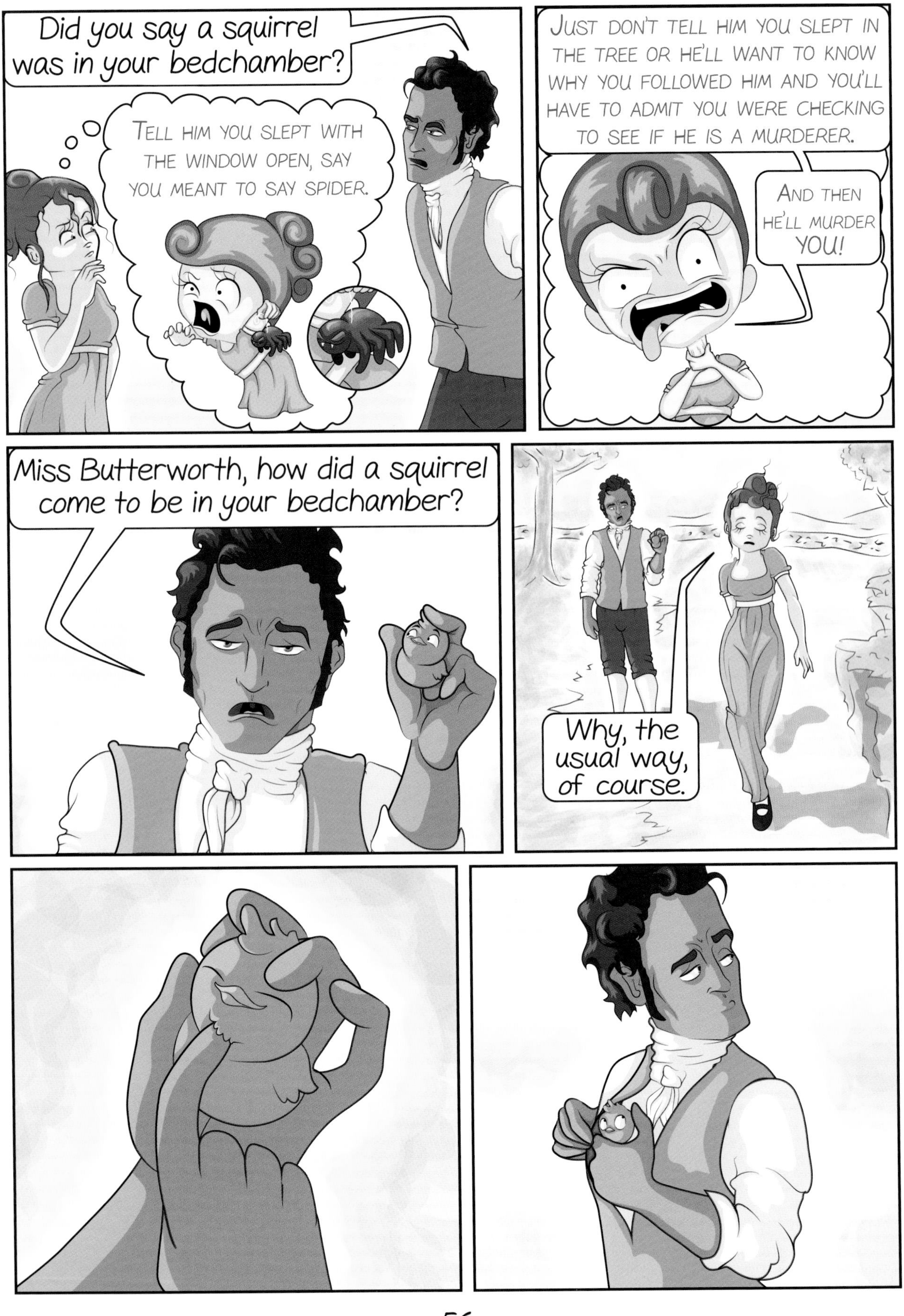
Did you say a squirrel was in your bedchamber?
TELL HIM YOU SLEPT WITH THE WINDOW OPEN, SAY YOU MEANT TO SAY SPIDER.
JUST DON'T TELL HIM YOU SLEPT IN THE TREE OR HE'LL WANT TO KNOW WHY YOU FOLLOWED HIM AND YOU'LL HAVE TO ADMIT YOU WERE CHECKING TO SEE IF HE IS A MURDERER.
AND THEN HE'LL MURDER YOU!
Miss Butterworth, how did a squirrel come to be in your bedchamber?
Why, the usual way, of course.

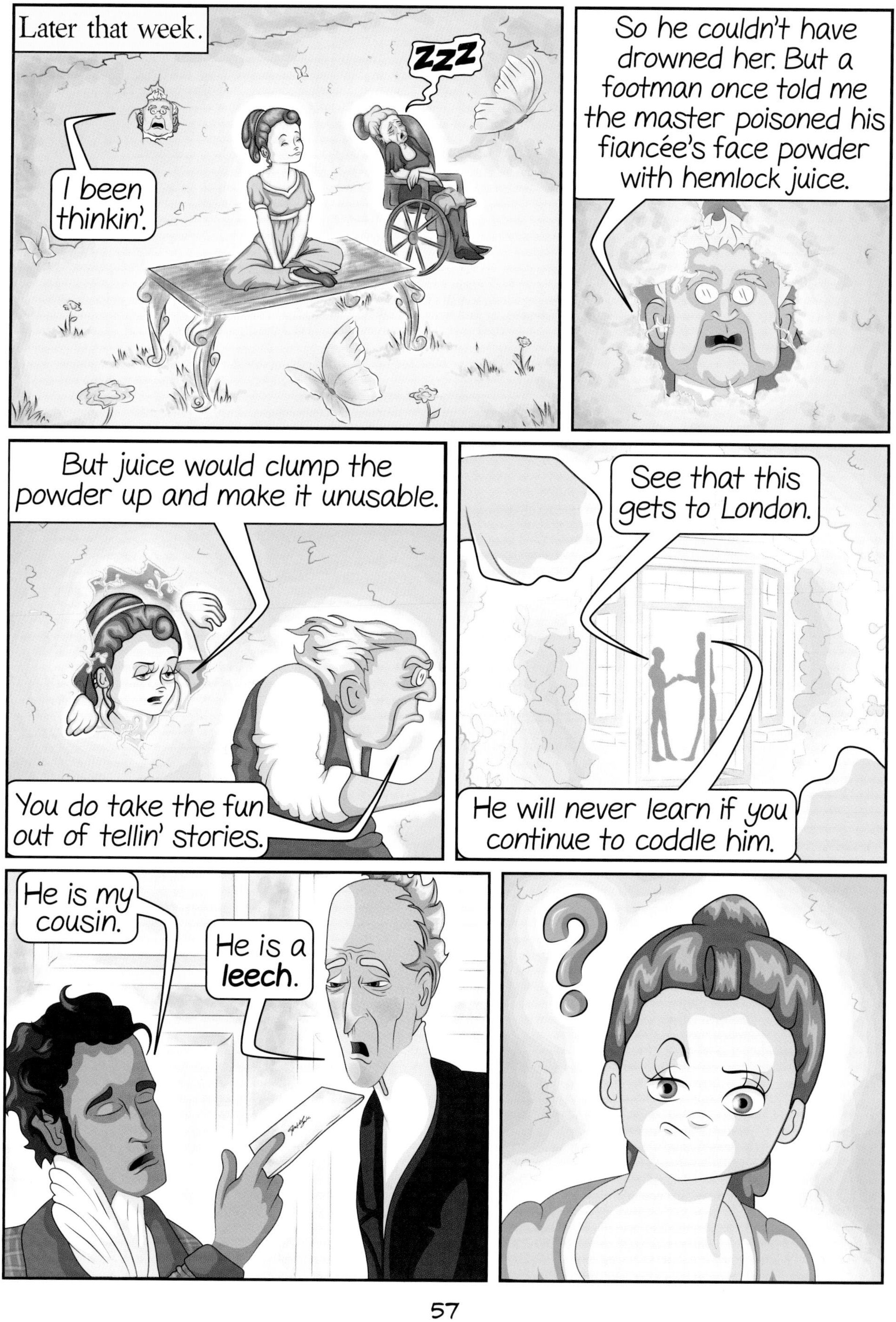
Later that week.
ZZZ
I been thinkin'.
So he couldn't have drowned her. But a footman once told me the master poisoned his fiancée's face powder with hemlock juice.
But juice would clump the powder up and make it unusable.
You do take the fun out of tellin' stories.
See that this gets to London.
He will never learn if you continue to coddle him.
He is my cousin.
He is a **leech**.
?

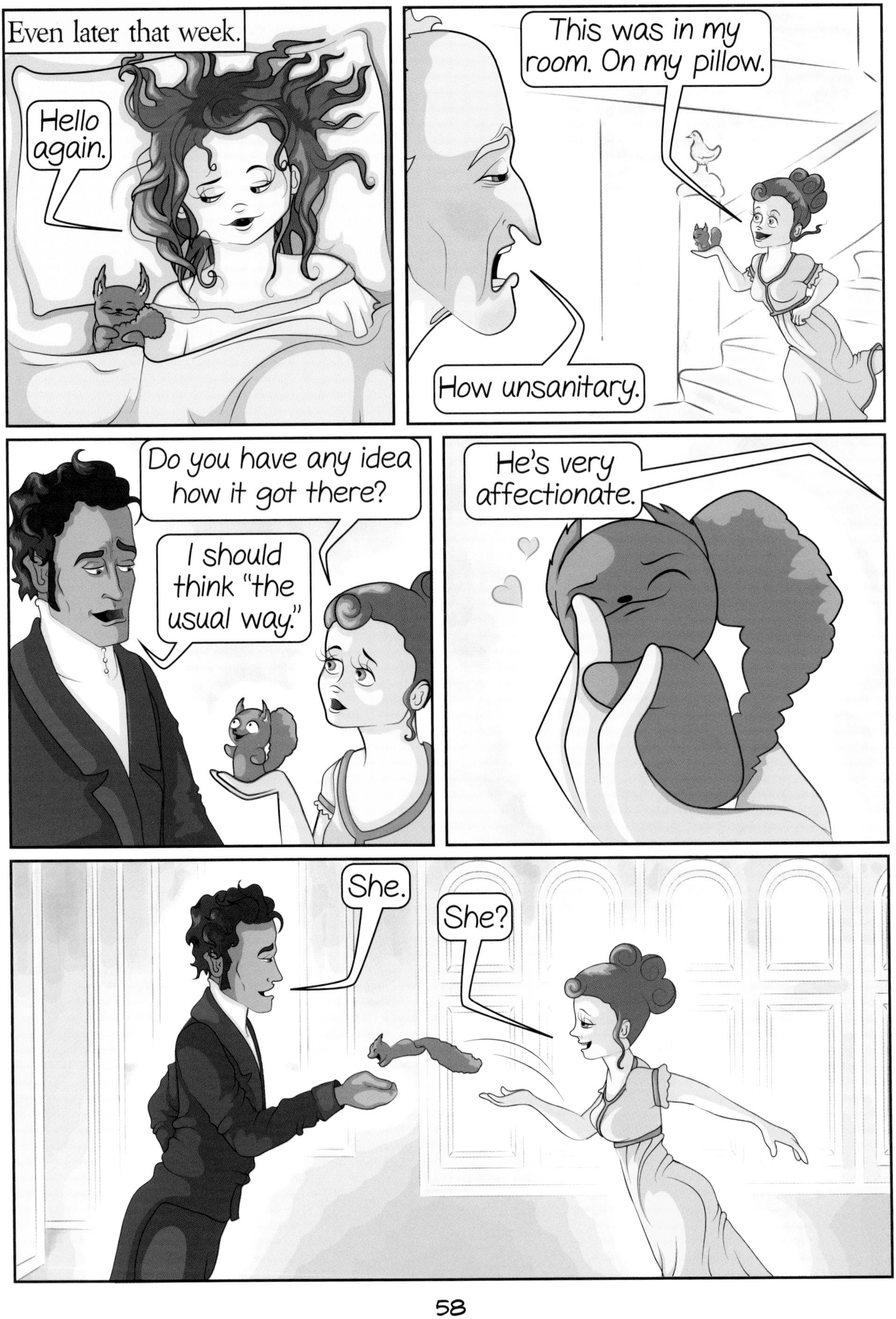
Even later that week.
Hello again.
This was in my room. On my pillow.
How unsanitary.
Do you have any idea how it got there?
I should think "the usual way."
He's very affectionate.
She.
She?

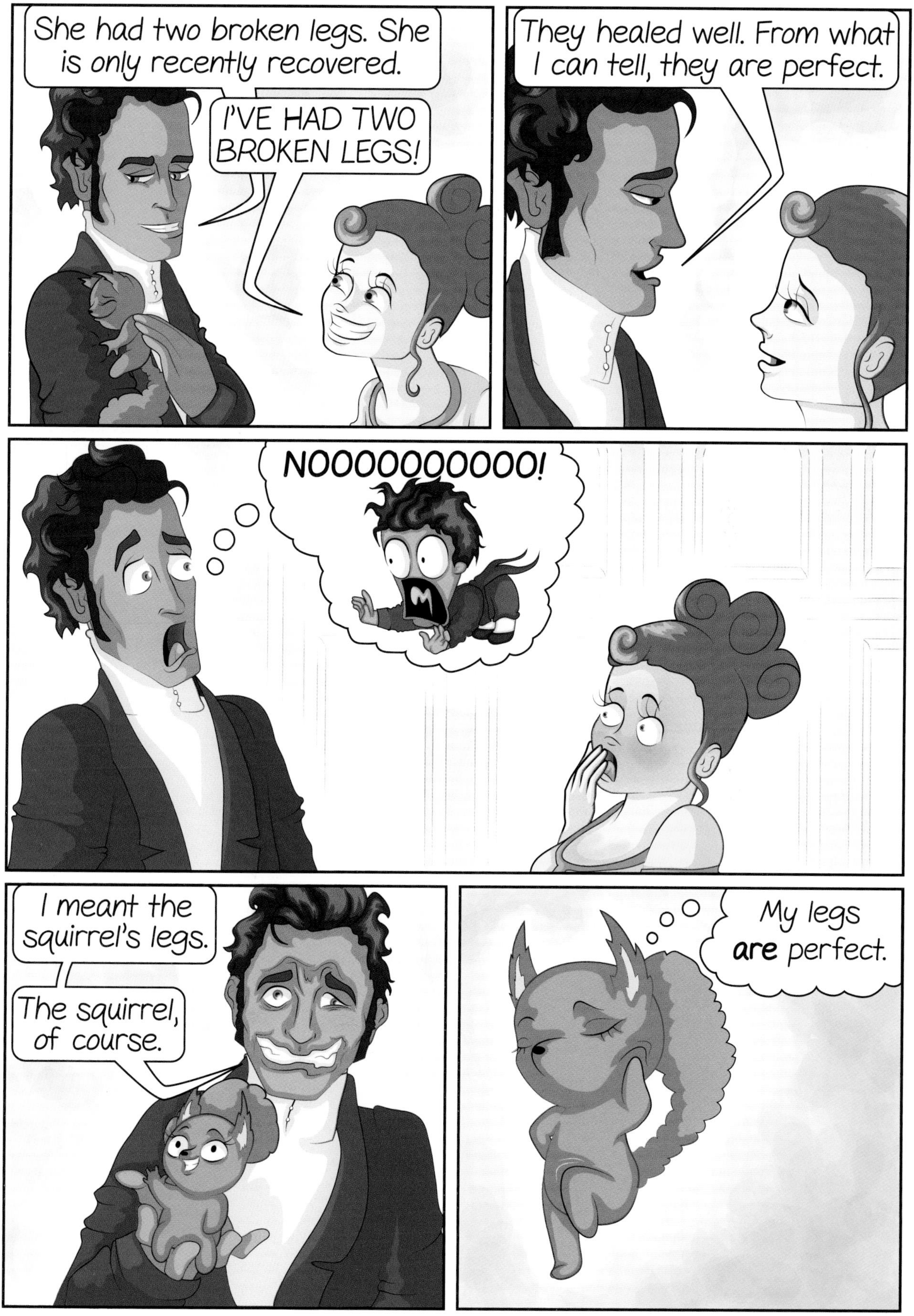
She had two broken legs. She is only recently recovered.
I'VE HAD TWO BROKEN LEGS!
They healed well. From what I can tell, they are perfect.
NOOOOOOOOOO!
I meant the squirrel's legs.
The squirrel, of course.
My legs **are** perfect.

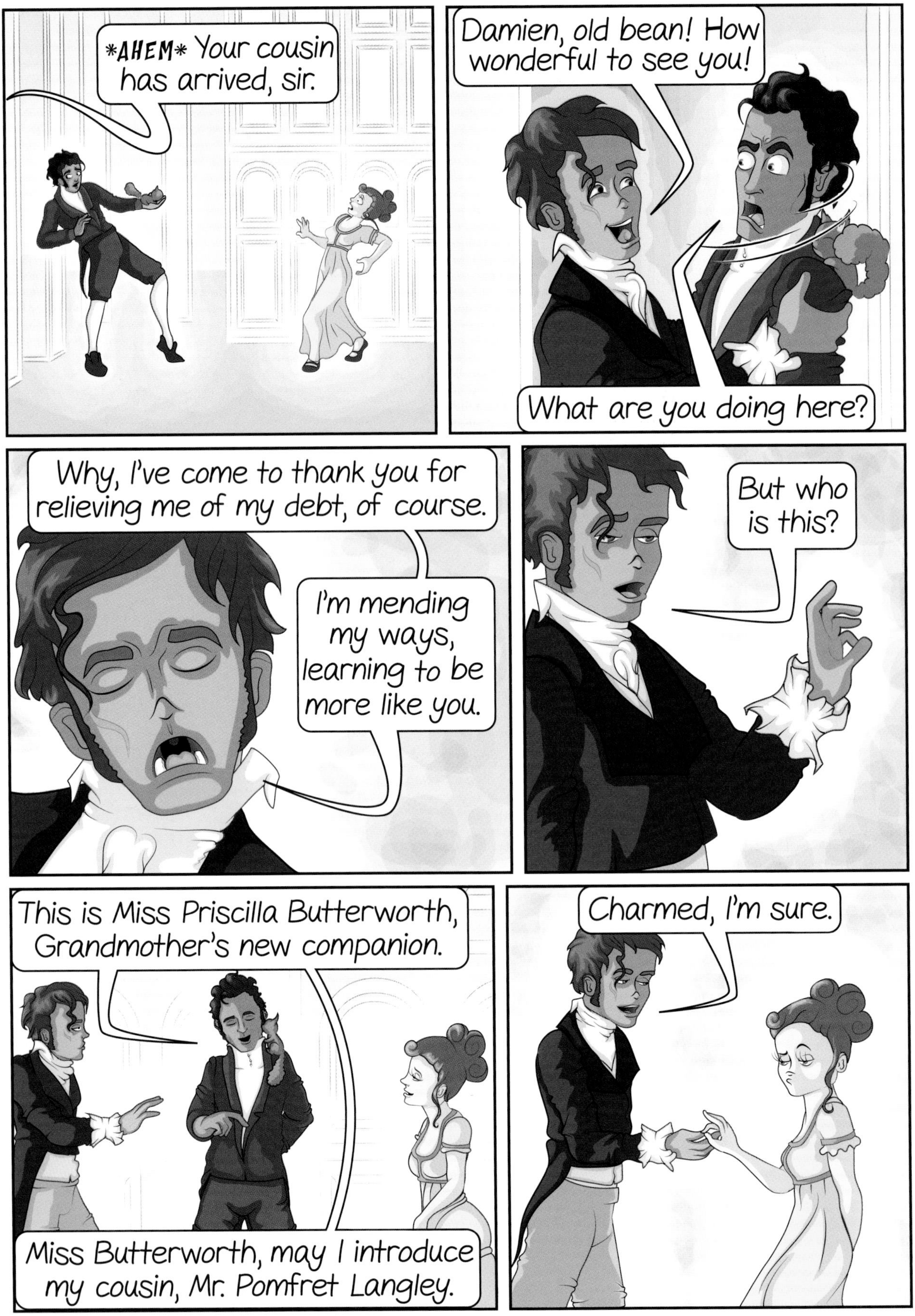
*AHEM* Your cousin has arrived, sir.
Damien, old bean! How wonderful to see you!
What are you doing here?
Why, I've come to thank you for relieving me of my debt, of course.
I'm mending my ways, learning to be more like you.
But who is this?
This is Miss Priscilla Butterworth, Grandmother's new companion.
Miss Butterworth, may I introduce my cousin, Mr. Pomfret Langley.
Charmed, I'm sure.

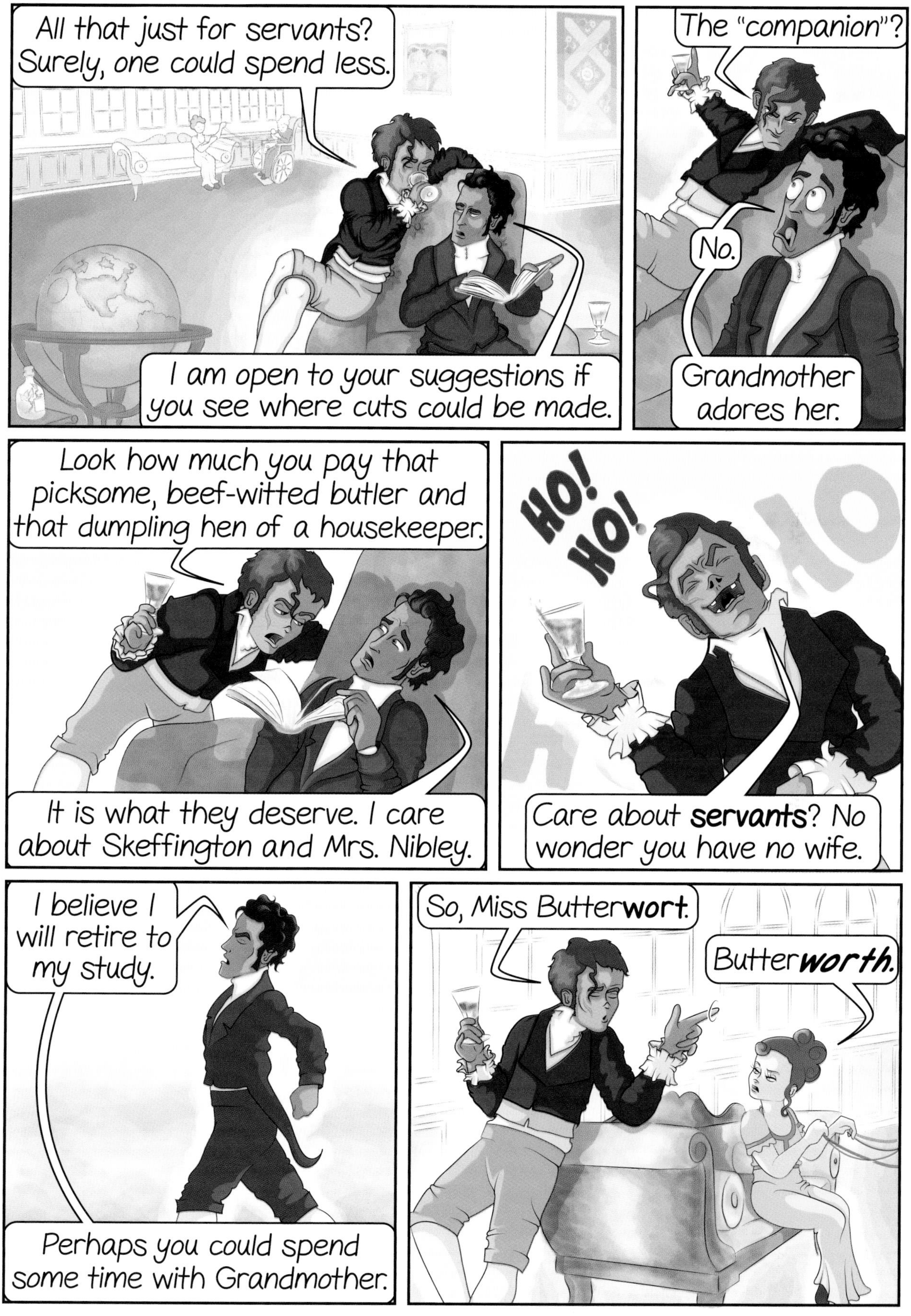
All that just for servants? Surely, one could spend less.
I am open to your suggestions if you see where cuts could be made.
The "companion"?
No.
Grandmother adores her.
Look how much you pay that picksome, beef-witted butler and that dumpling hen of a housekeeper.
It is what they deserve. I care about Skeffington and Mrs. Nibley.
HO! HO!
HO
Care about **servants**? No wonder you have no wife.
I believe I will retire to my study.
Perhaps you could spend some time with Grandmother.
So, Miss Butter**wort**.
Butter***worth***.

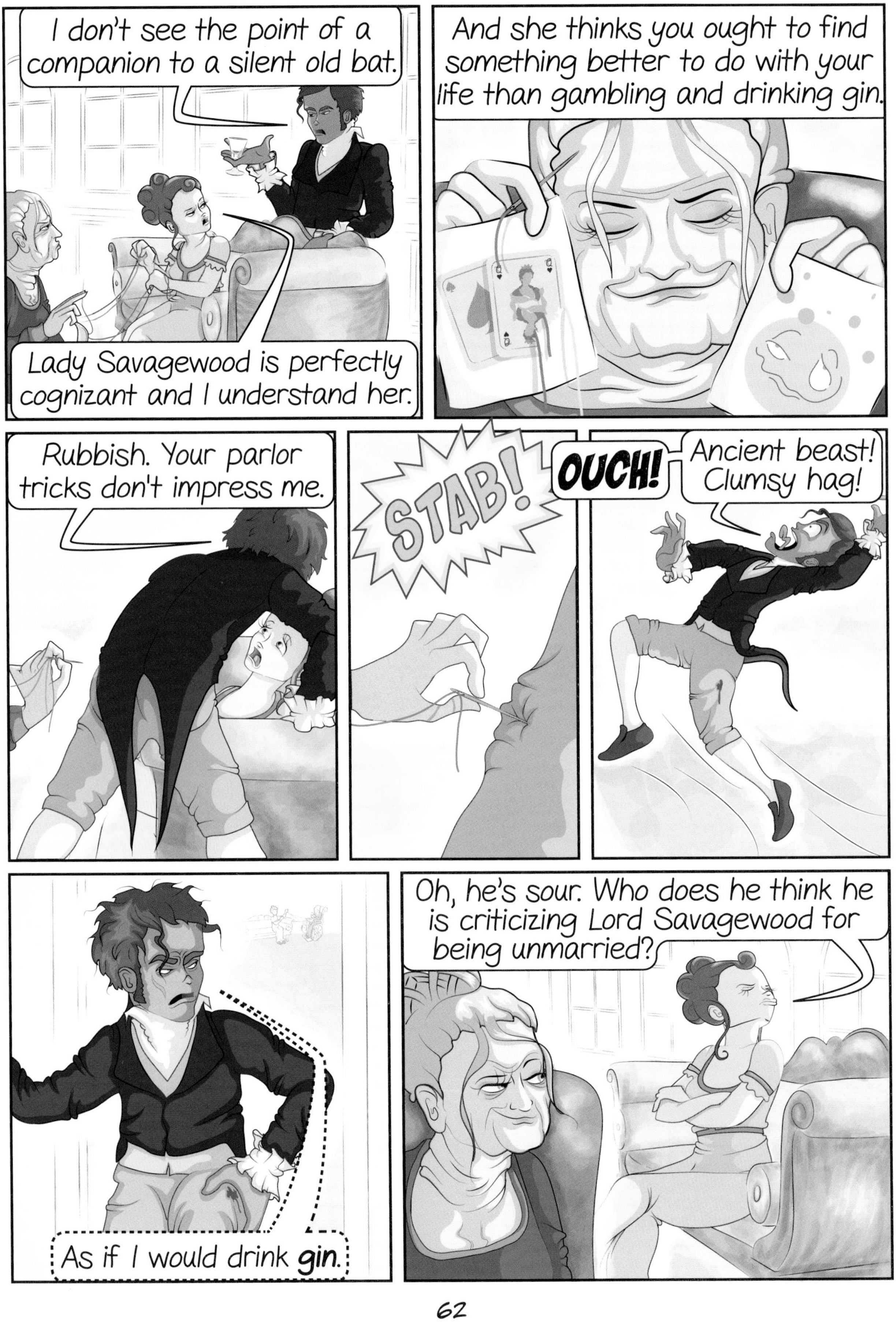
I don't see the point of a companion to a silent old bat.
Lady Savagewood is perfectly cognizant and I understand her.
And she thinks you ought to find something better to do with your life than gambling and drinking gin.
Rubbish. Your parlor tricks don't impress me.
STAB!
OUCH!
Ancient beast! Clumsy hag!
As if I would drink **gin**.
Oh, he's sour. Who does he think he is criticizing Lord Savagewood for being unmarried?

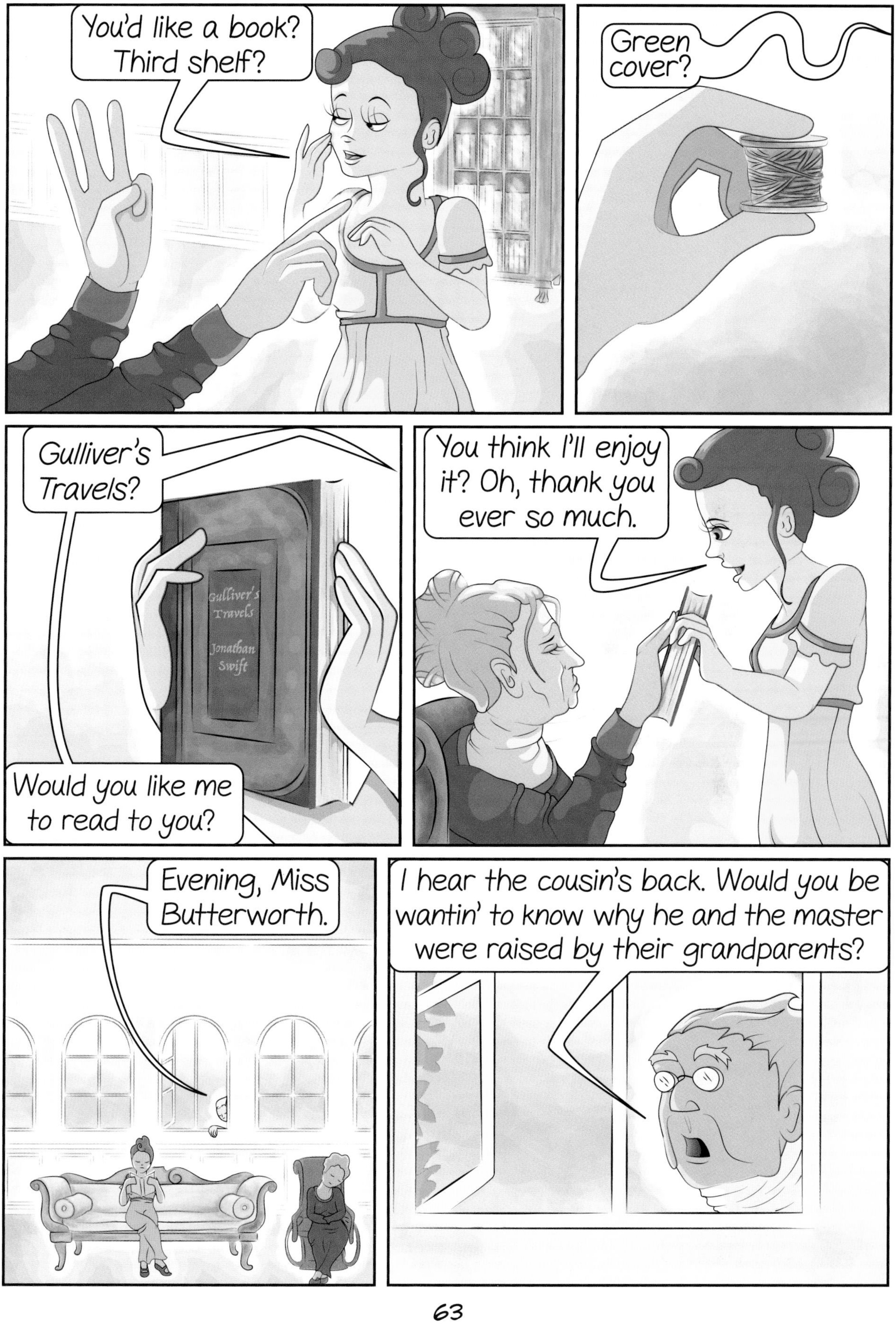
You'd like a book? Third shelf?
Green cover?
Gulliver's Travels?
Gulliver's Travels Jonathan Swift
Would you like me to read to you?
You think I'll enjoy it? Oh, thank you ever so much.
Evening, Miss Butterworth.
I hear the cousin's back. Would you be wantin' to know why he and the master were raised by their grandparents?

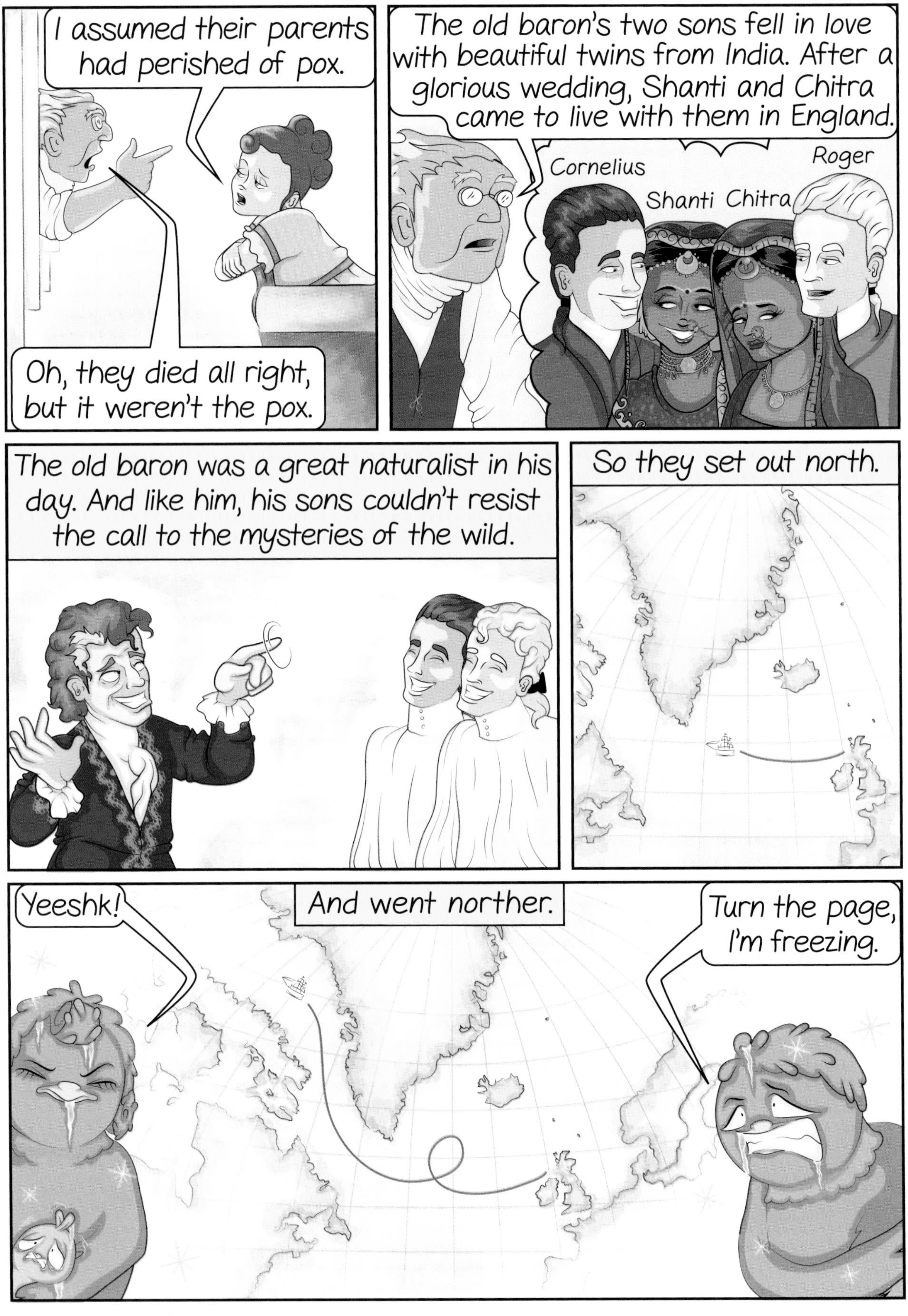
I assumed their parents had perished of pox.
Oh, they died all right, but it weren't the pox.
The old baron's two sons fell in love with beautiful twins from India. After a glorious wedding, Shanti and Chitra came to live with them in England.
Cornelius
Shanti
Chitra
Roger
The old baron was a great naturalist in his day. And like him, his sons couldn't resist the call to the mysteries of the wild.
So they set out north.
Yeeshk!
And went norther.
Turn the page, I'm freezing.

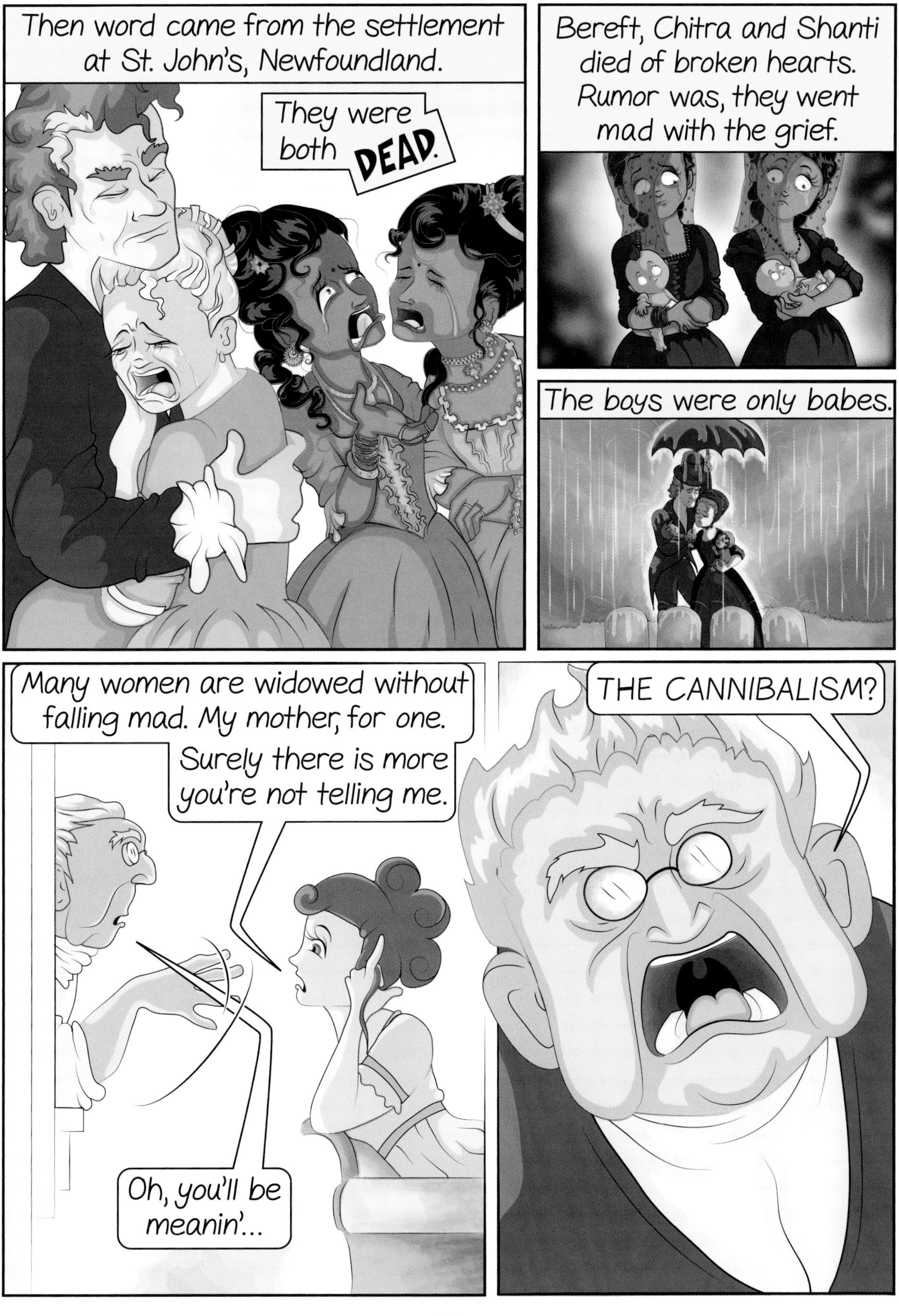
Then word came from the settlement at St. John's, Newfoundland.
They were both DEAD.
Bereft, Chitra and Shanti died of broken hearts. Rumor was, they went mad with the grief.
The boys were only babes.
Many women are widowed without falling mad. My mother, for one.
Surely there is more you're not telling me.
Oh, you'll be meanin'...
THE CANNIBALISM?

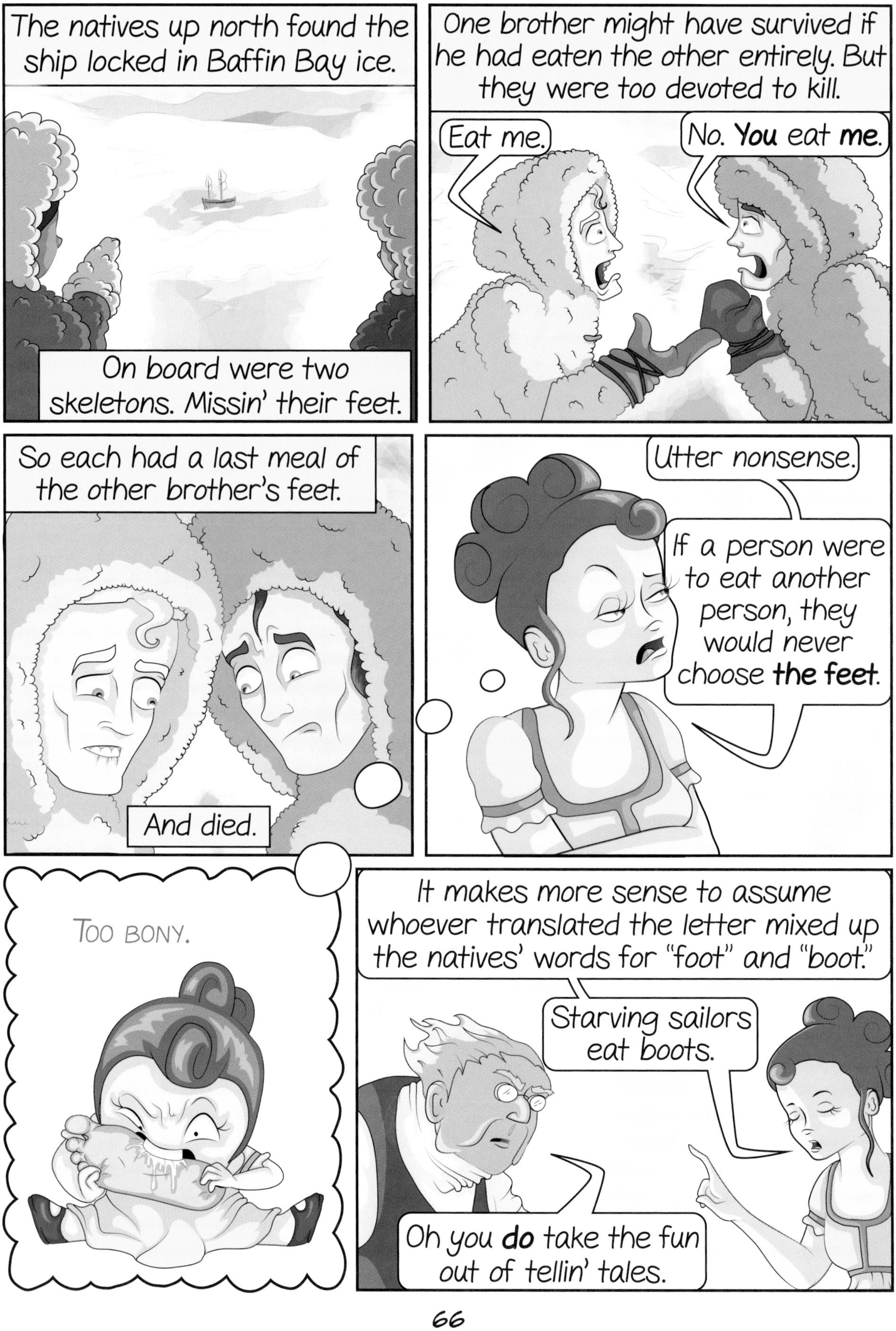
The natives up north found the ship locked in Baffin Bay ice.
On board were two skeletons. Missin' their feet.
One brother might have survived if he had eaten the other entirely. But they were too devoted to kill.
Eat me.
No. **You** eat **me**.
So each had a last meal of the other brother's feet.
And died.
Utter nonsense.
If a person were to eat another person, they would never choose **the feet**.
TOO BONY.
It makes more sense to assume whoever translated the letter mixed up the natives' words for "foot" and "boot."
Starving sailors eat boots.
Oh you **do** take the fun out of tellin' tales.

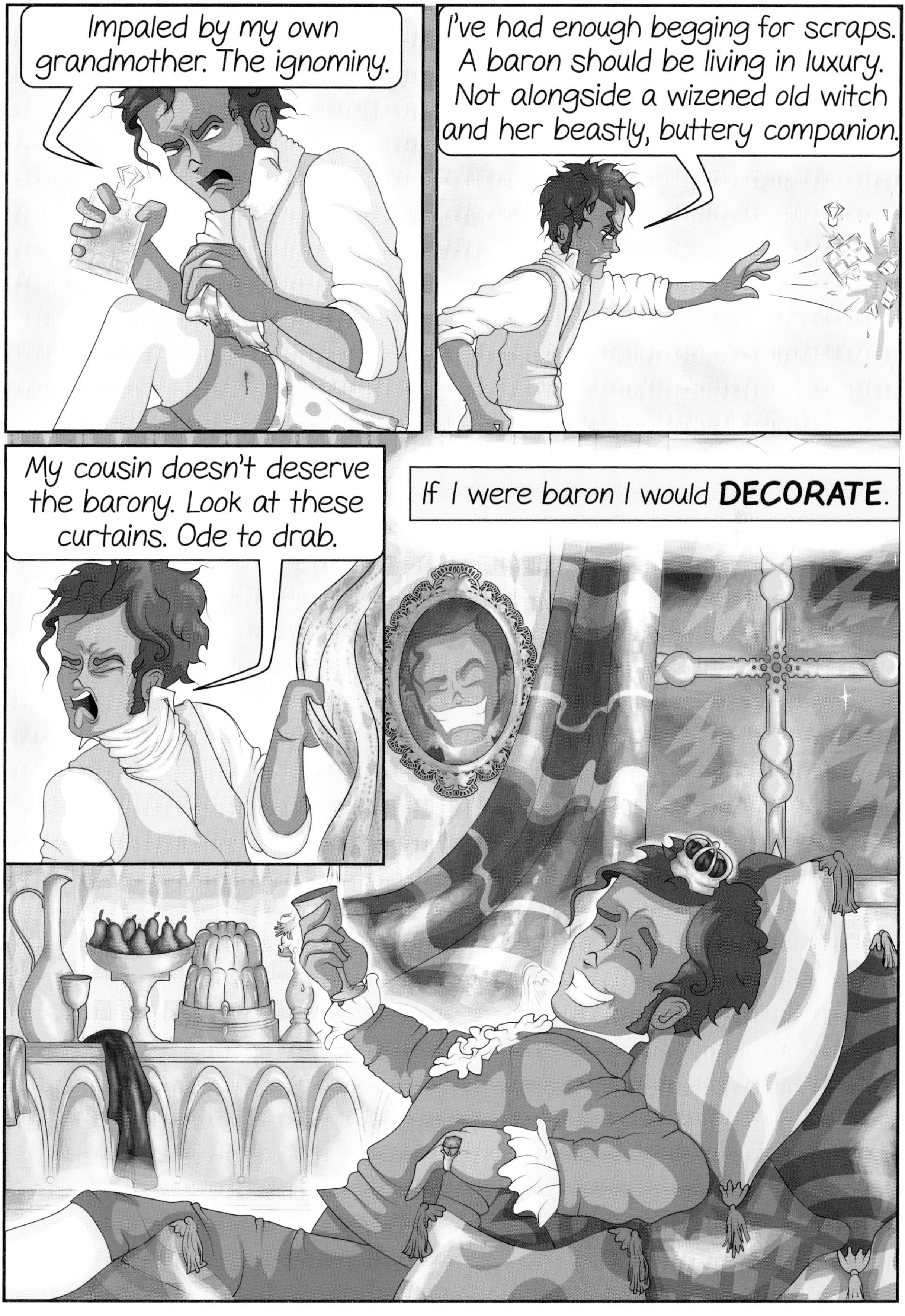
Impaled by my own grandmother. The ignominy.
I've had enough begging for scraps. A baron should be living in luxury. Not alongside a wizened old witch and her beastly, buttery companion.
My cousin doesn't deserve the barony. Look at these curtains. Ode to drab.
If I were baron I would **DECORATE**.

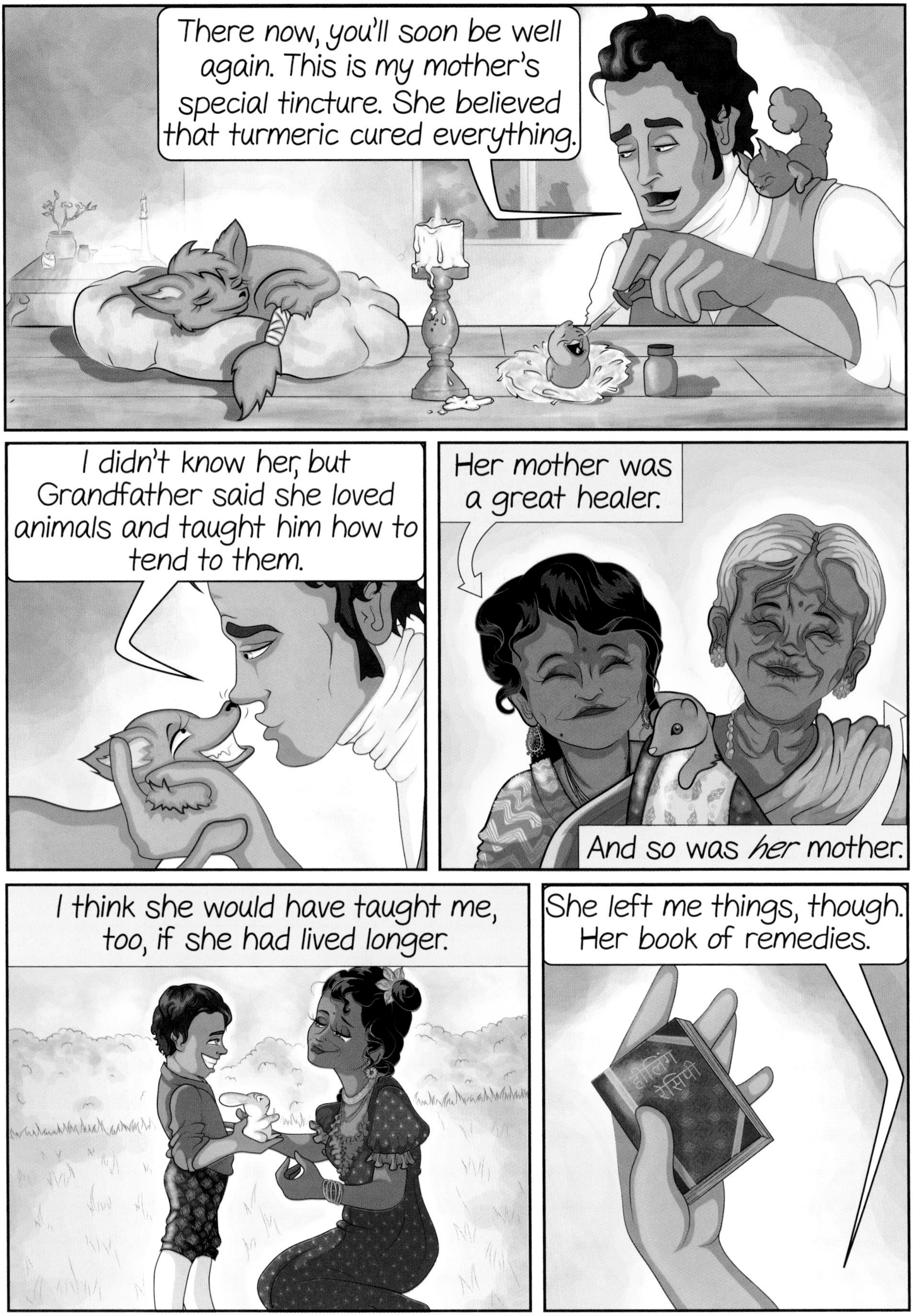
There now, you'll soon be well again. This is my mother's special tincture. She believed that turmeric cured everything.
I didn't know her, but Grandfather said she loved animals and taught him how to tend to them.
Her mother was a great healer.
And so was *her* mother.
I think she would have taught me, too, if she had lived longer.
She left me things, though. Her book of remedies.

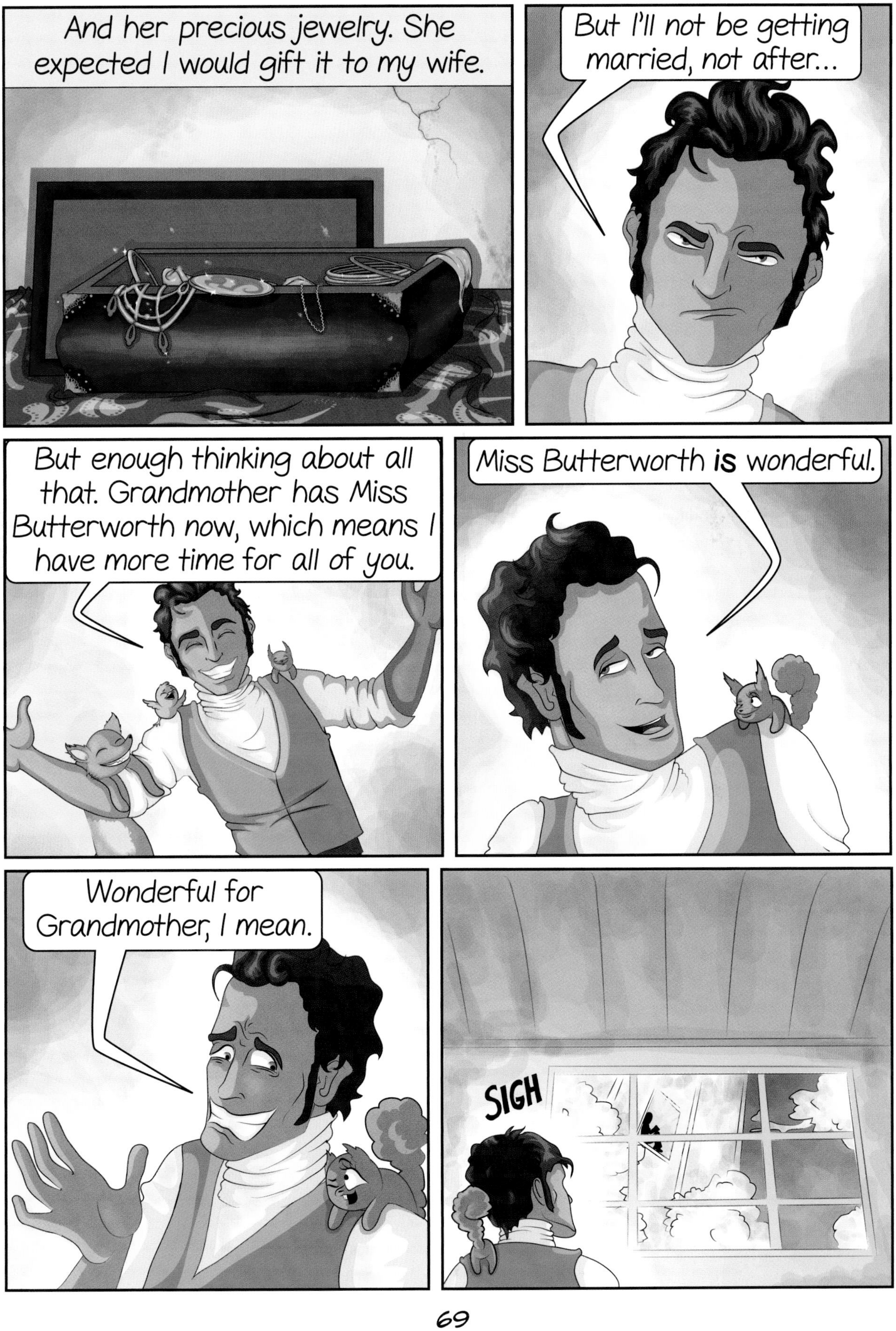
And her precious jewelry. She expected I would gift it to my wife.
But I'll not be getting married, not after...
But enough thinking about all that. Grandmother has Miss Butterworth now, which means I have more time for all of you.
Miss Butterworth **is** wonderful.
Wonderful for Grandmother, I mean.
SIGH

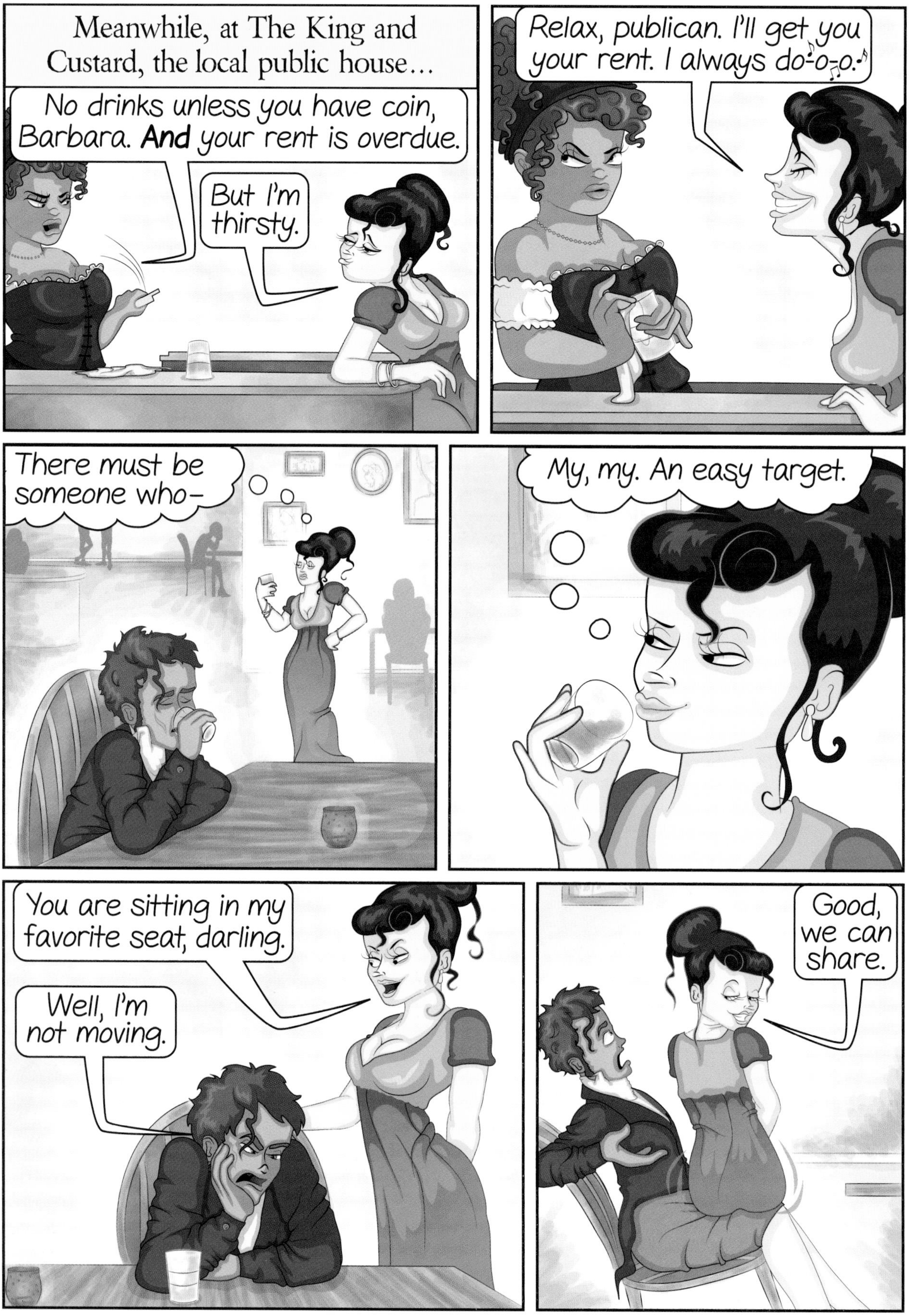

Meanwhile, at The King and Custard, the local public house...
No drinks unless you have coin, Barbara. **And** your rent is overdue.
But I'm thirsty.
Relax, publican. I'll get you your rent. I always do-o-o.
There must be someone who–
My, my. An easy target.
You are sitting in my favorite seat, darling.
Well, I'm not moving.
Good, we can share.

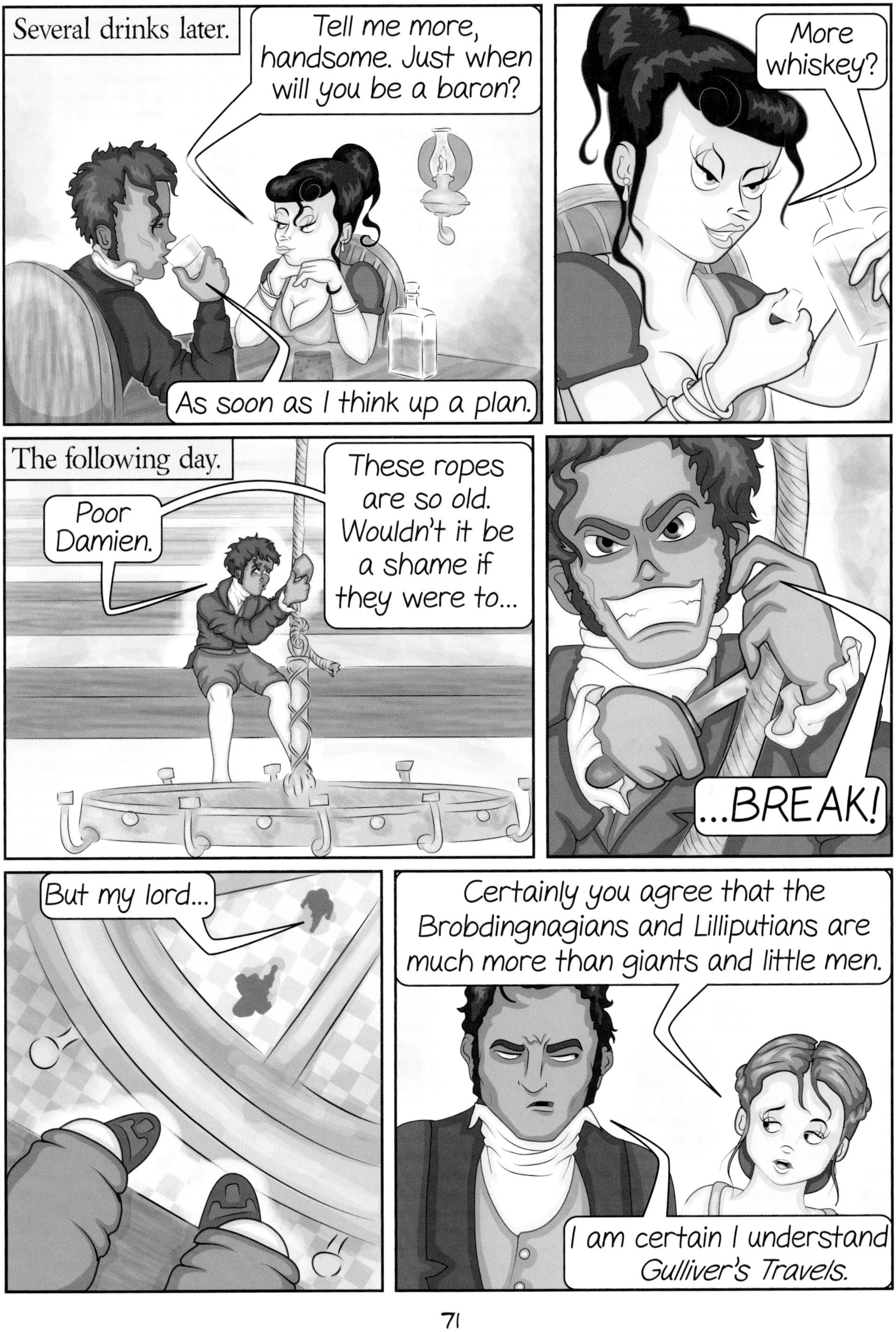
Several drinks later.
Tell me more, handsome. Just when will you be a baron?
As soon as I think up a plan.
More whiskey?
The following day.
Poor Damien.
These ropes are so old. Wouldn't it be a shame if they were to...
...BREAK!
But my lord...
Certainly you agree that the Brobdingnagians and Lilliputians are much more than giants and little men.
I am certain I understand *Gulliver's Travels.*

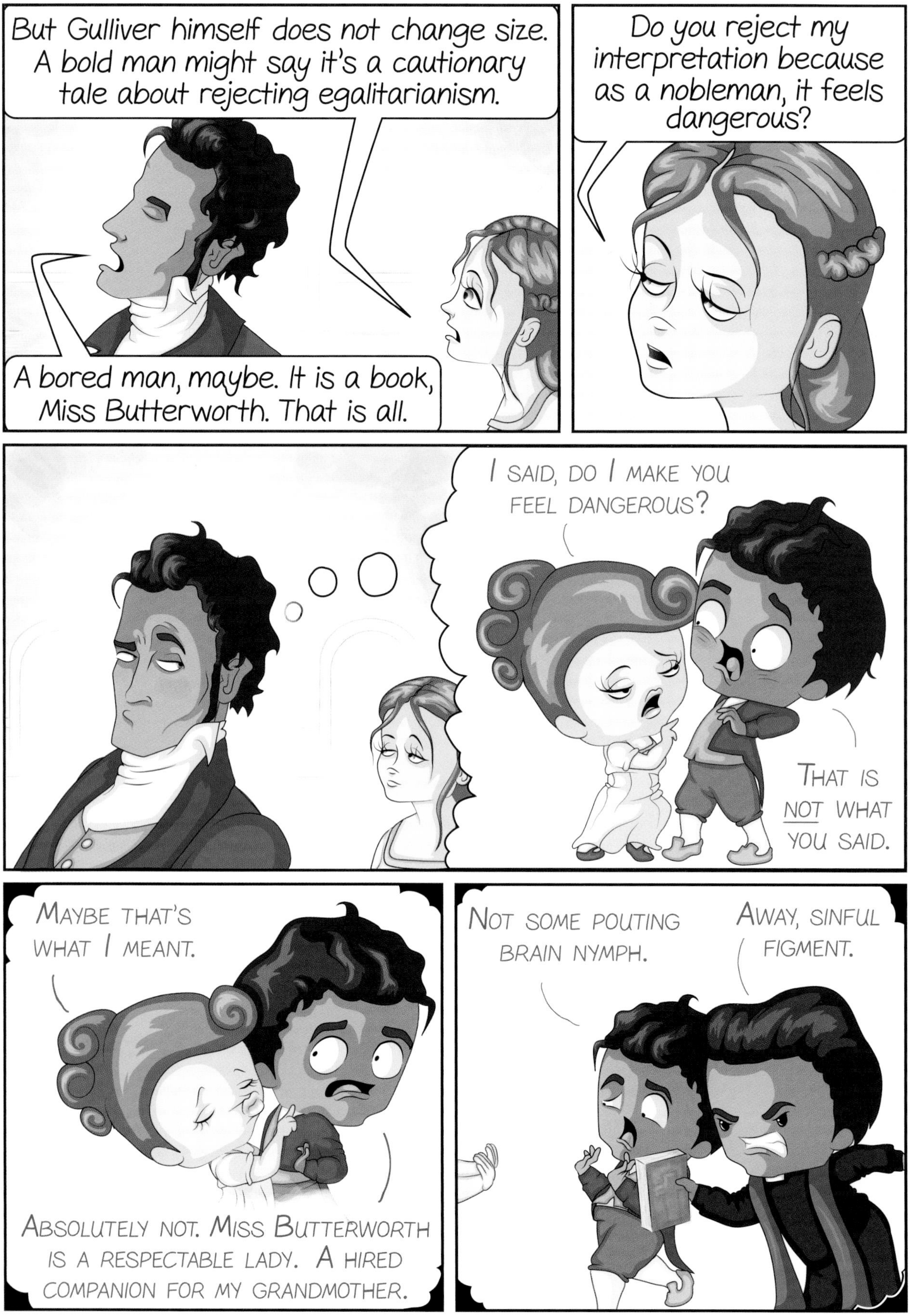

But Gulliver himself does not change size. A bold man might say it's a cautionary tale about rejecting egalitarianism.
A bored man, maybe. It is a book, Miss Butterworth. That is all.
Do you reject my interpretation because as a nobleman, it feels dangerous?
I SAID, DO I MAKE YOU FEEL DANGEROUS?
THAT IS NOT WHAT YOU SAID.
MAYBE THAT'S WHAT I MEANT.
ABSOLUTELY NOT. MISS BUTTERWORTH IS A RESPECTABLE LADY. A HIRED COMPANION FOR MY GRANDMOTHER.
NOT SOME POUTING BRAIN NYMPH.
AWAY, SINFUL FIGMENT.

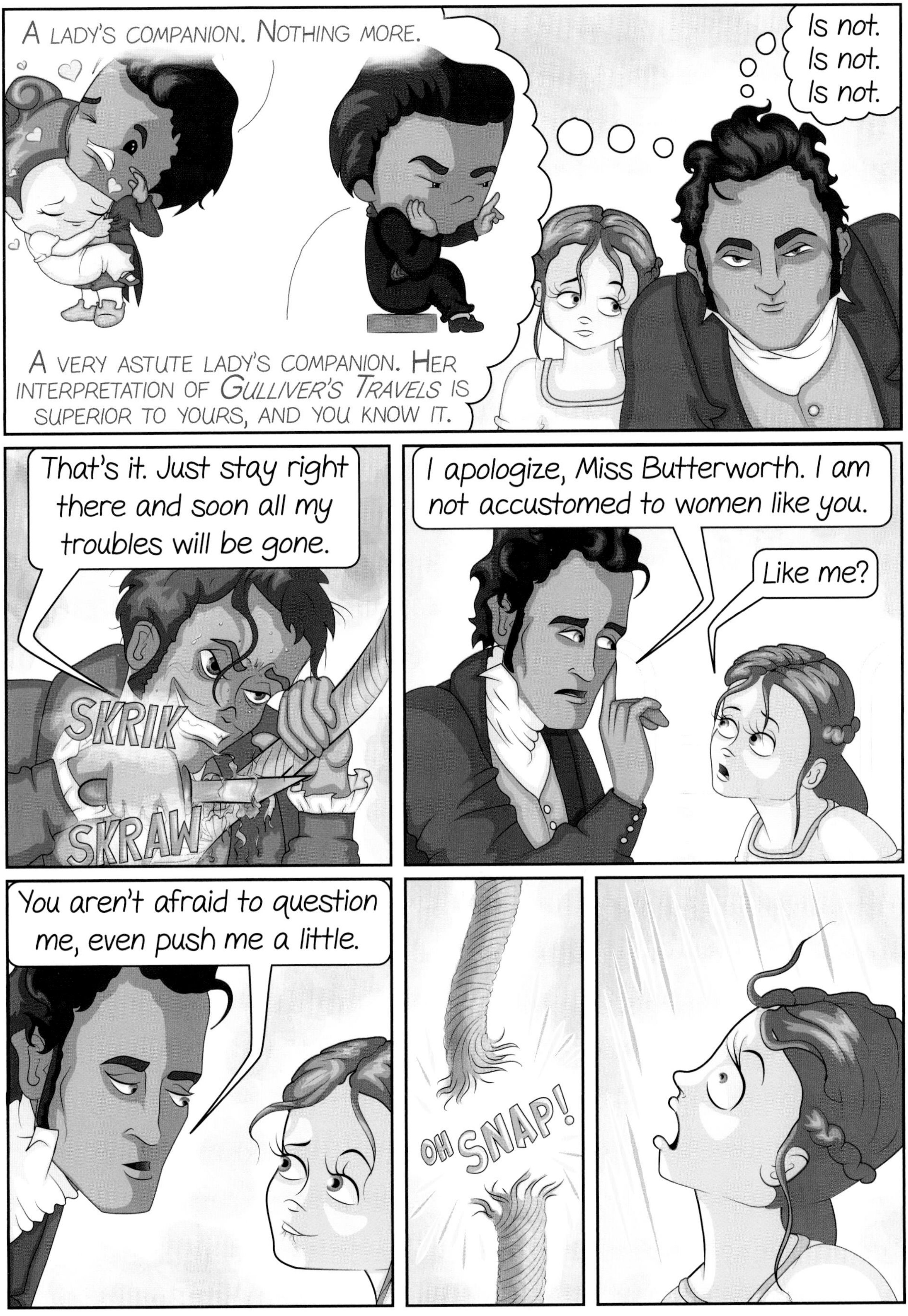

A LADY'S COMPANION. NOTHING MORE.
A VERY ASTUTE LADY'S COMPANION. HER INTERPRETATION OF GULLIVER'S TRAVELS IS SUPERIOR TO YOURS, AND YOU KNOW IT.
Is not. Is not. Is not.
That's it. Just stay right there and soon all my troubles will be gone.
SKRIK
SKRAW
I apologize, Miss Butterworth. I am not accustomed to women like you.
Like me?
You aren't afraid to question me, even push me a little.
OH SNAP!

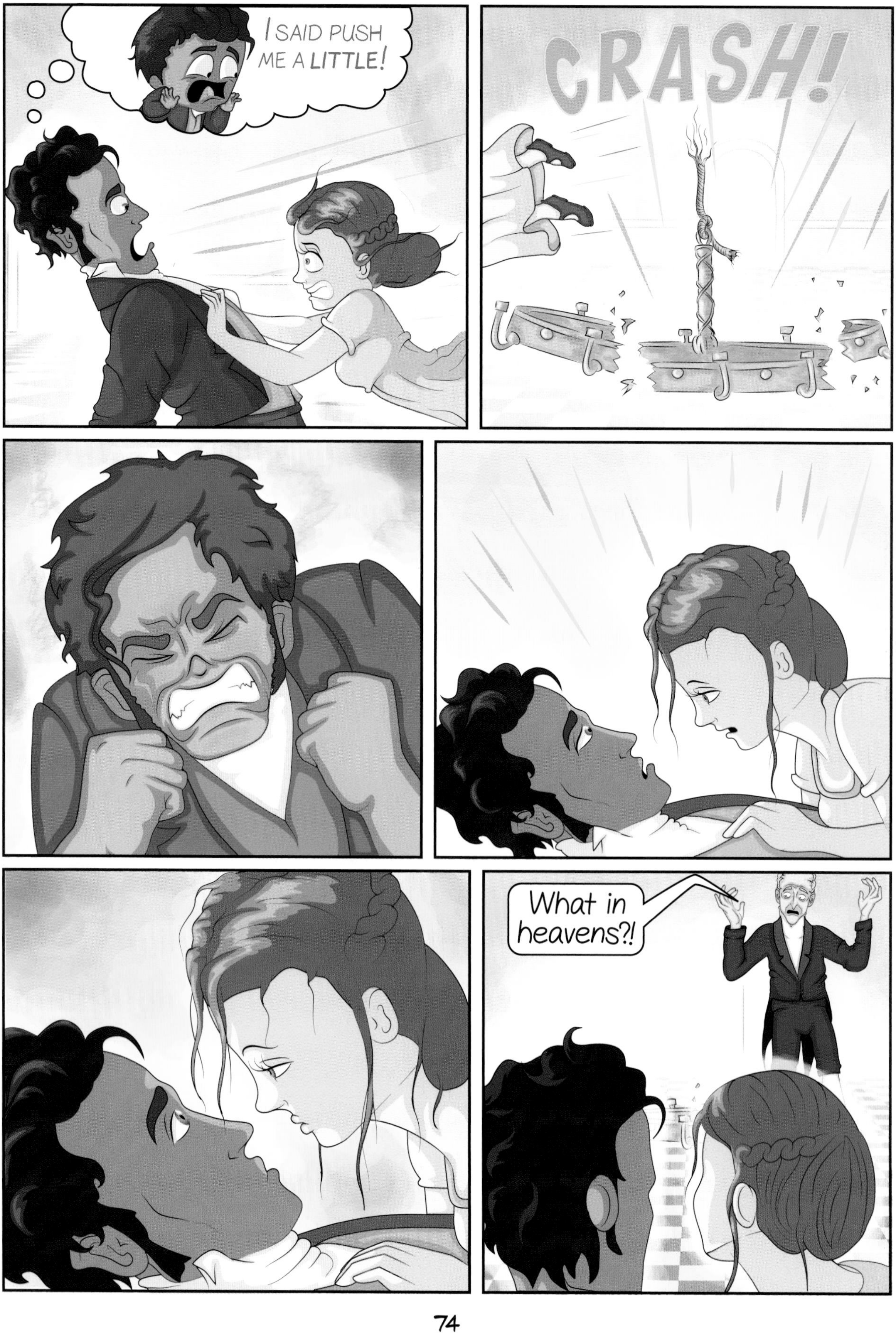
I SAID PUSH ME A **LITTLE**!
CRASH!
What in heavens?!

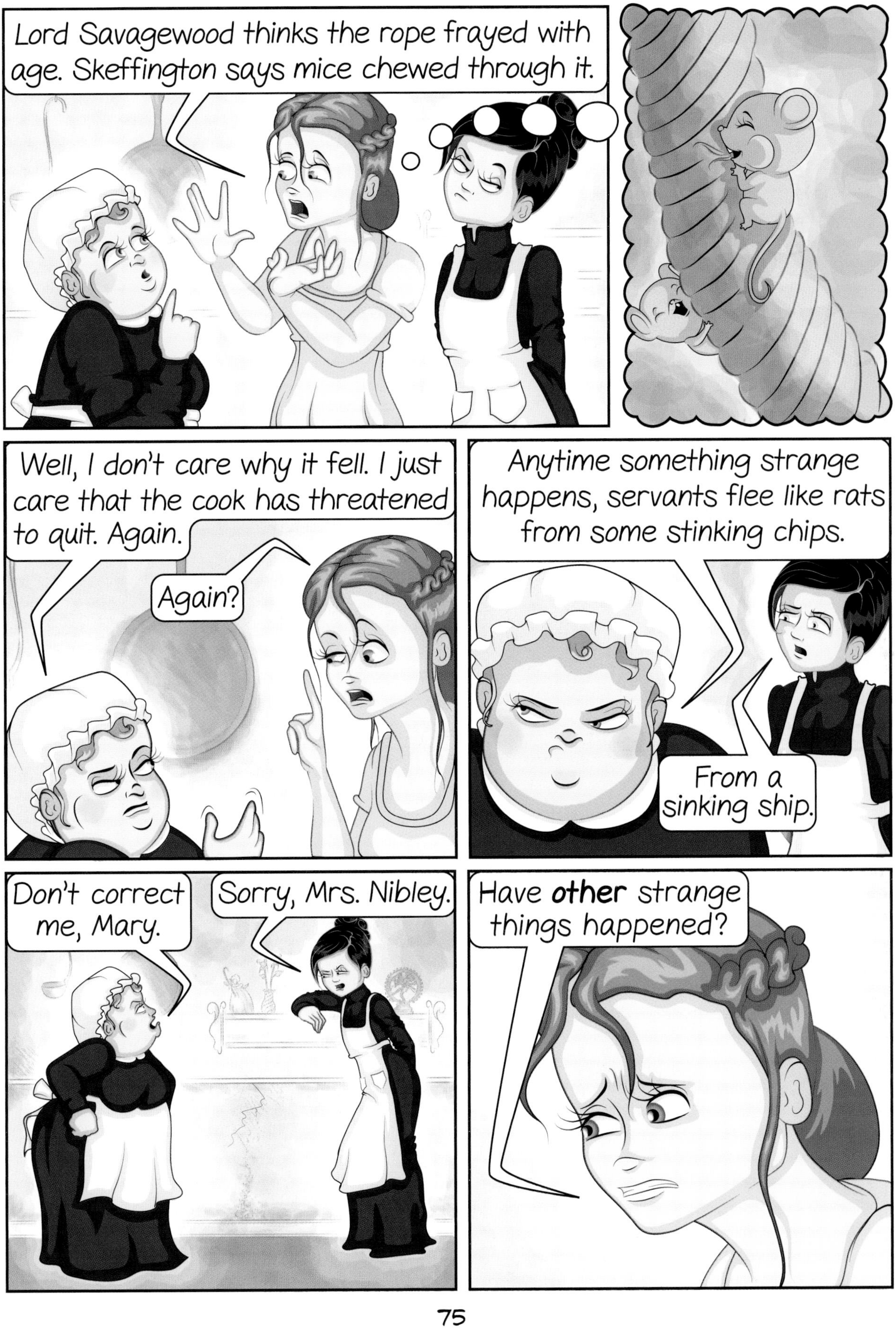
Lord Savagewood thinks the rope frayed with age. Skeffington says mice chewed through it.
Well, I don't care why it fell. I just care that the cook has threatened to quit. Again.
Again?
Anytime something strange happens, servants flee like rats from some stinking chips.
From a sinking ship.
Don't correct me, Mary.
Sorry, Mrs. Nibley.
Have **other** strange things happened?

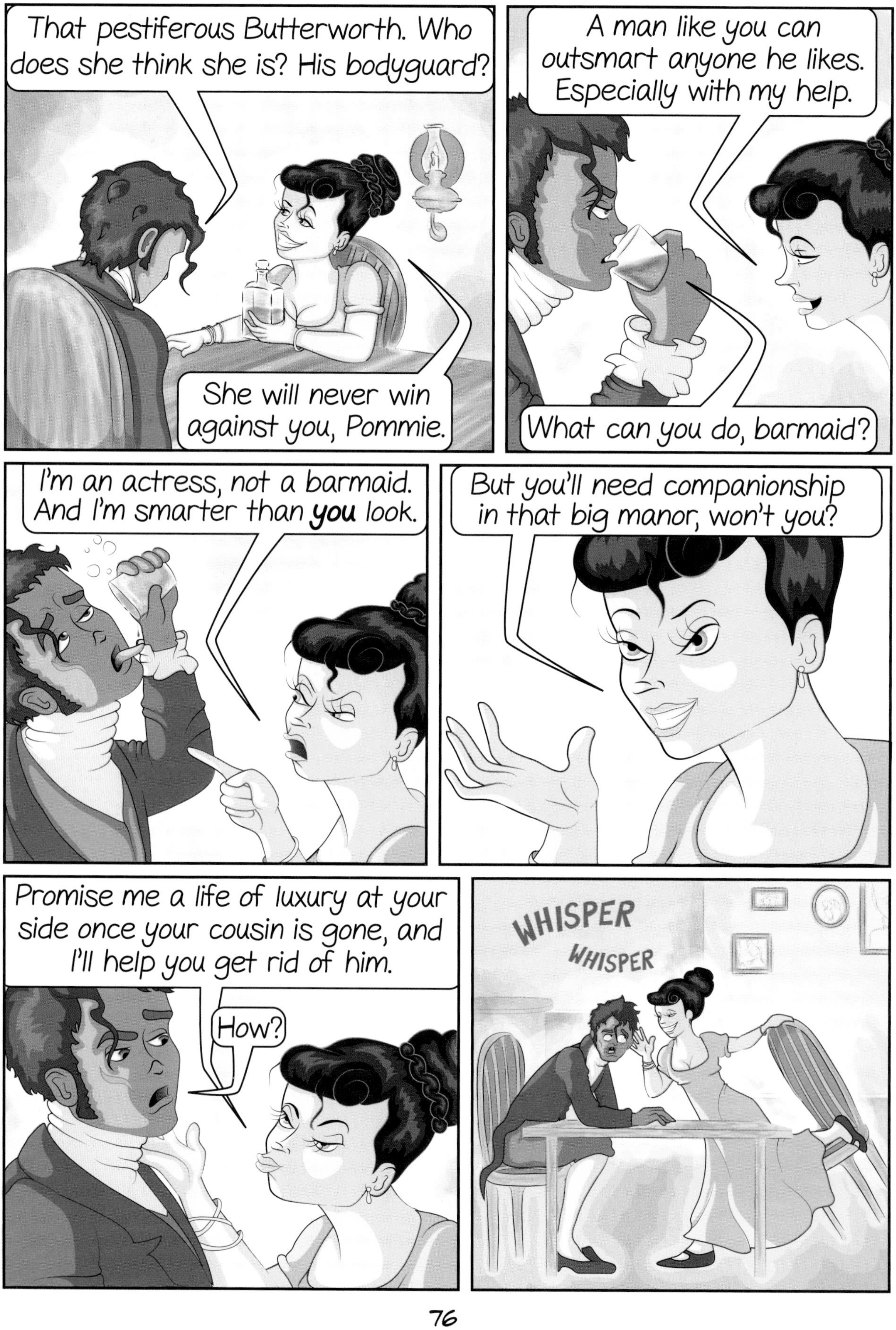
That pestiferous Butterworth. Who does she think she is? His bodyguard?
She will never win against you, Pommie.
A man like you can outsmart anyone he likes. Especially with my help.
What can you do, barmaid?
I'm an actress, not a barmaid. And I'm smarter than **you** look.
But you'll need companionship in that big manor, won't you?
Promise me a life of luxury at your side once your cousin is gone, and I'll help you get rid of him.
How?
WHISPER
WHISPER

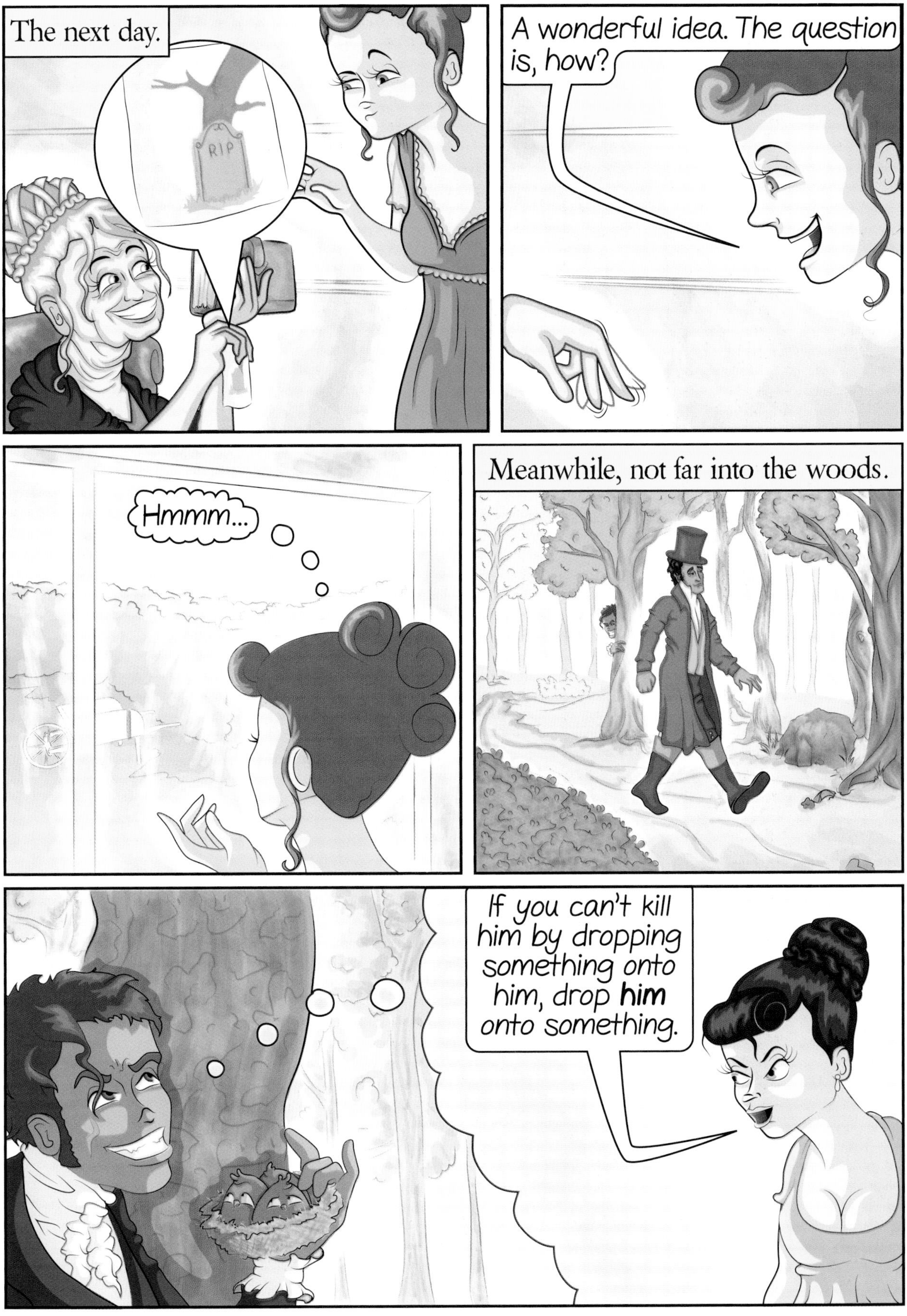

The next day.
RIP
A wonderful idea. The question is, how?
Hmmm...
Meanwhile, not far into the woods.
If you can't kill him by dropping something onto him, drop **him** onto something.

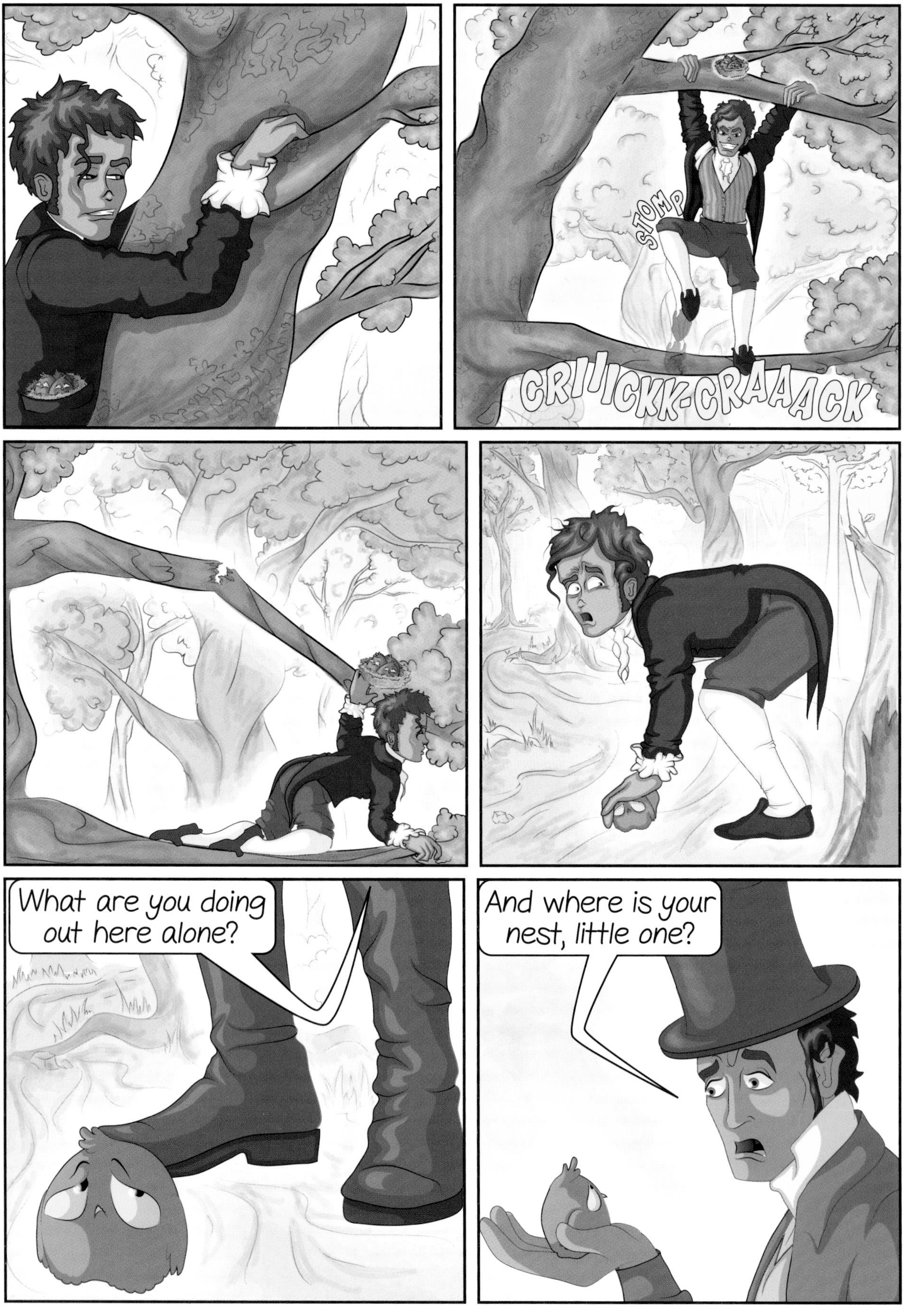
STOMP
CRIIICKK-CRAAACK
What are you doing out here alone?
And where is your nest, little one?

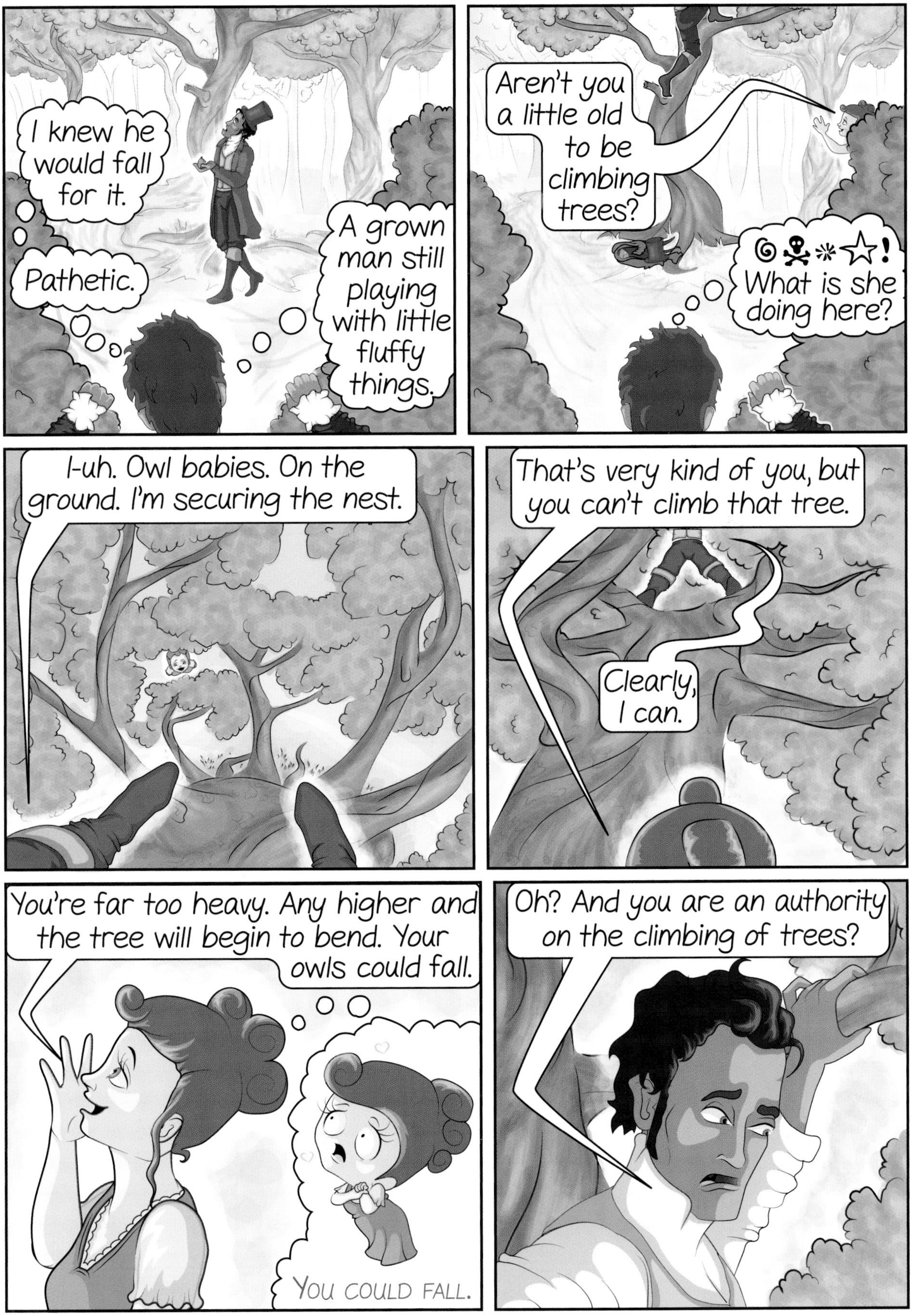
I knew he would fall for it.
Pathetic.
A grown man still playing with little fluffy things.
Aren't you a little old to be climbing trees?
@☠*☆! What is she doing here?
I-uh. Owl babies. On the ground. I'm securing the nest.
That's very kind of you, but you can't climb that tree.
Clearly, I can.
You're far too heavy. Any higher and the tree will begin to bend. Your owls could fall.
YOU COULD FALL.
Oh? And you are an authority on the climbing of trees?

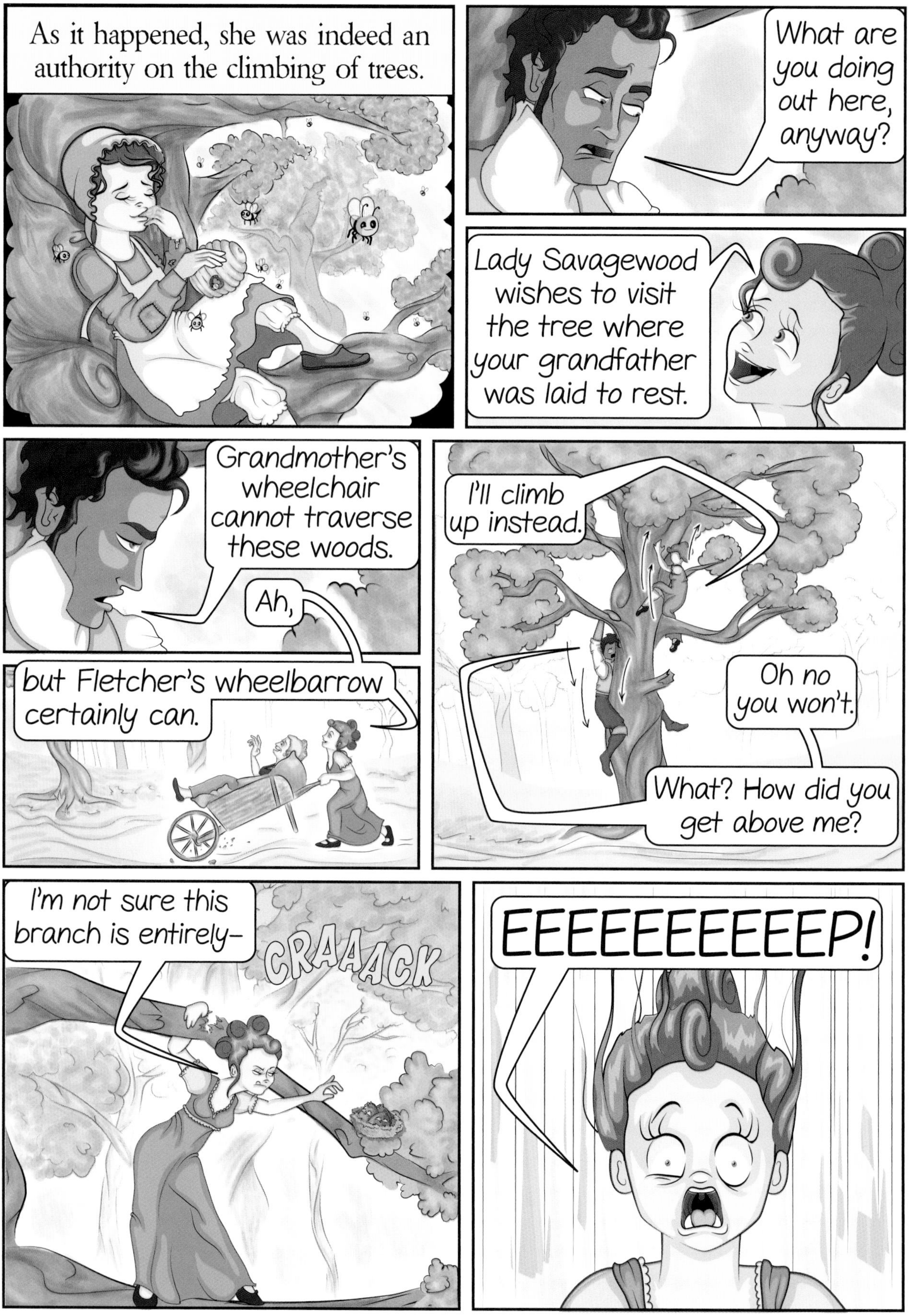

As it happened, she was indeed an authority on the climbing of trees.
What are you doing out here, anyway?
Lady Savagewood wishes to visit the tree where your grandfather was laid to rest.
Grandmother's wheelchair cannot traverse these woods.
Ah,
but Fletcher's wheelbarrow certainly can.
I'll climb up instead.
Oh no you won't.
What? How did you get above me?
I'm not sure this branch is entirely–
CRAAACK
EEEEEEEEEEEP!

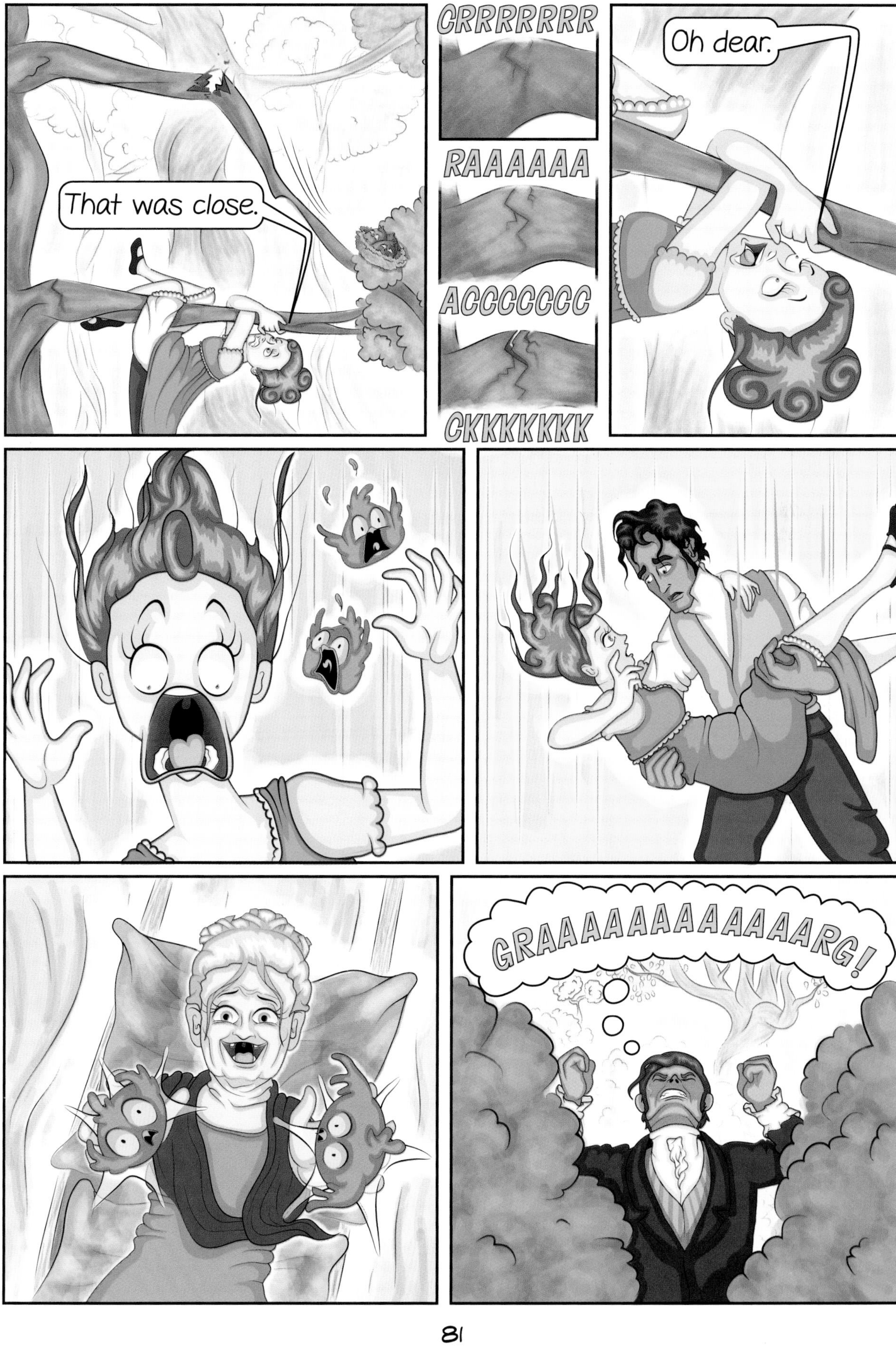
That was close.
CRRRRRRR
RAAAAAA
ACCCCCCC
CKKKKKK
Oh dear.
GRAAAAAAAAAAAARG!

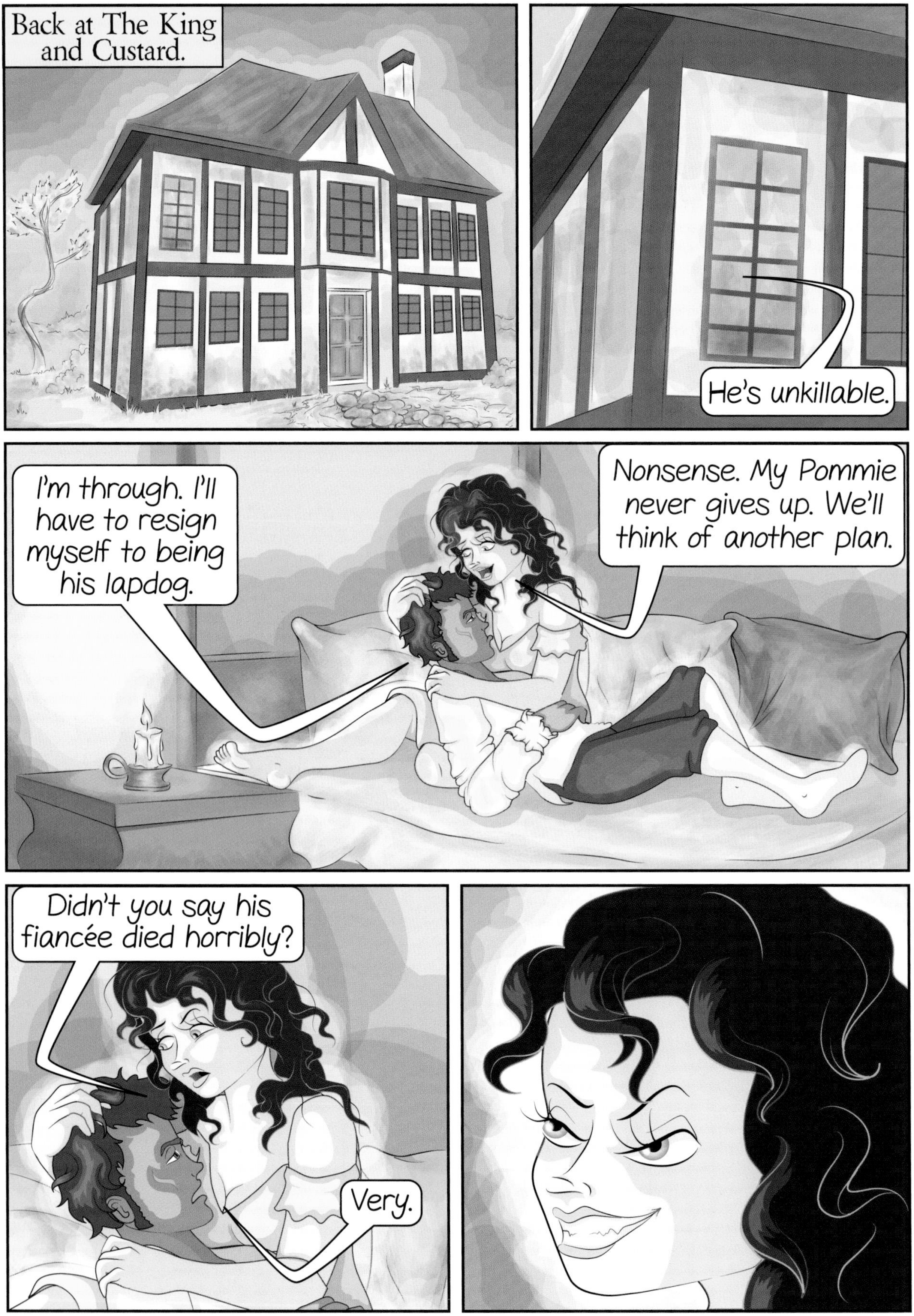
Back at The King and Custard.
He's unkillable.
I'm through. I'll have to resign myself to being his lapdog.
Nonsense. My Pommie never gives up. We'll think of another plan.
Didn't you say his fiancée died horribly?
Very.

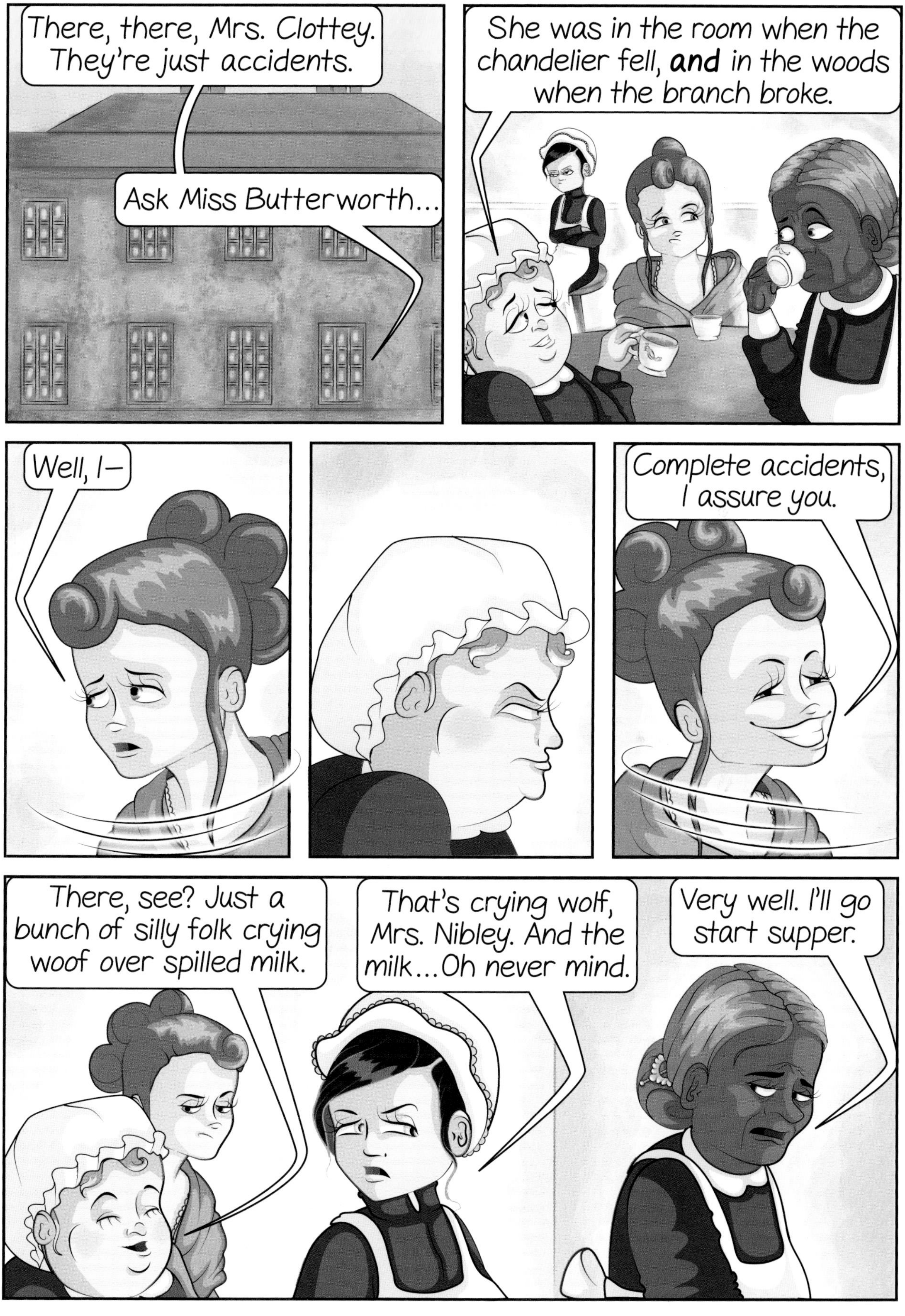

There, there, Mrs. Clottey. They're just accidents.
Ask Miss Butterworth...
She was in the room when the chandelier fell, **and** in the woods when the branch broke.
Well, I–
Complete accidents, I assure you.
There, see? Just a bunch of silly folk crying woof over spilled milk.
That's crying wolf, Mrs. Nibley. And the milk...Oh never mind.
Very well. I'll go start supper.

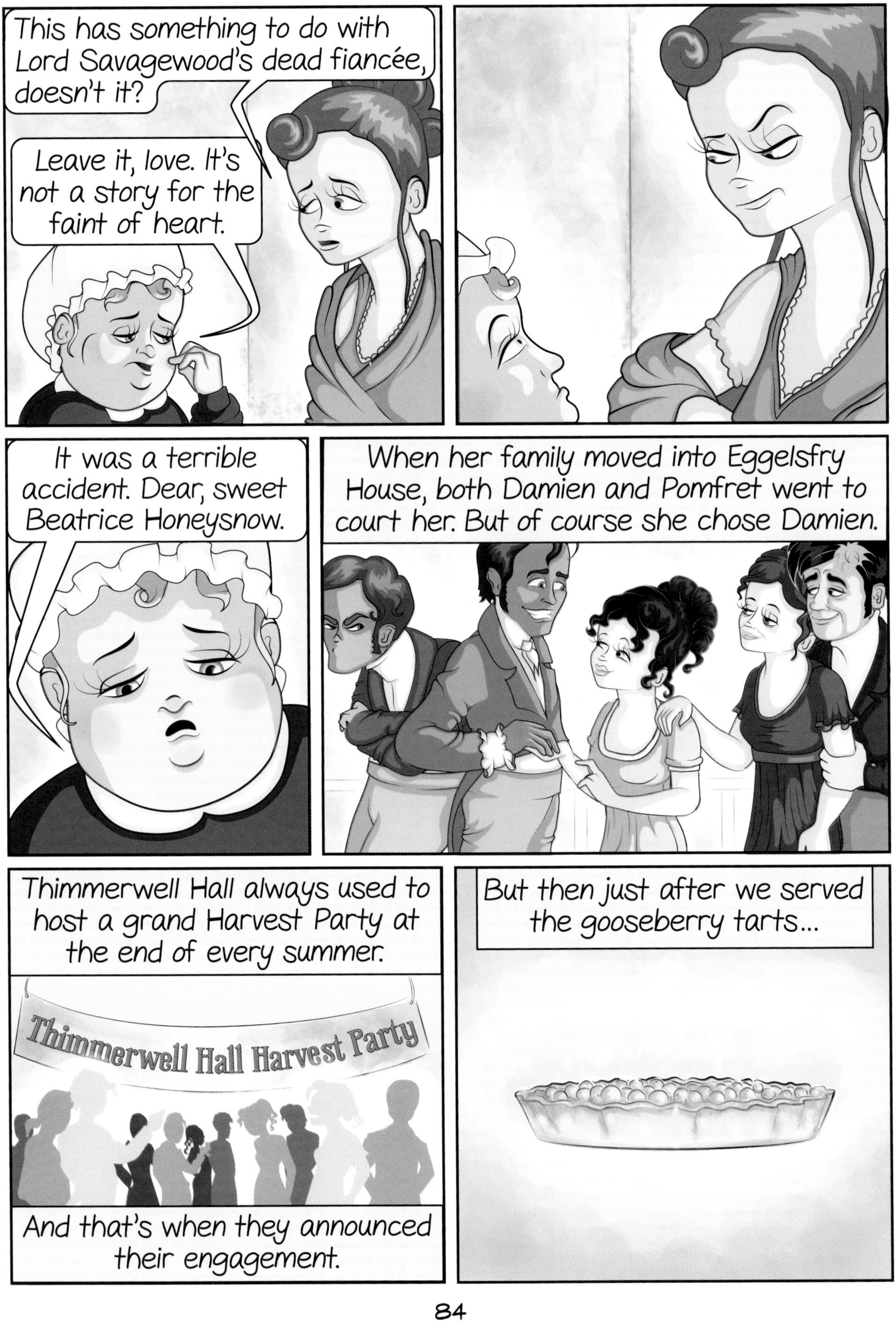
This has something to do with Lord Savagewood's dead fiancée, doesn't it?
Leave it, love. It's not a story for the faint of heart.
It was a terrible accident. Dear, sweet Beatrice Honeysnow.
When her family moved into Eggelsfry House, both Damien and Pomfret went to court her. But of course she chose Damien.
Thimmerwell Hall always used to host a grand Harvest Party at the end of every summer.
Thimmerwell Hall Harvest Party
And that's when they announced their engagement.
But then just after we served the gooseberry tarts...

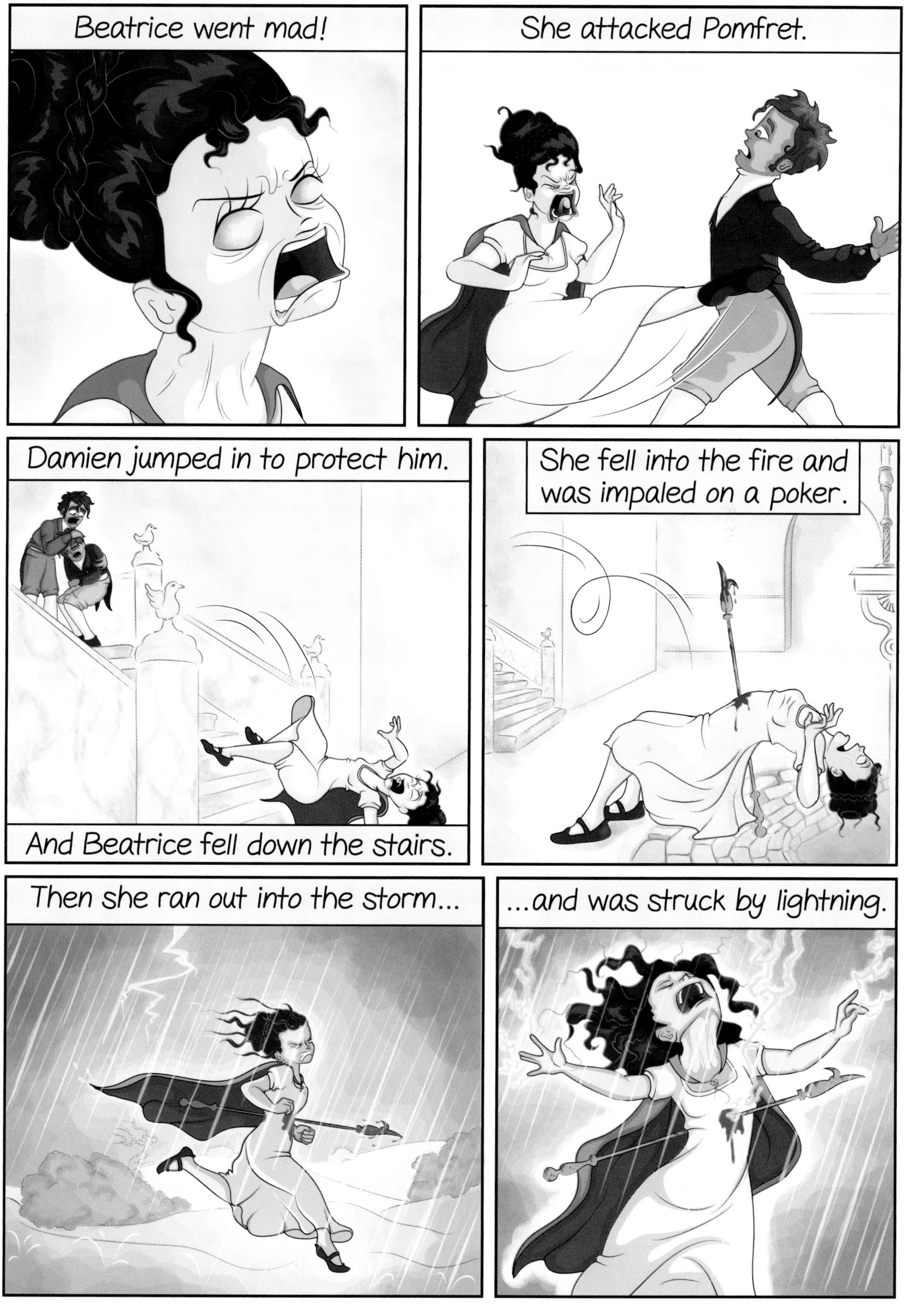
Beatrice went mad!
She attacked Pomfret.
Damien jumped in to protect him.
And Beatrice fell down the stairs.
She fell into the fire and was impaled on a poker.
Then she ran out into the storm...
...and was struck by lightning.

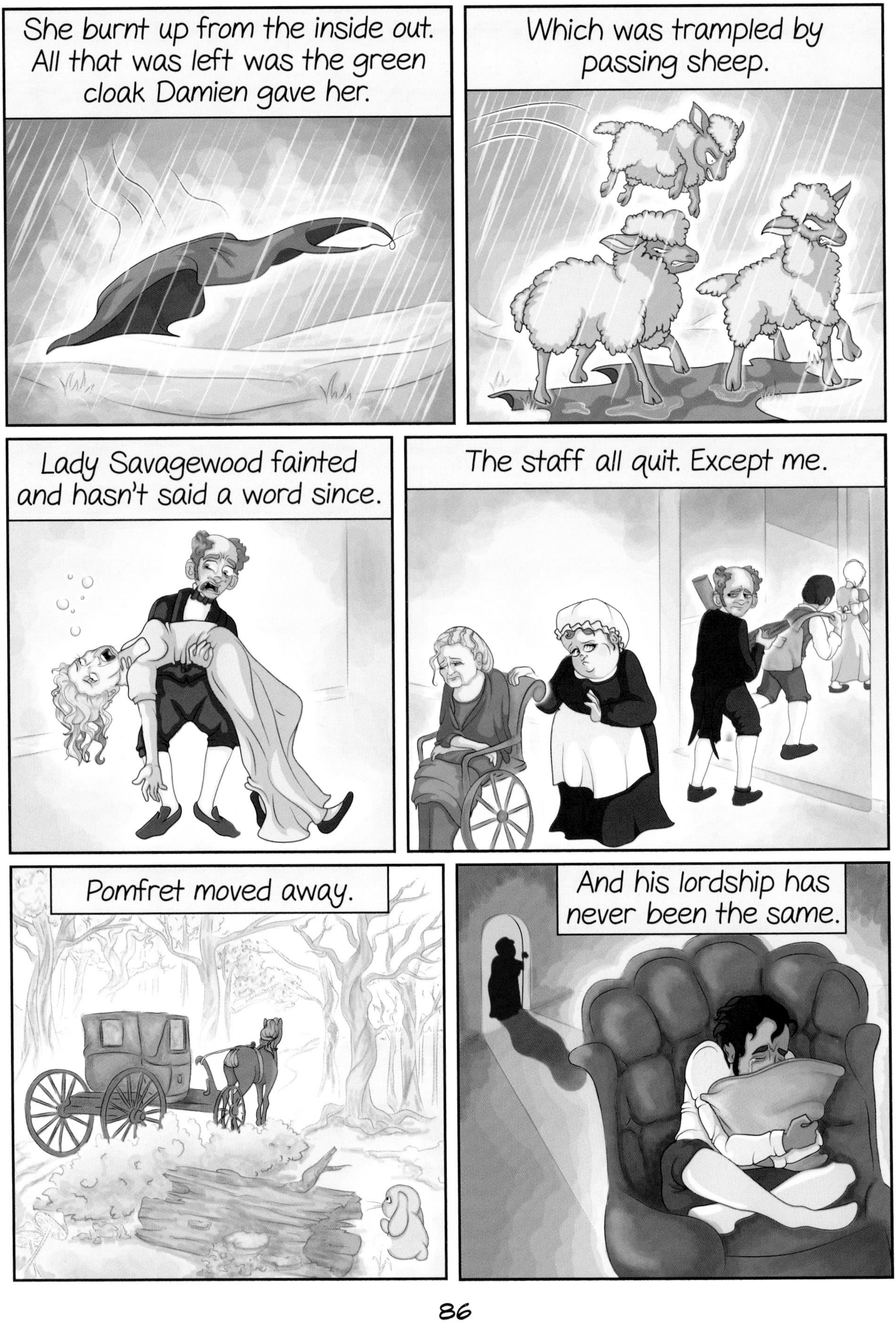
She burnt up from the inside out. All that was left was the green cloak Damien gave her.
Which was trampled by passing sheep.
Lady Savagewood fainted and hasn't said a word since.
The staff all quit. Except me.
Pomfret moved away.
And his lordship has never been the same.

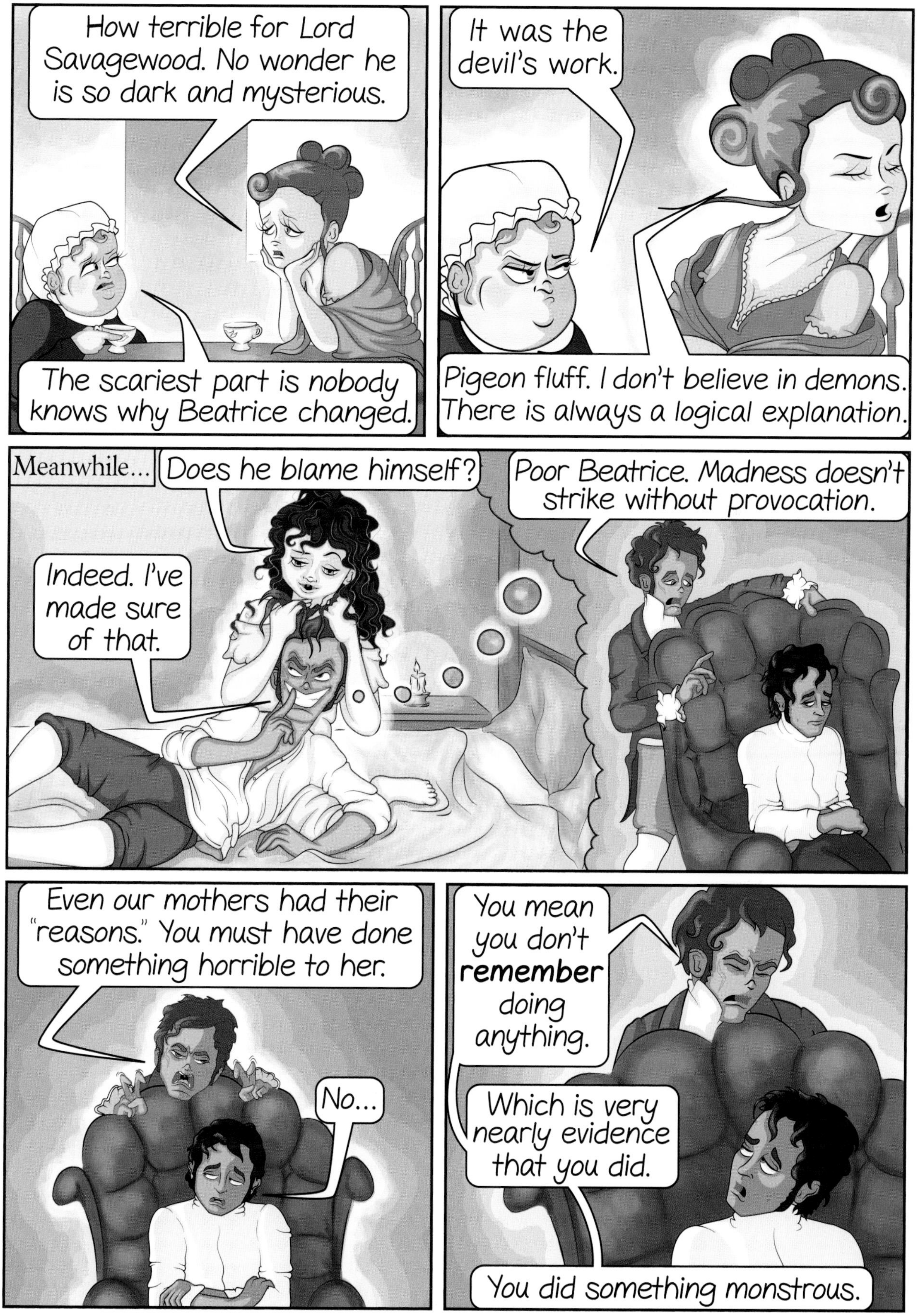
How terrible for Lord Savagewood. No wonder he is so dark and mysterious.
The scariest part is nobody knows why Beatrice changed.
It was the devil's work.
Pigeon fluff. I don't believe in demons. There is always a logical explanation.
Meanwhile...
Does he blame himself?
Indeed. I've made sure of that.
Poor Beatrice. Madness doesn't strike without provocation.
Even our mothers had their "reasons." You must have done something horrible to her.
No...
You mean you don't **remember** doing anything.
Which is very nearly evidence that you did.
You did something monstrous.

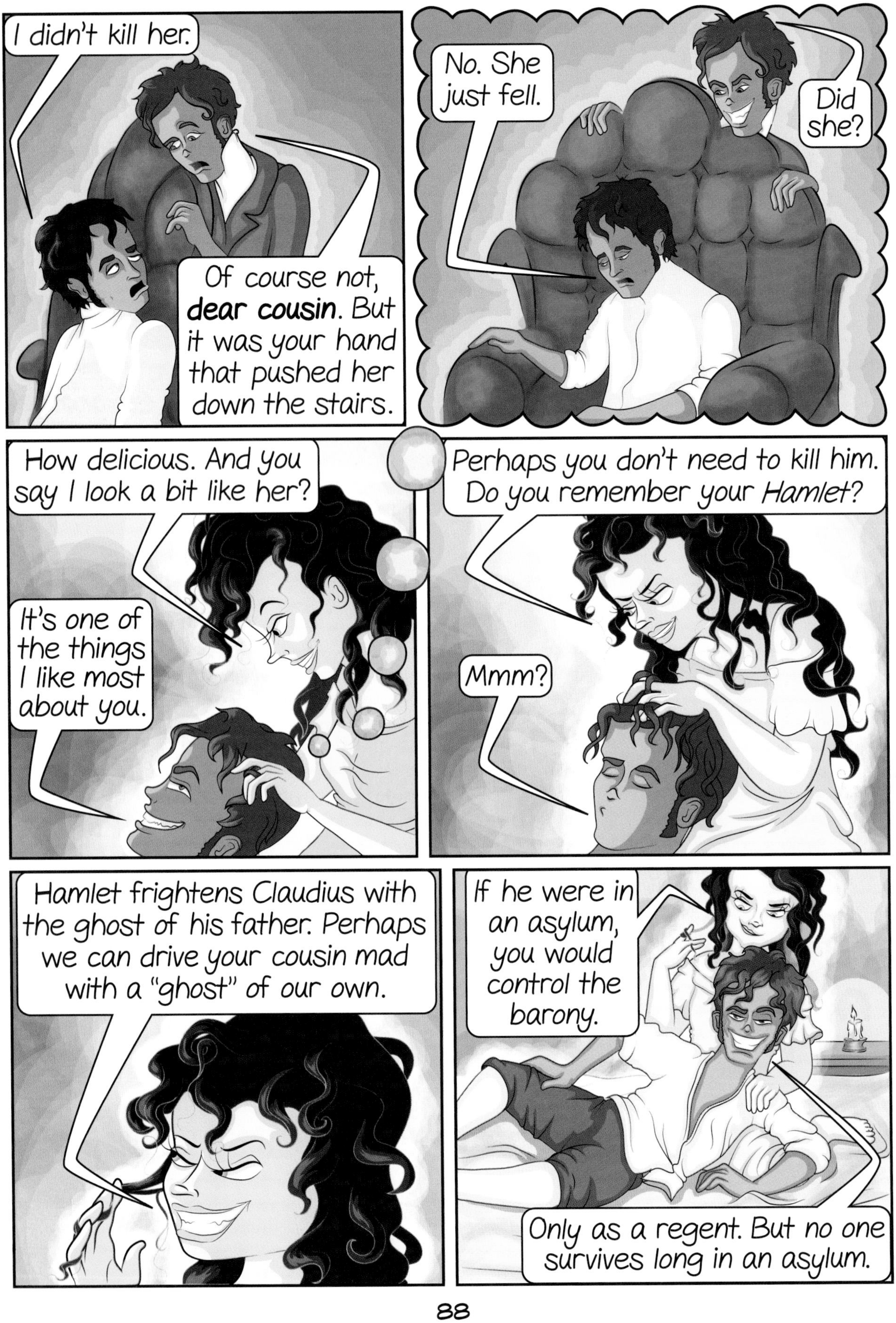
I didn't kill her.
Of course not, **dear cousin**. But it was your hand that pushed her down the stairs.
No. She just fell.
Did she?
How delicious. And you say I look a bit like her?
It's one of the things I like most about you.
Perhaps you don't need to kill him. Do you remember your *Hamlet*?
Mmm?
Hamlet frightens Claudius with the ghost of his father. Perhaps we can drive your cousin mad with a "ghost" of our own.
If he were in an asylum, you would control the barony.
Only as a regent. But no one survives long in an asylum.

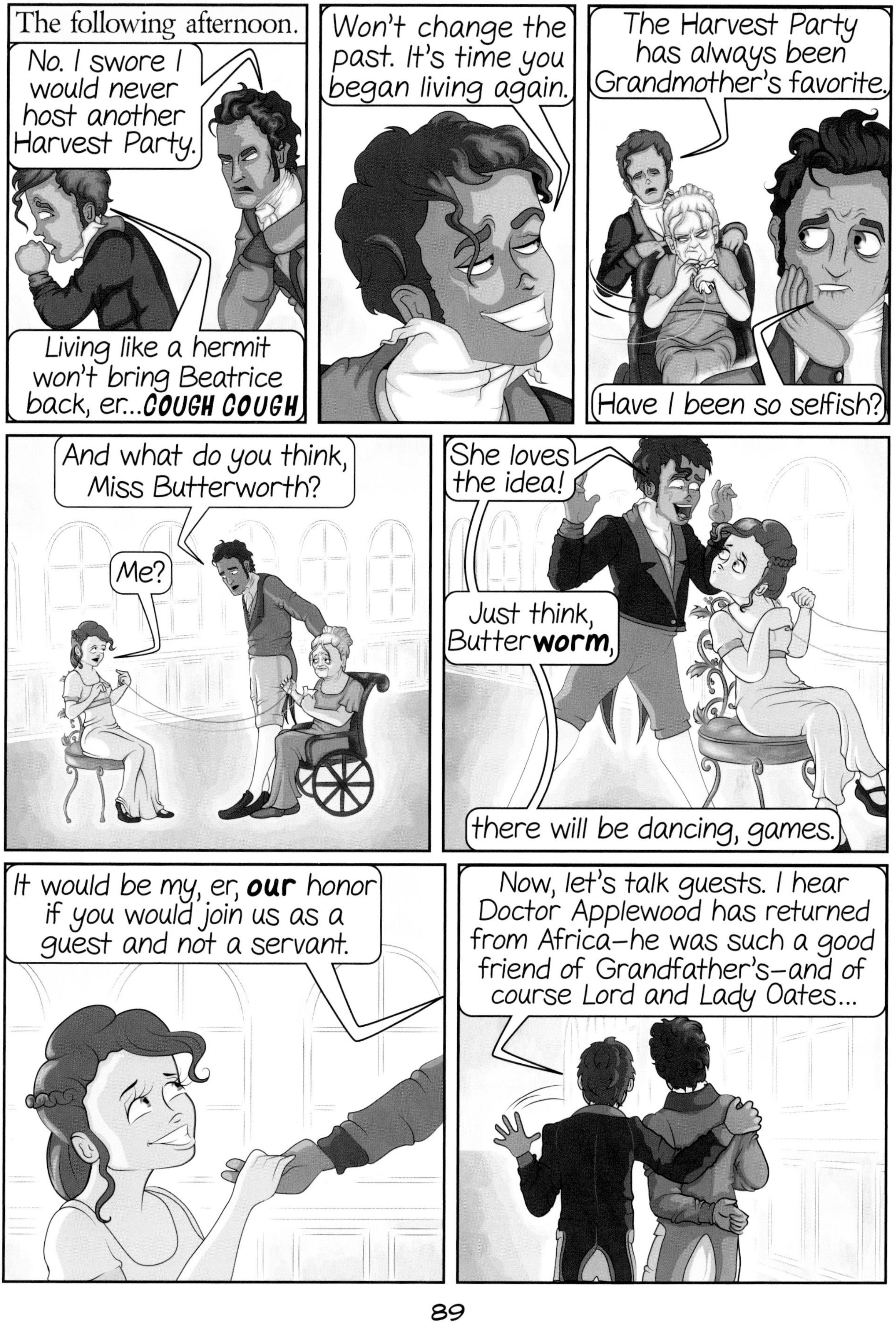
The following afternoon.
No. I swore I would never host another Harvest Party.
Living like a hermit won't bring Beatrice back, er...COUGH COUGH
Won't change the past. It's time you began living again.
The Harvest Party has always been Grandmother's favorite.
Have I been so selfish?
And what do you think, Miss Butterworth?
Me?
She loves the idea!
Just think, Butter**worm**,
there will be dancing, games.
It would be my, er, **our** honor if you would join us as a guest and not a servant.
Now, let's talk guests. I hear Doctor Applewood has returned from Africa—he was such a good friend of Grandfather's—and of course Lord and Lady Oates...

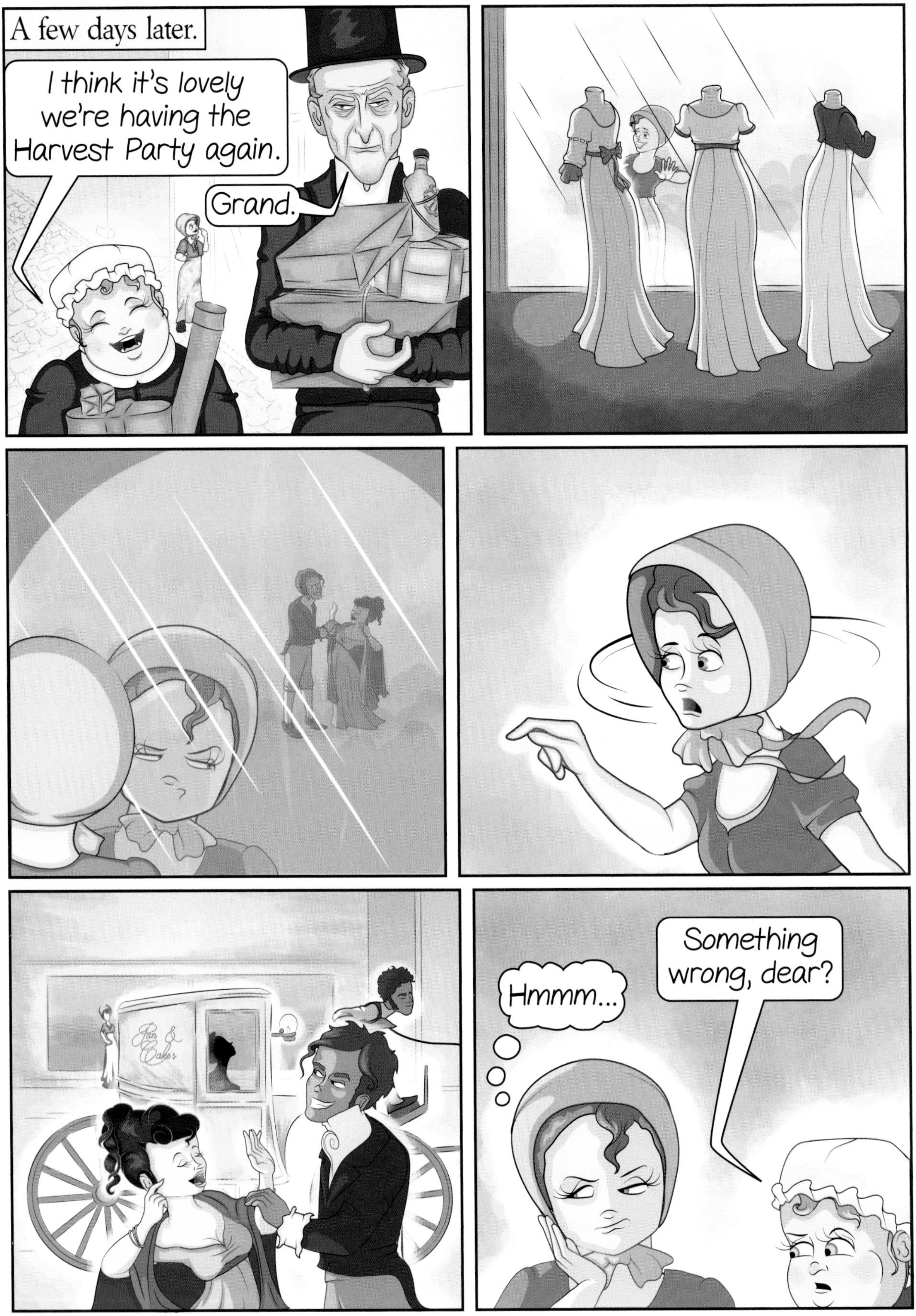
A few days later.
I think it's lovely we're having the Harvest Party again.
Grand.
Hmmm...
Something wrong, dear?

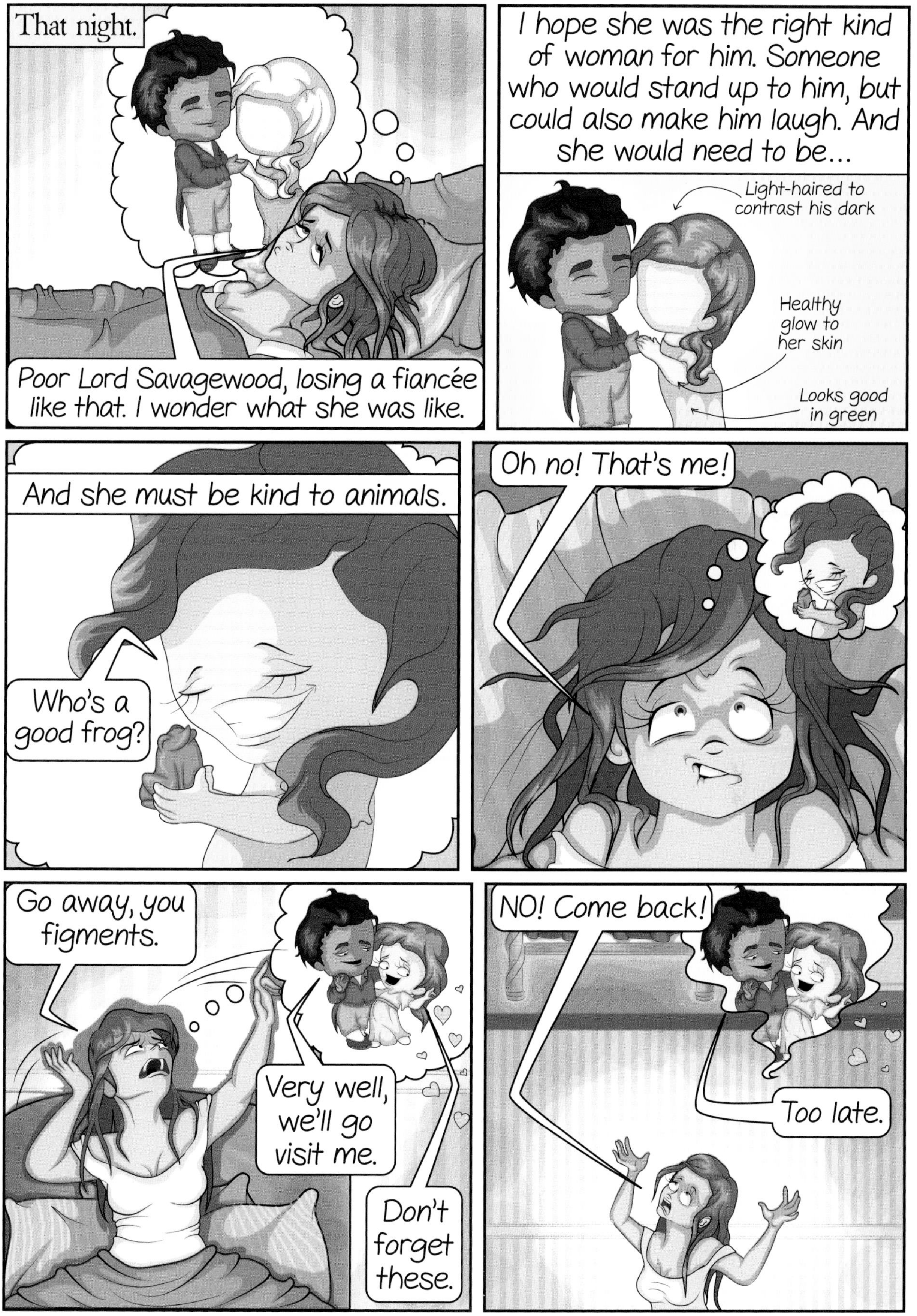
That night.
Poor Lord Savagewood, losing a fiancée like that. I wonder what she was like.
I hope she was the right kind of woman for him. Someone who would stand up to him, but could also make him laugh. And she would need to be...
Light-haired to contrast his dark
Healthy glow to her skin
Looks good in green
And she must be kind to animals.
Who's a good frog?
Oh no! That's me!
Go away, you figments.
Very well, we'll go visit me.
Don't forget these.
NO! Come back!
Too late.

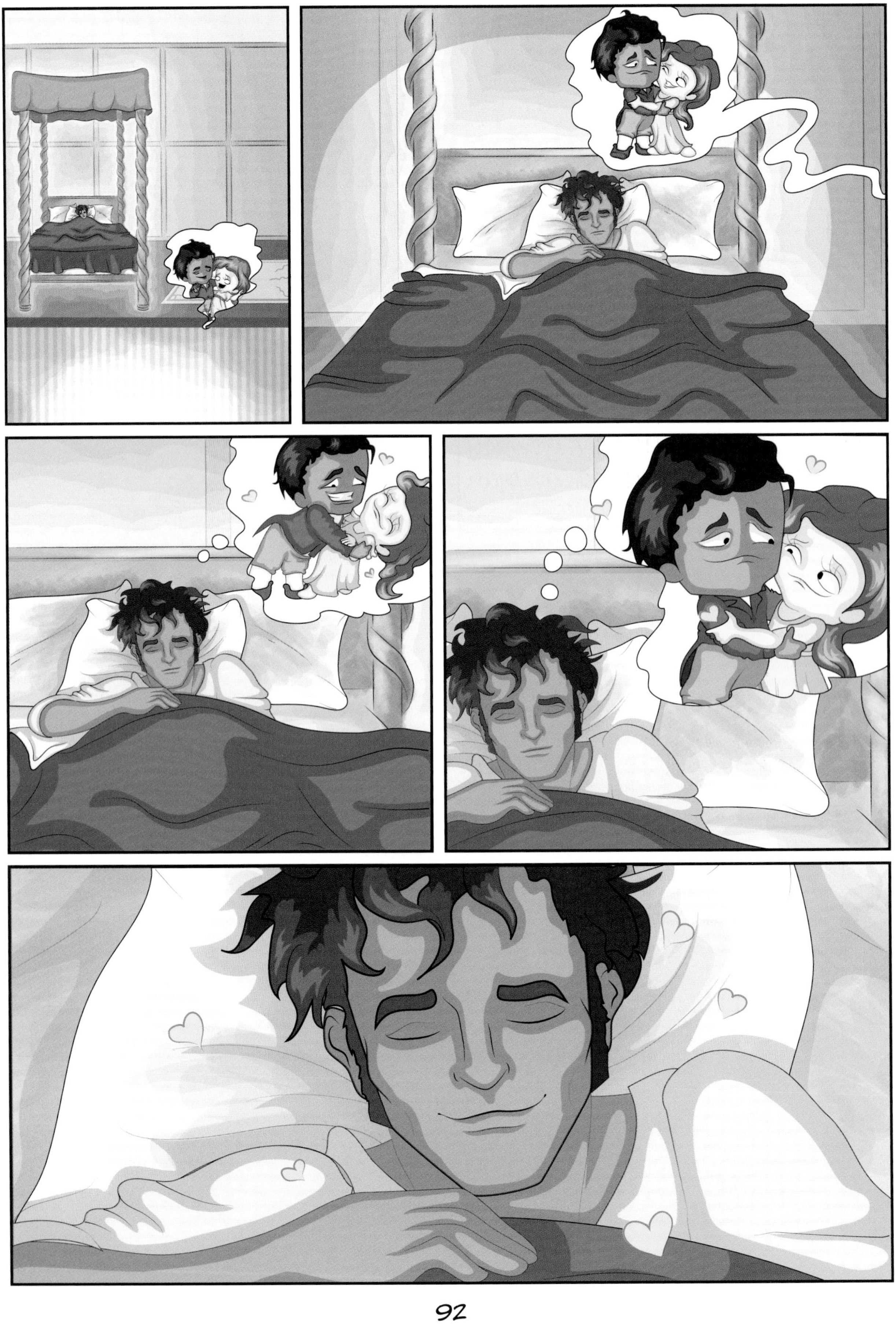

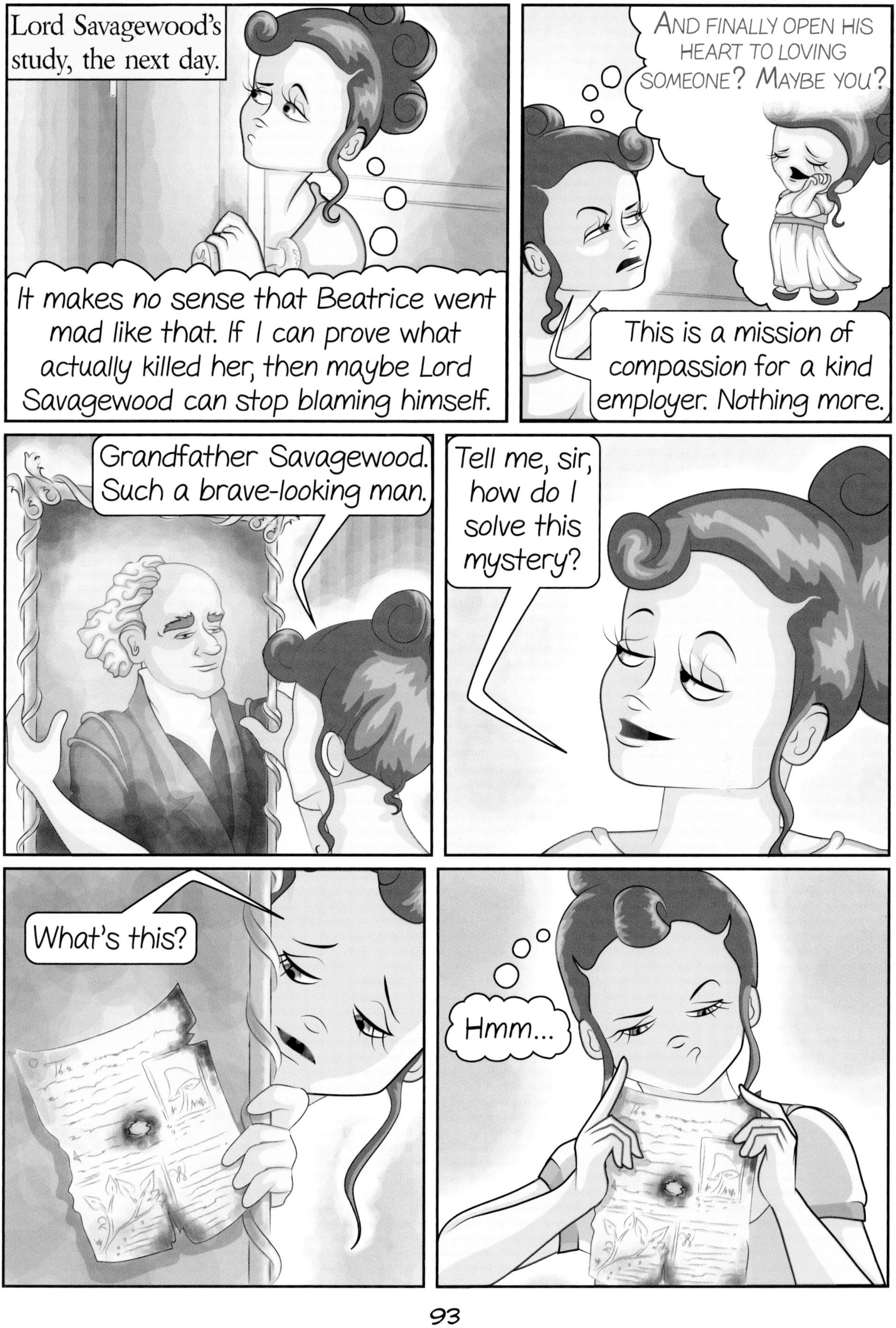

Lord Savagewood's study, the next day.
It makes no sense that Beatrice went mad like that. If I can prove what actually killed her, then maybe Lord Savagewood can stop blaming himself.
AND FINALLY OPEN HIS HEART TO LOVING SOMEONE? MAYBE YOU?
This is a mission of compassion for a kind employer. Nothing more.
Grandfather Savagewood. Such a brave-looking man.
Tell me, sir, how do I solve this mystery?
What's this?
Hmm...

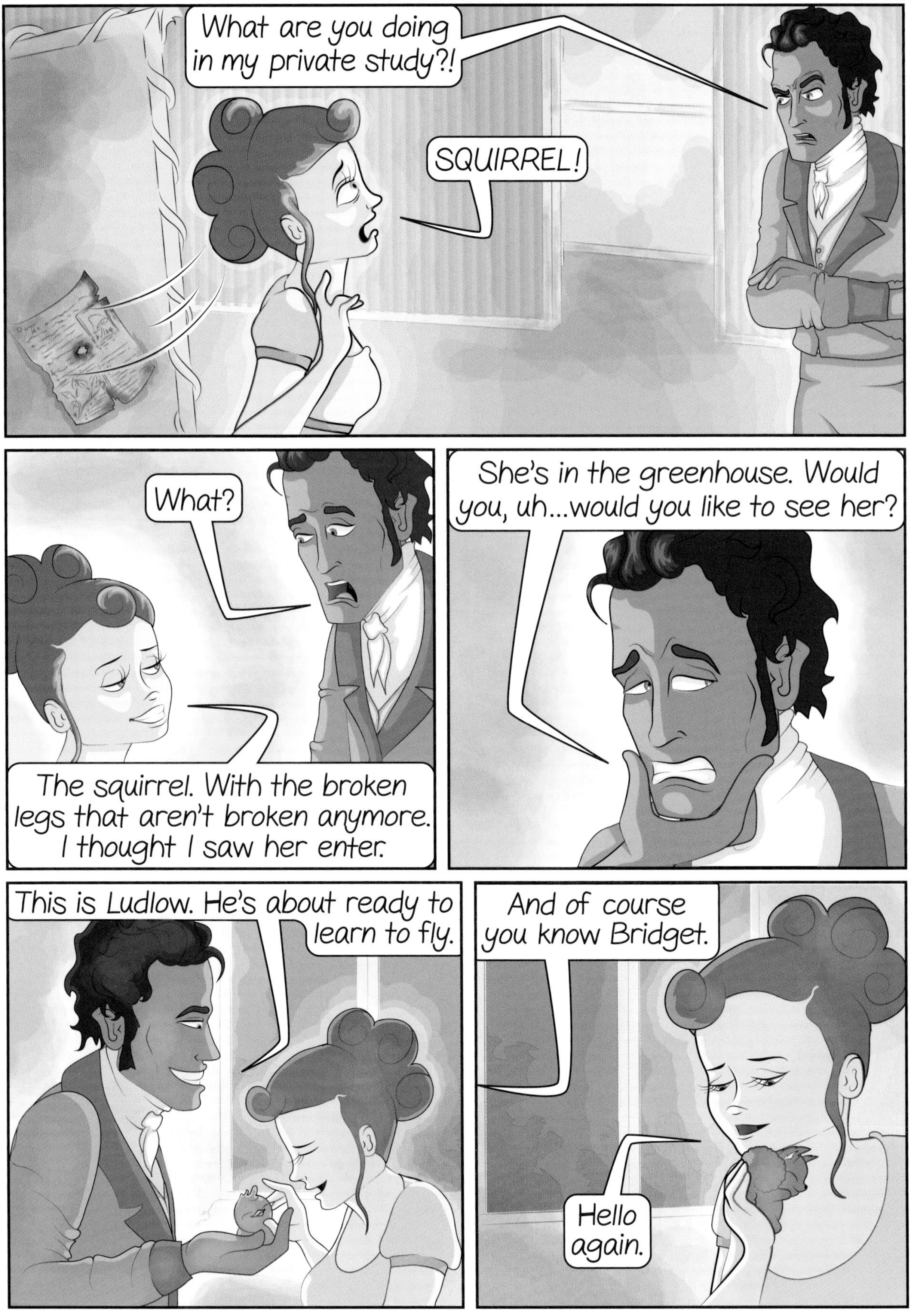
What are you doing in my private study?!
SQUIRREL!
What?
The squirrel. With the broken legs that aren't broken anymore. I thought I saw her enter.
She's in the greenhouse. Would you, uh...would you like to see her?
This is Ludlow. He's about ready to learn to fly.
And of course you know Bridget.
Hello again.

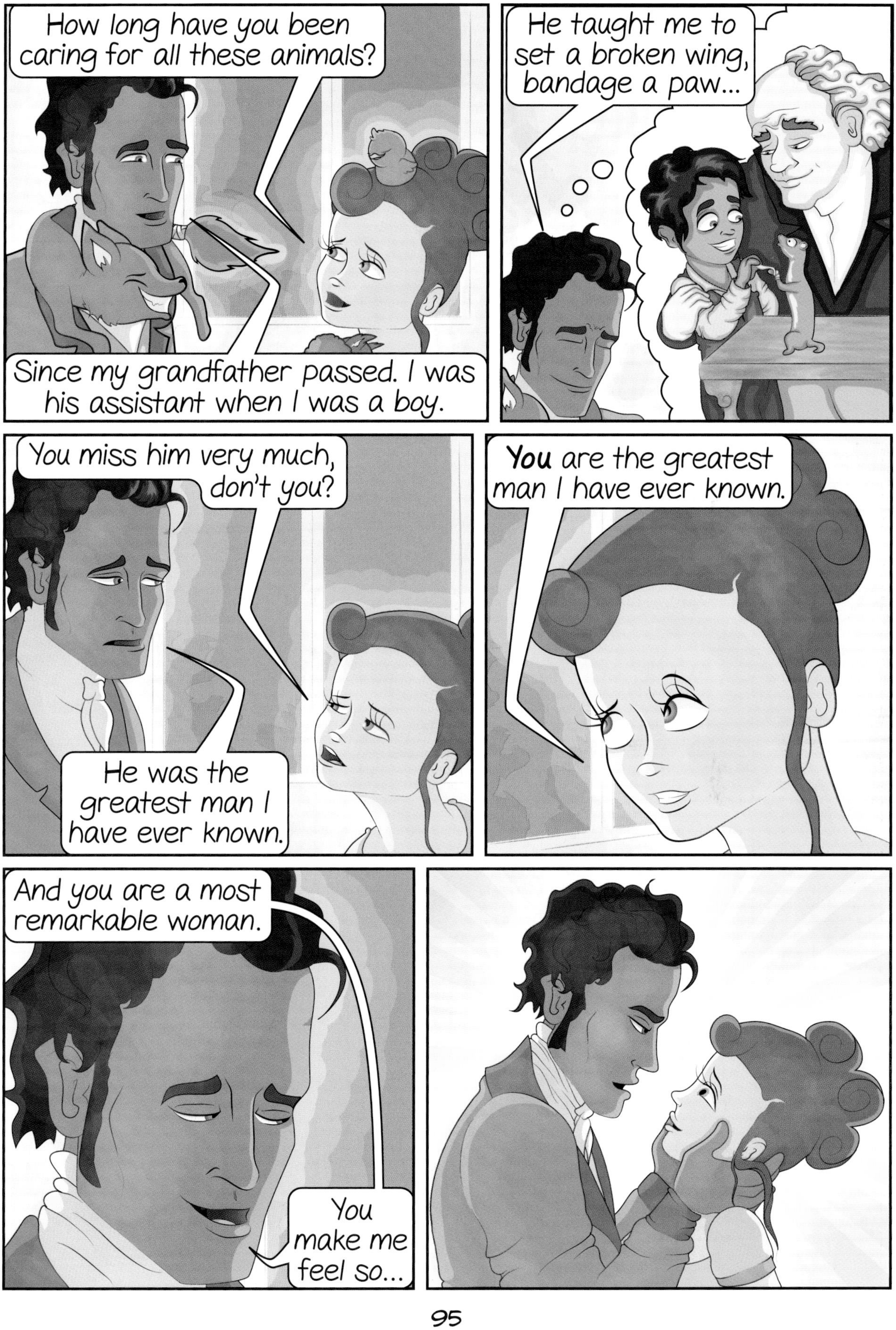
How long have you been caring for all these animals?
Since my grandfather passed. I was his assistant when I was a boy.
He taught me to set a broken wing, bandage a paw...
You miss him very much, don't you?
He was the greatest man I have ever known.
**You** are the greatest man I have ever known.
And you are a most remarkable woman.
You make me feel so...

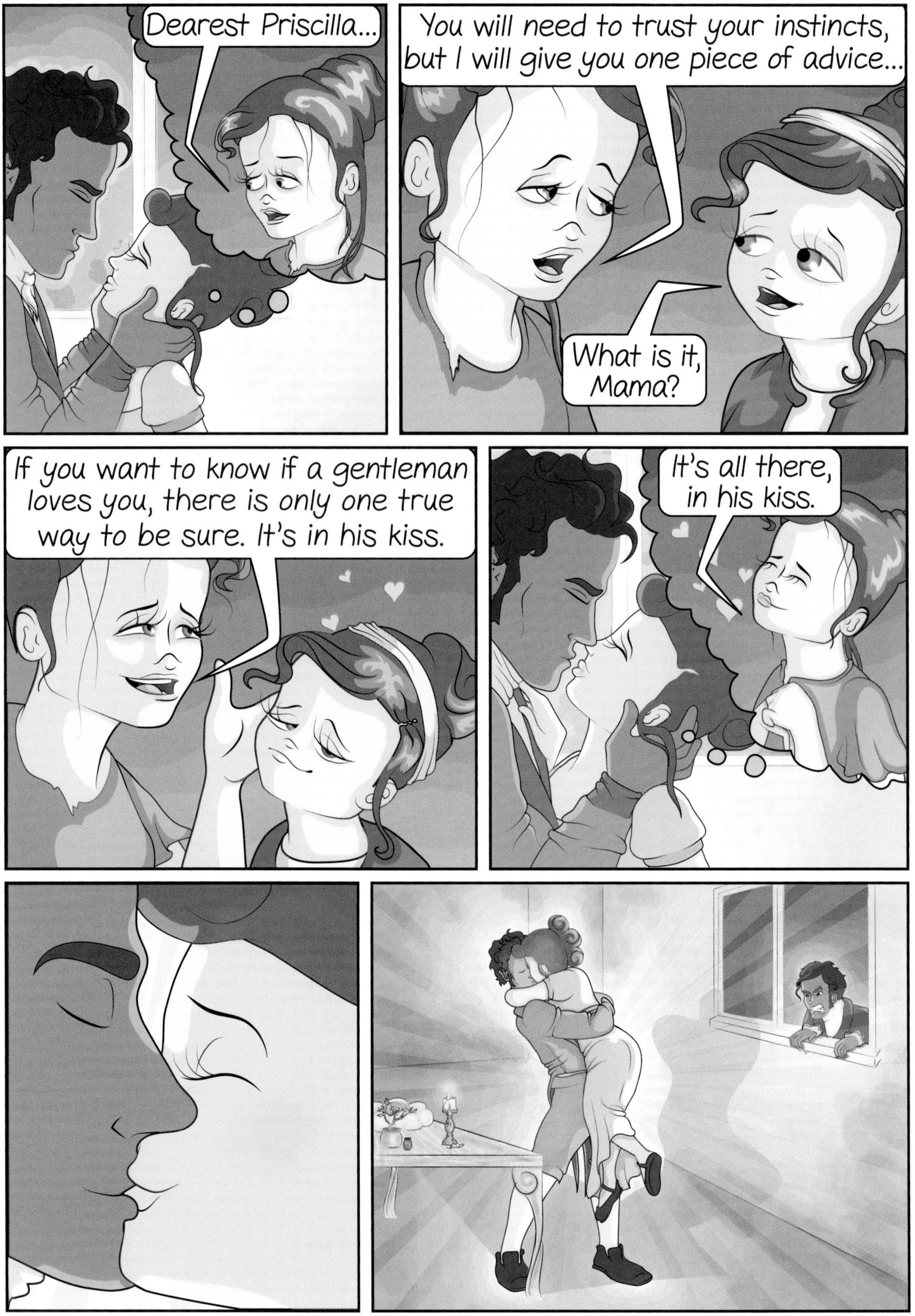
Dearest Priscilla...
You will need to trust your instincts, but I will give you one piece of advice...
What is it, Mama?
If you want to know if a gentleman loves you, there is only one true way to be sure. It's in his kiss.
It's all there, in his kiss.

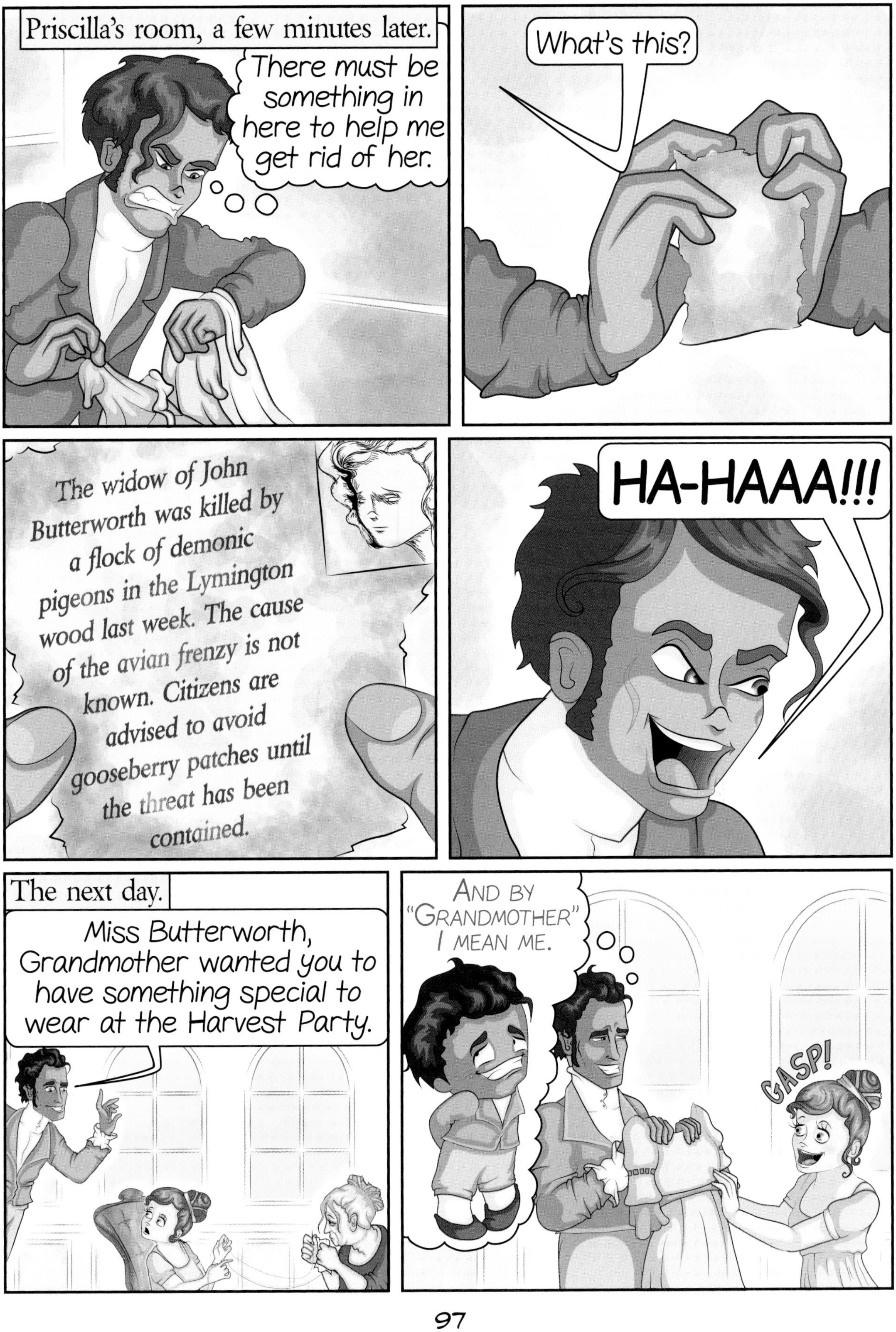

Priscilla's room, a few minutes later.
There must be something in here to help me get rid of her.
What's this?
The widow of John Butterworth was killed by a flock of demonic pigeons in the Lymington wood last week. The cause of the avian frenzy is not known. Citizens are advised to avoid gooseberry patches until the threat has been contained.
HA-HAAA!!!
The next day.
Miss Butterworth, Grandmother wanted you to have something special to wear at the Harvest Party.
AND BY "GRANDMOTHER" I MEAN ME.
GASP!

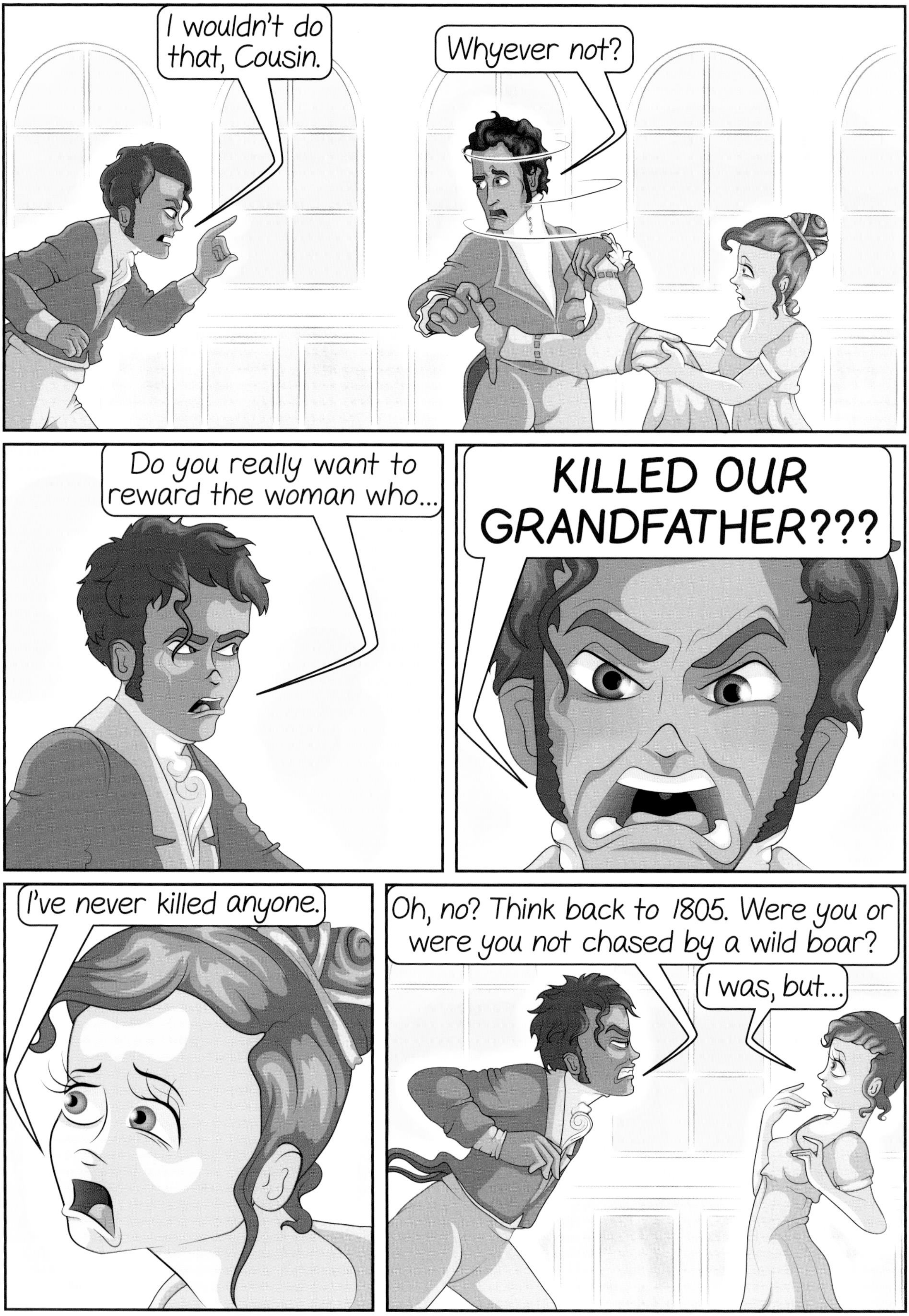
I wouldn't do that, Cousin.
Whyever not?
Do you really want to reward the woman who...
KILLED OUR GRANDFATHER???
I've never killed anyone.
Oh, no? Think back to 1805. Were you or were you not chased by a wild boar?
I was, but...

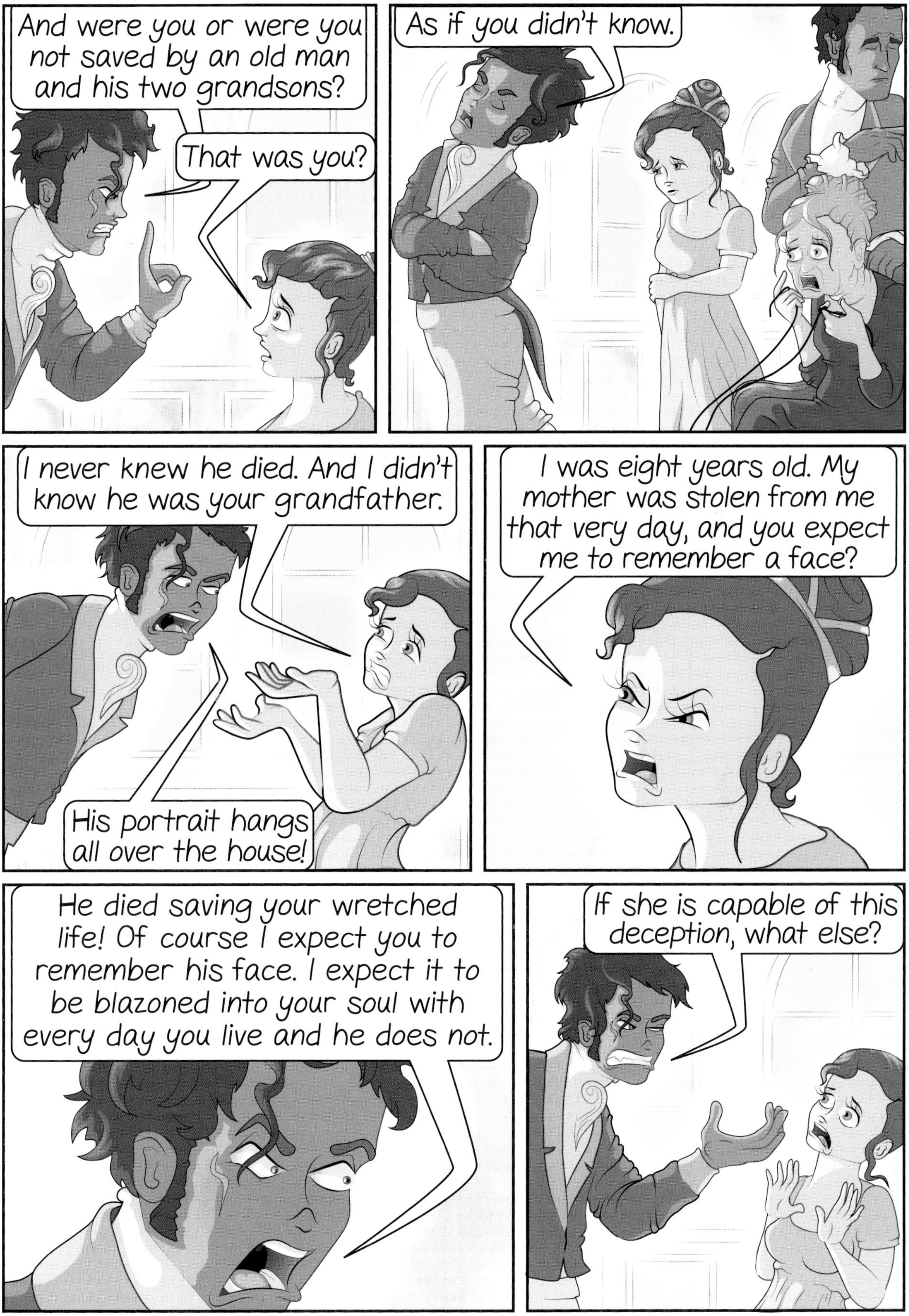
And were you or were you not saved by an old man and his two grandsons?
That was you?
As if you didn't know.
I never knew he died. And I didn't know he was your grandfather.
His portrait hangs all over the house!
I was eight years old. My mother was stolen from me that very day, and you expect me to remember a face?
He died saving your wretched life! Of course I expect you to remember his face. I expect it to be blazoned into your soul with every day you live and he does not.
If she is capable of this deception, what else?

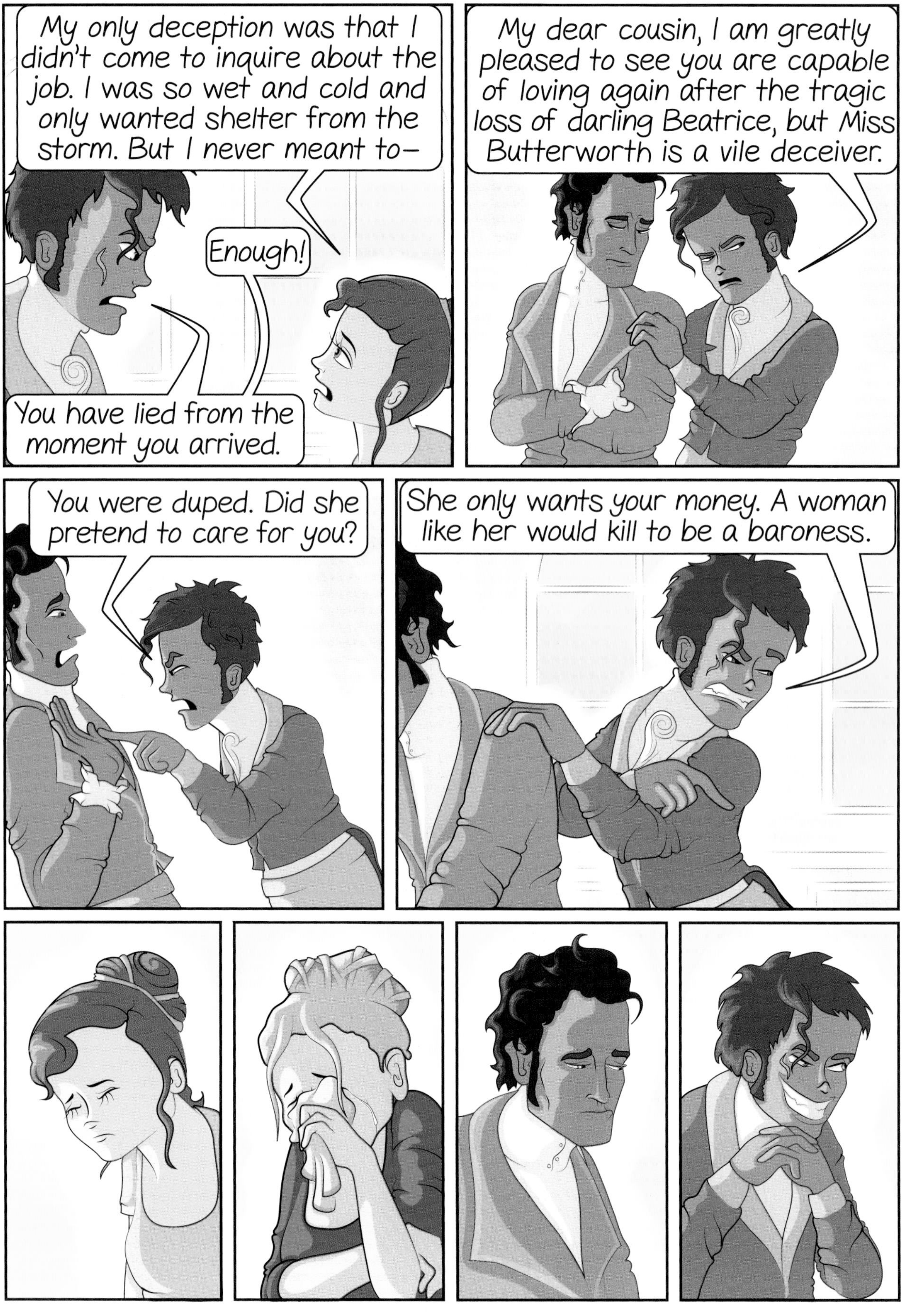
My only deception was that I didn't come to inquire about the job. I was so wet and cold and only wanted shelter from the storm. But I never meant to–
Enough!
You have lied from the moment you arrived.
My dear cousin, I am greatly pleased to see you are capable of loving again after the tragic loss of darling Beatrice, but Miss Butterworth is a vile deceiver.
You were duped. Did she pretend to care for you?
She only wants your money. A woman like her would kill to be a baroness.

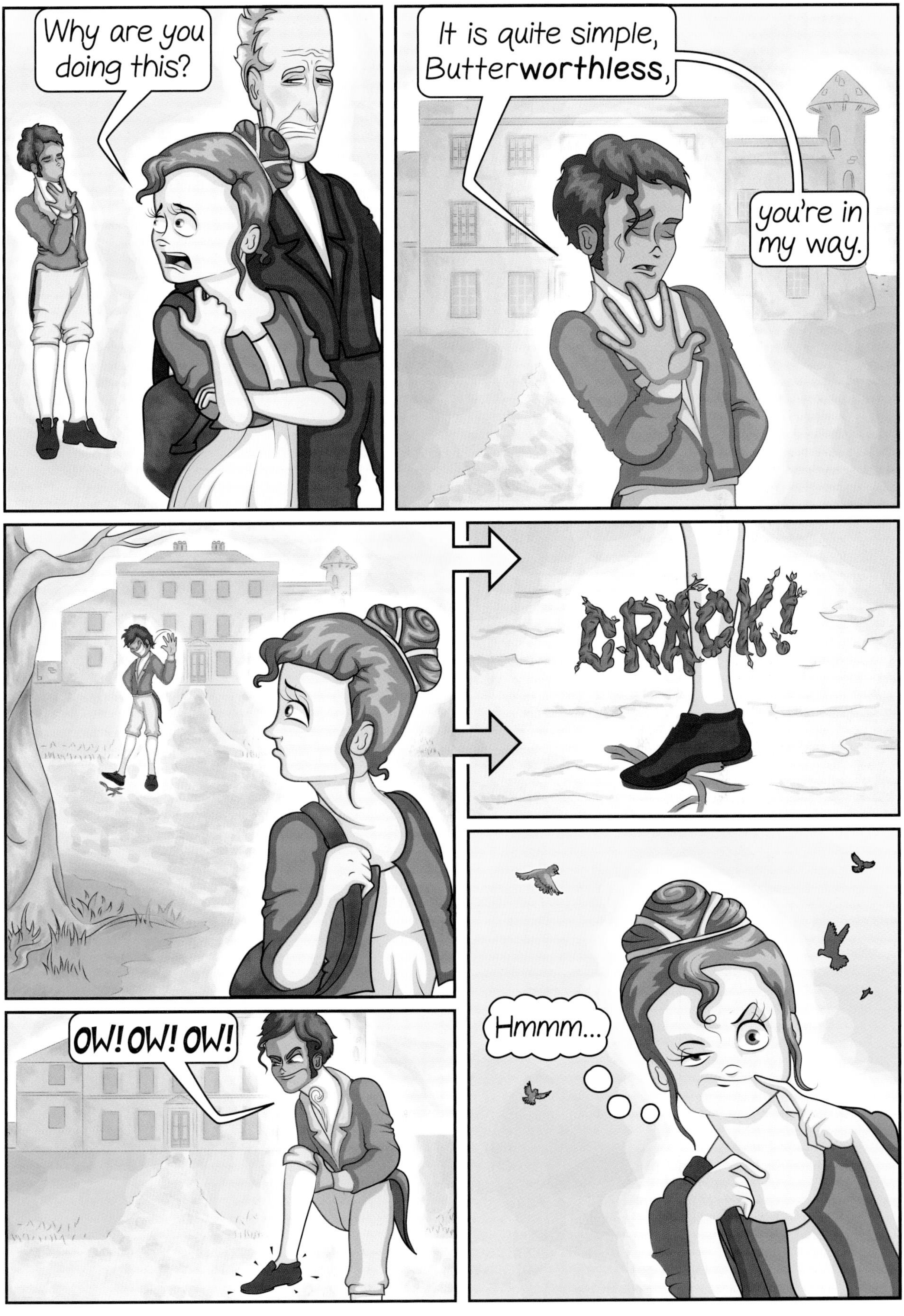
Why are you doing this?
It is quite simple, Butter**worthless**,
you're in my way.
CRACK!
OW! OW! OW!
Hmmm...

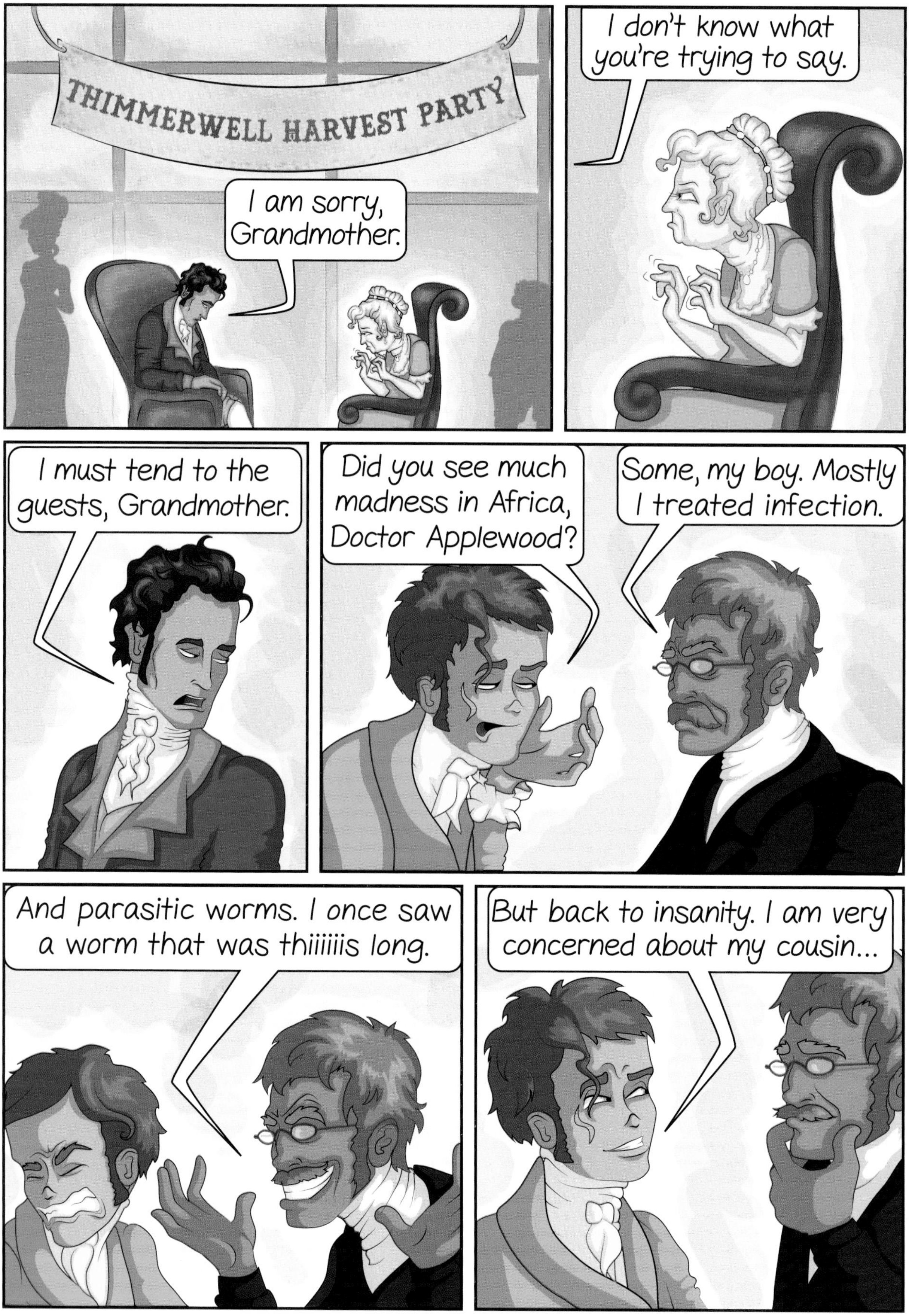
THIMMERWELL HARVEST PARTY
I am sorry, Grandmother.
I don't know what you're trying to say.
I must tend to the guests, Grandmother.
Did you see much madness in Africa, Doctor Applewood?
Some, my boy. Mostly I treated infection.
And parasitic worms. I once saw a worm that was thiiiiiis long.
But back to insanity. I am very concerned about my cousin...

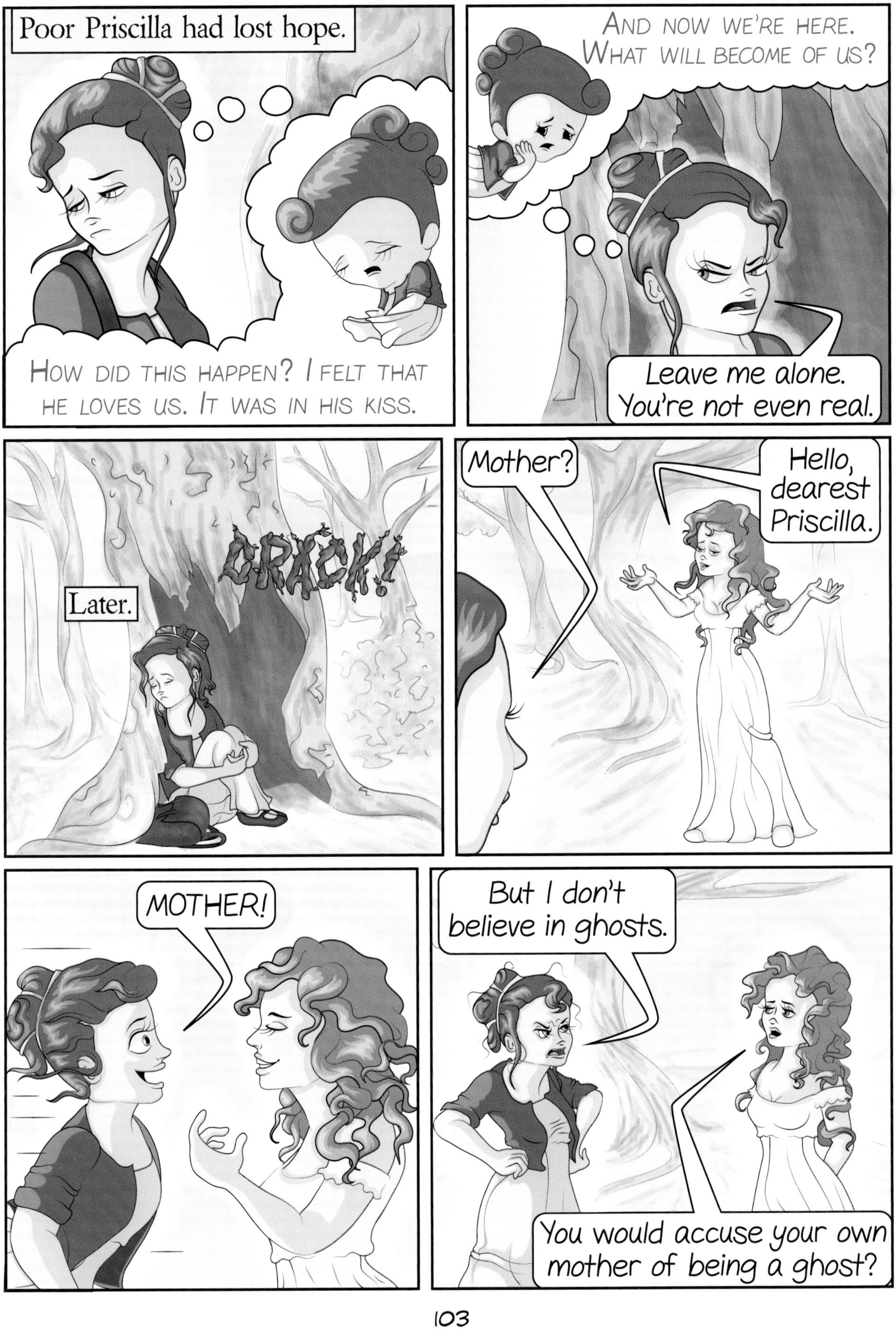

Poor Priscilla had lost hope.
HOW DID THIS HAPPEN? I FELT THAT HE LOVES US. IT WAS IN HIS KISS.
AND NOW WE'RE HERE. WHAT WILL BECOME OF US?
Leave me alone. You're not even real.
Later.
CRACK!
Mother?
Hello, dearest Priscilla.
MOTHER!
But I don't believe in ghosts.
You would accuse your own mother of being a ghost?

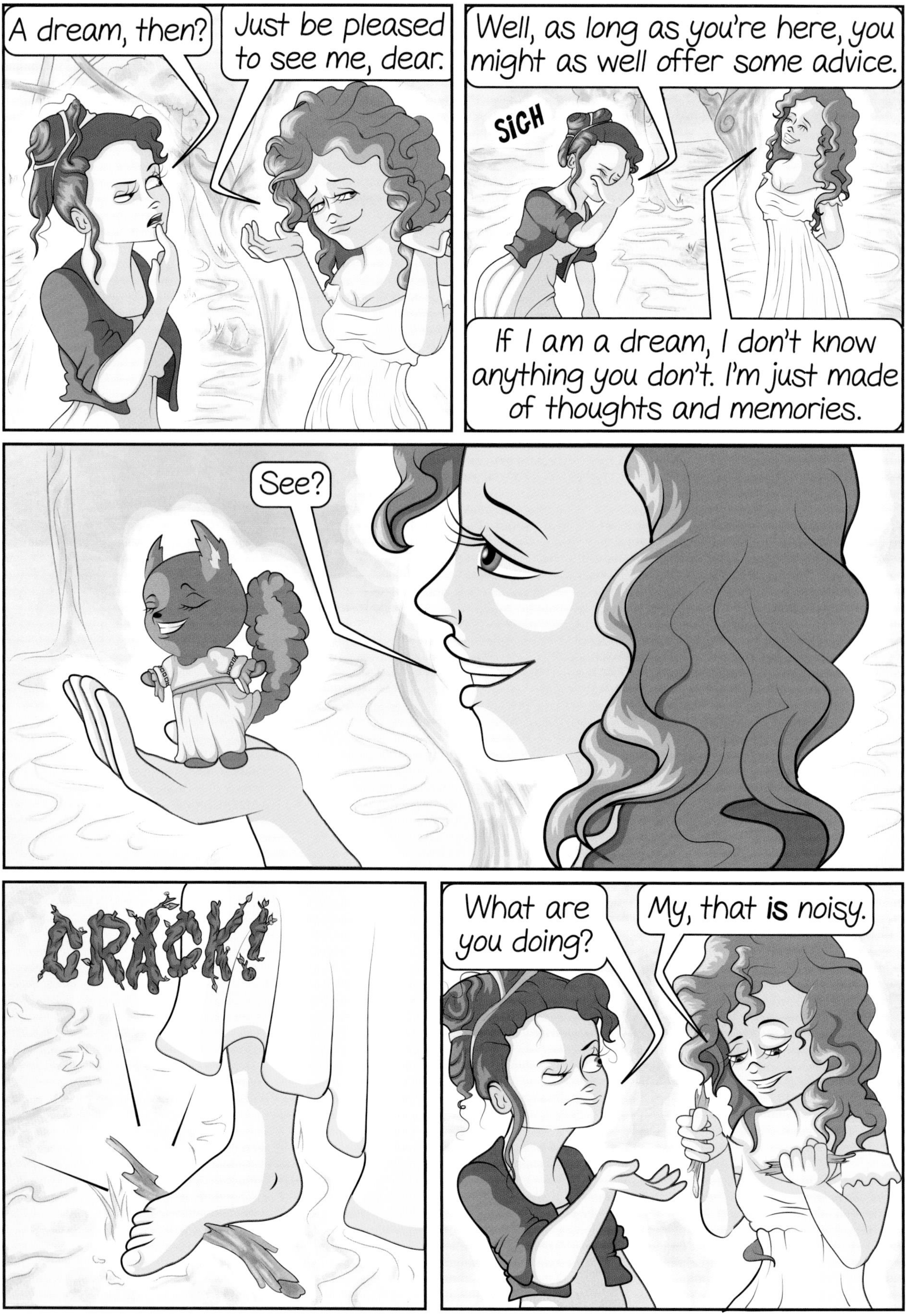
A dream, then?
Just be pleased to see me, dear.
Well, as long as you're here, you might as well offer some advice.
SIGH
If I am a dream, I don't know anything you don't. I'm just made of thoughts and memories.
See?
CRACK!
What are you doing?
My, that **is** noisy.

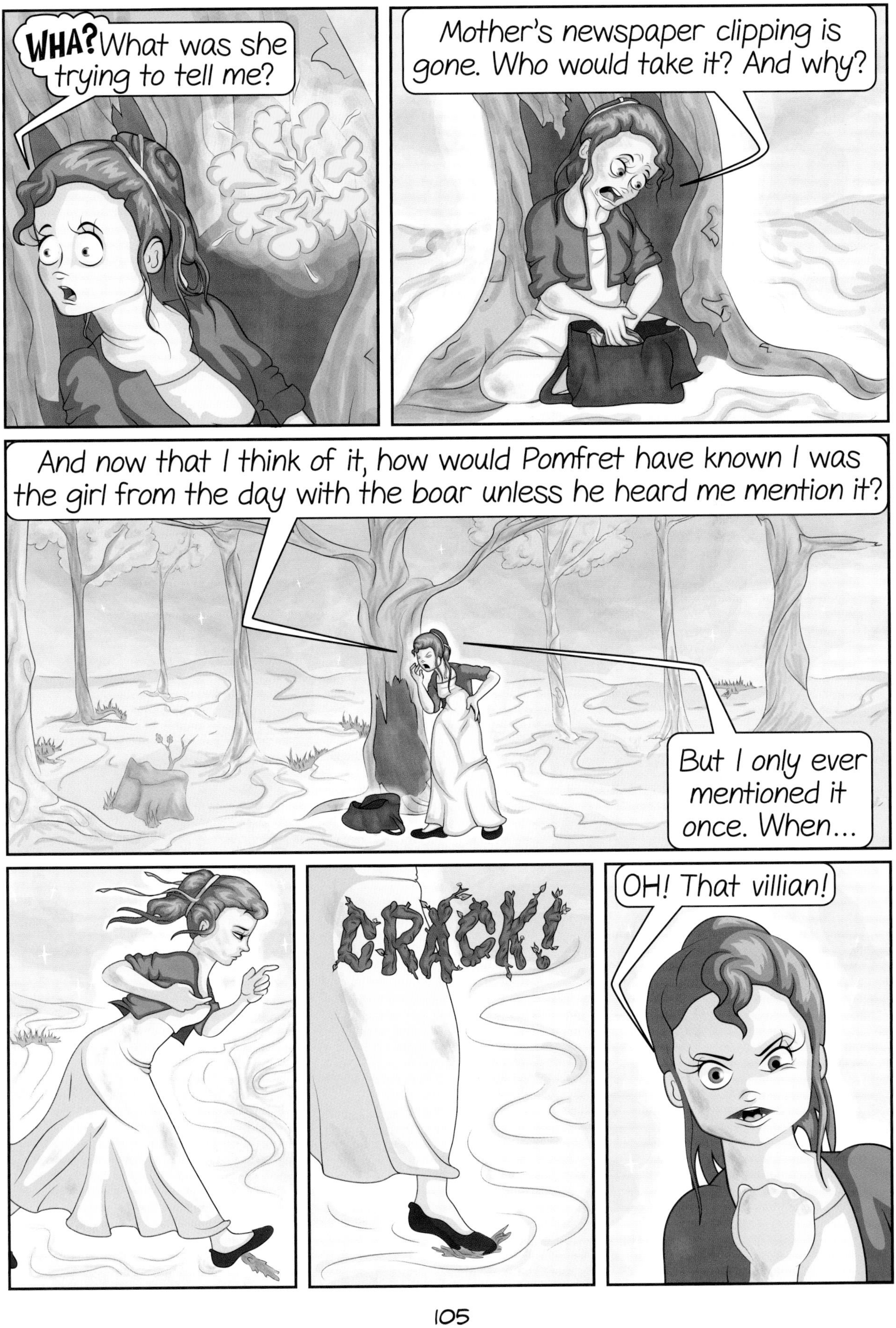
WHA? What was she trying to tell me?
Mother's newspaper clipping is gone. Who would take it? And why?
And now that I think of it, how would Pomfret have known I was the girl from the day with the boar unless he heard me mention it?
But I only ever mentioned it once. When...
CRACK!
OH! That villian!

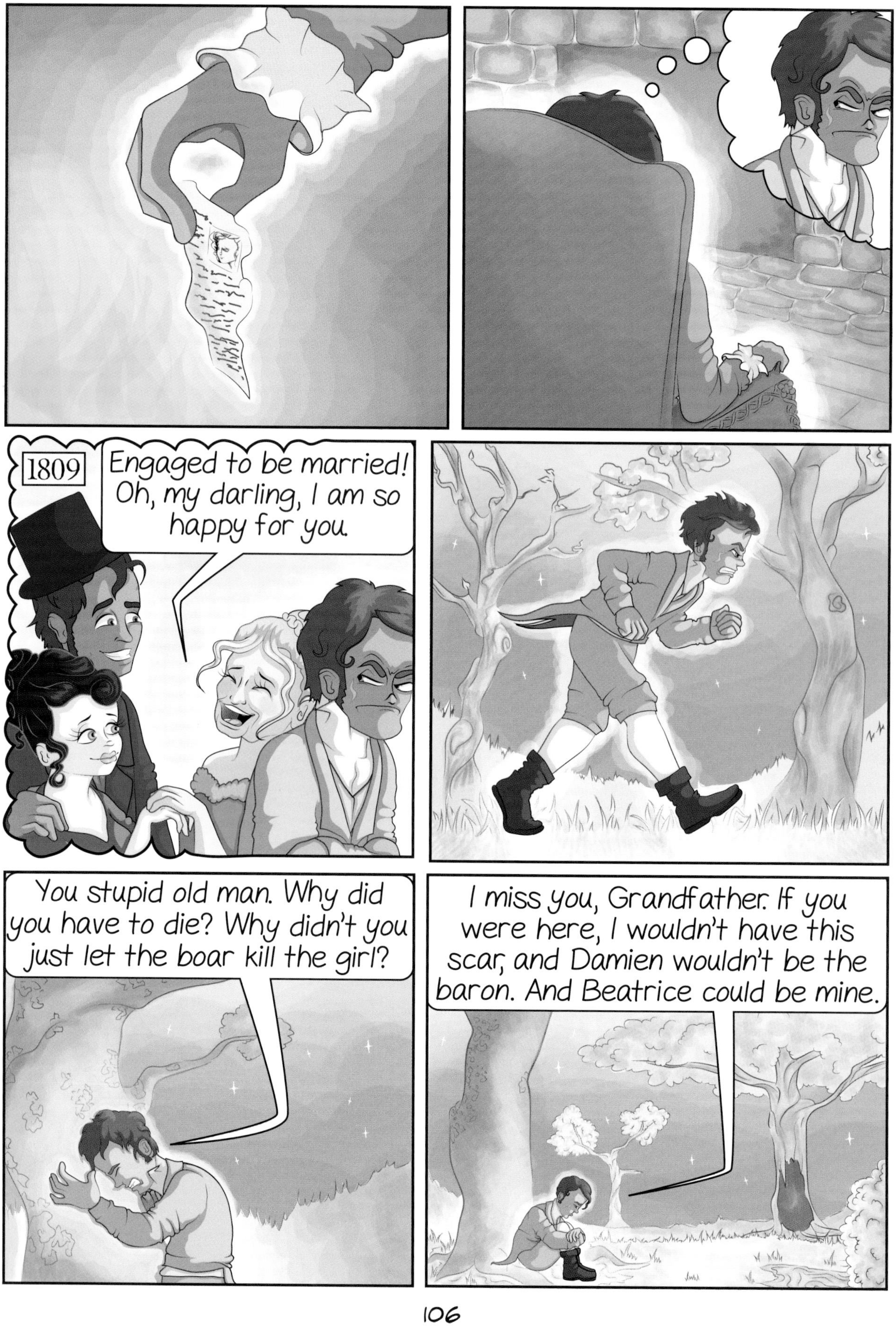
1809
Engaged to be married! Oh, my darling, I am so happy for you.
You stupid old man. Why did you have to die? Why didn't you just let the boar kill the girl?
I miss you, Grandfather. If you were here, I wouldn't have this scar, and Damien wouldn't be the baron. And Beatrice could be mine.

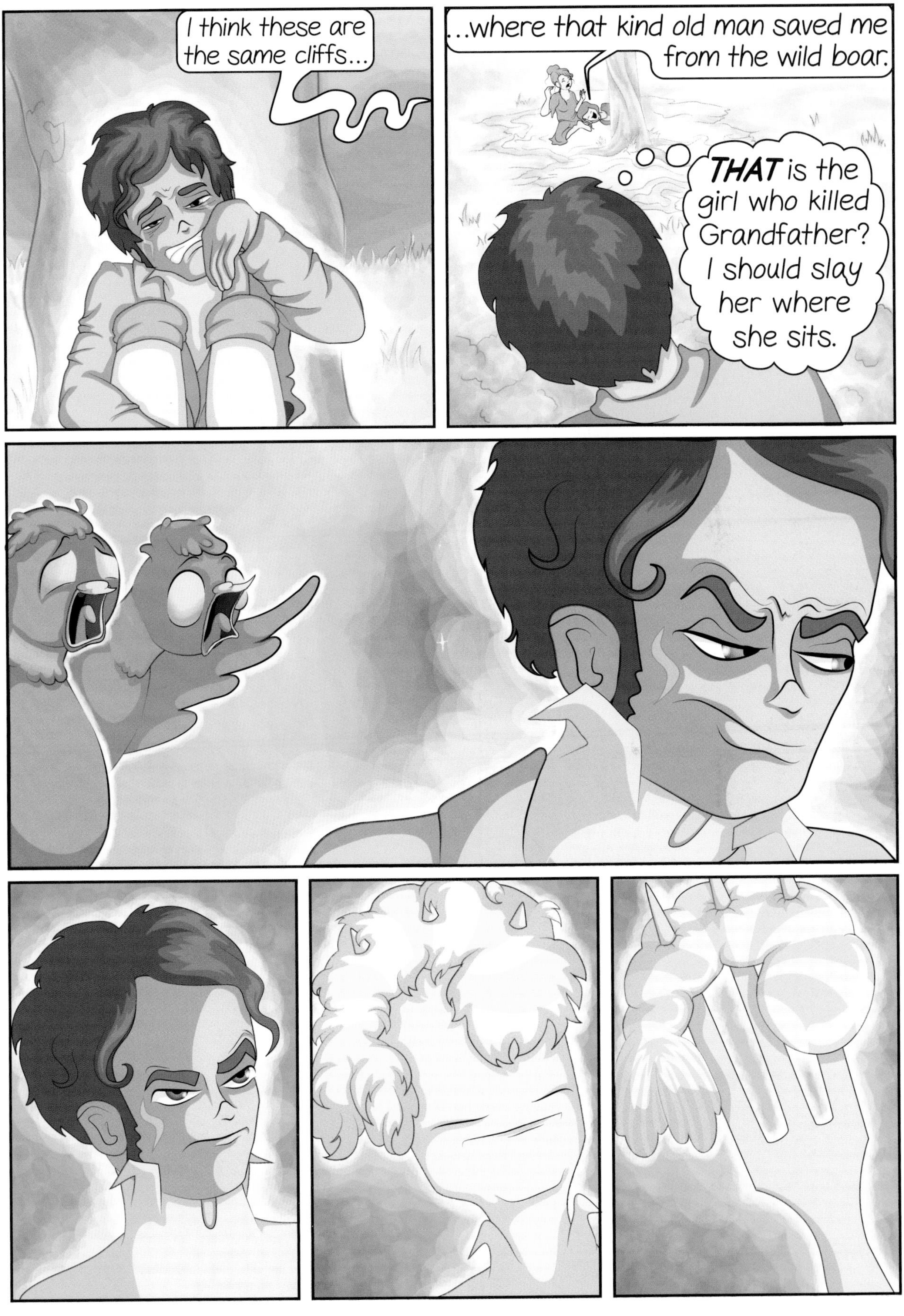
I think these are the same cliffs...
...where that kind old man saved me from the wild boar.
**THAT** is the girl who killed Grandfather? I should slay her where she sits.

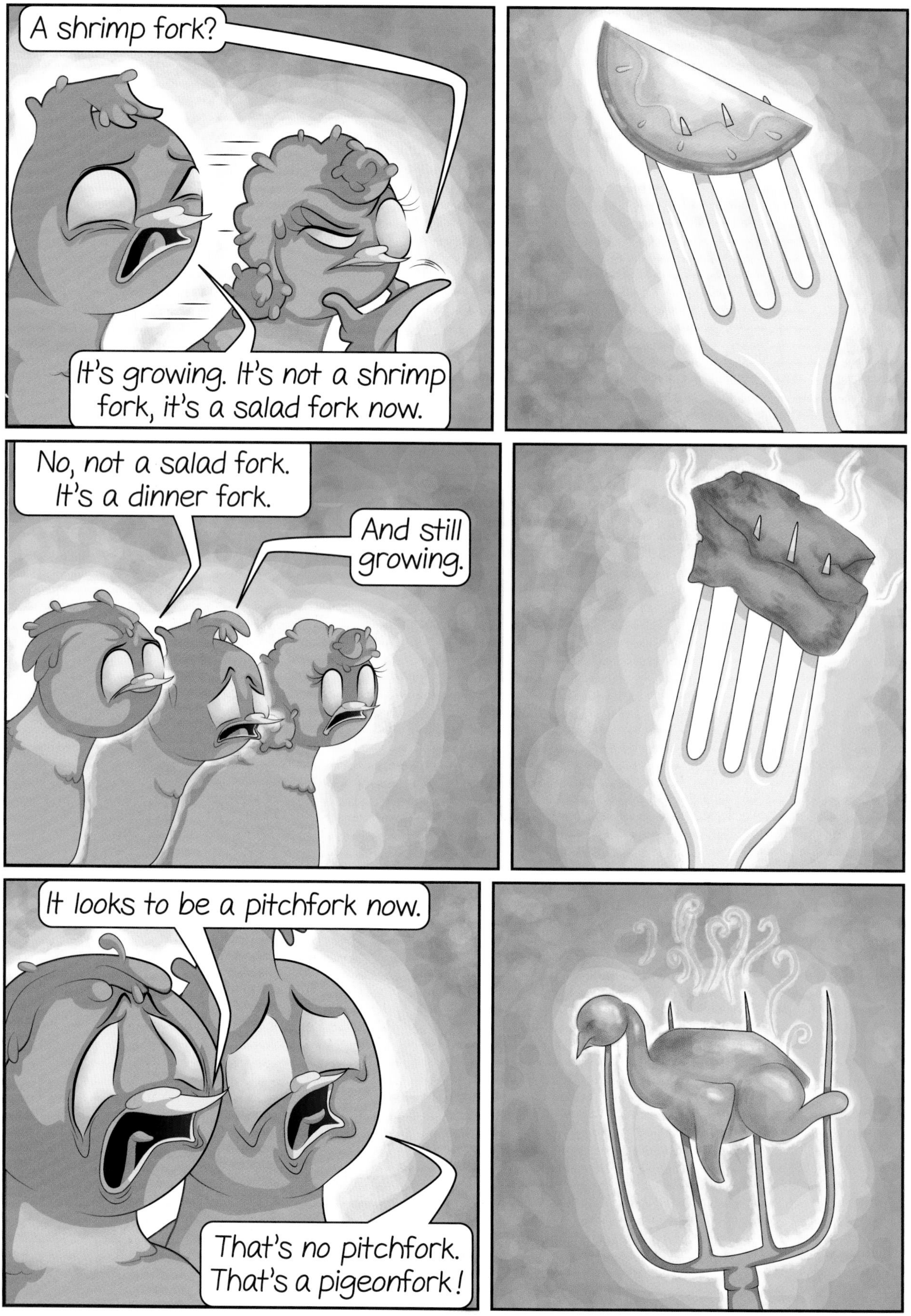
A shrimp fork?
It's growing. It's not a shrimp fork, it's a salad fork now.
No, not a salad fork. It's a dinner fork.
And still growing.
It looks to be a pitchfork now.
That's no pitchfork. That's a pigeonfork!

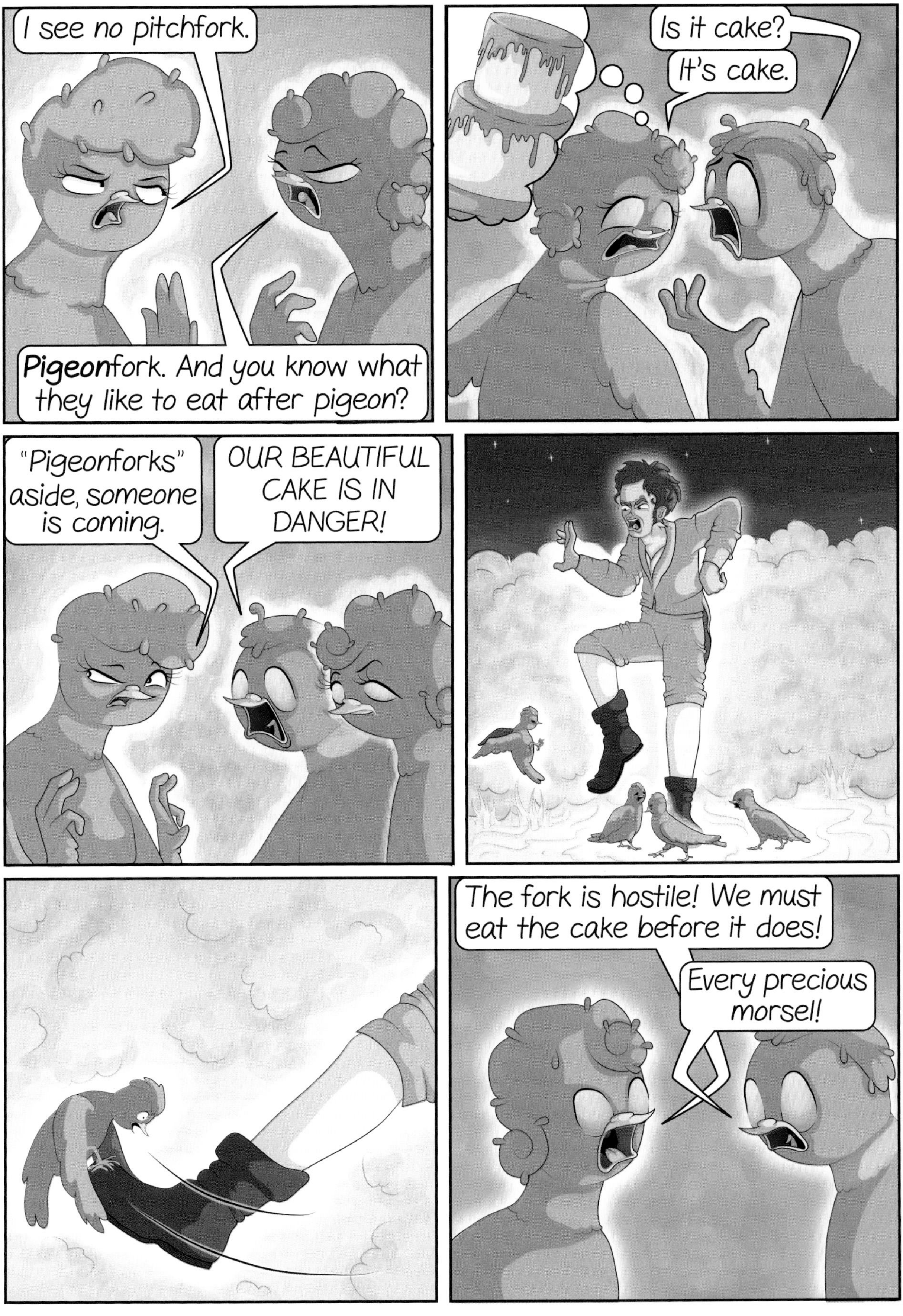
I see no pitchfork.
Pigeonfork. And you know what they like to eat after pigeon?
Is it cake?
It's cake.
"Pigeonforks" aside, someone is coming.
OUR BEAUTIFUL CAKE IS IN DANGER!
The fork is hostile! We must eat the cake before it does!
Every precious morsel!

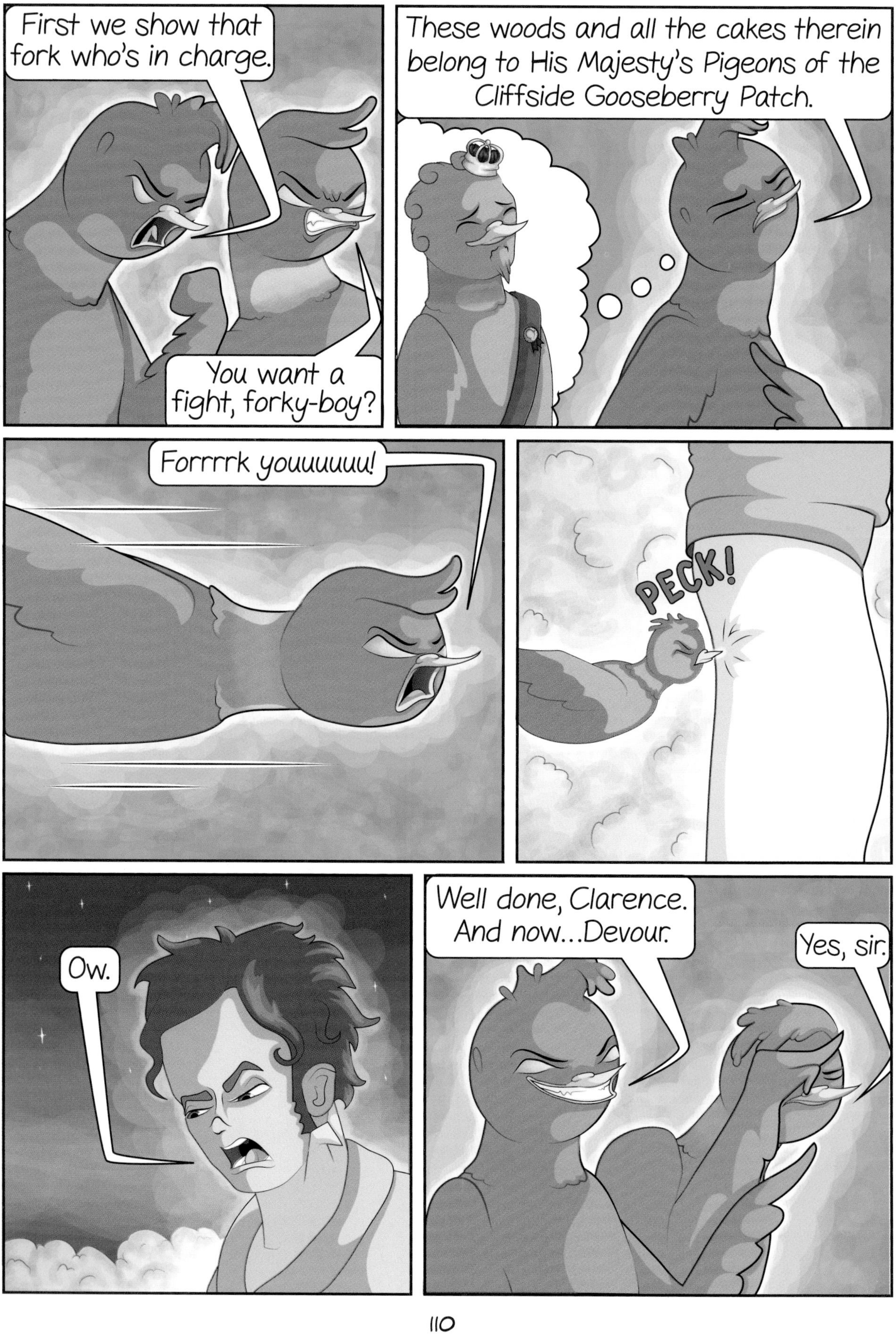
First we show that fork who's in charge.
You want a fight, forky-boy?
These woods and all the cakes therein belong to His Majesty's Pigeons of the Cliffside Gooseberry Patch.
Forrrrk youuuuuu!
PECK!
Ow.
Well done, Clarence. And now...Devour.
Yes, sir.

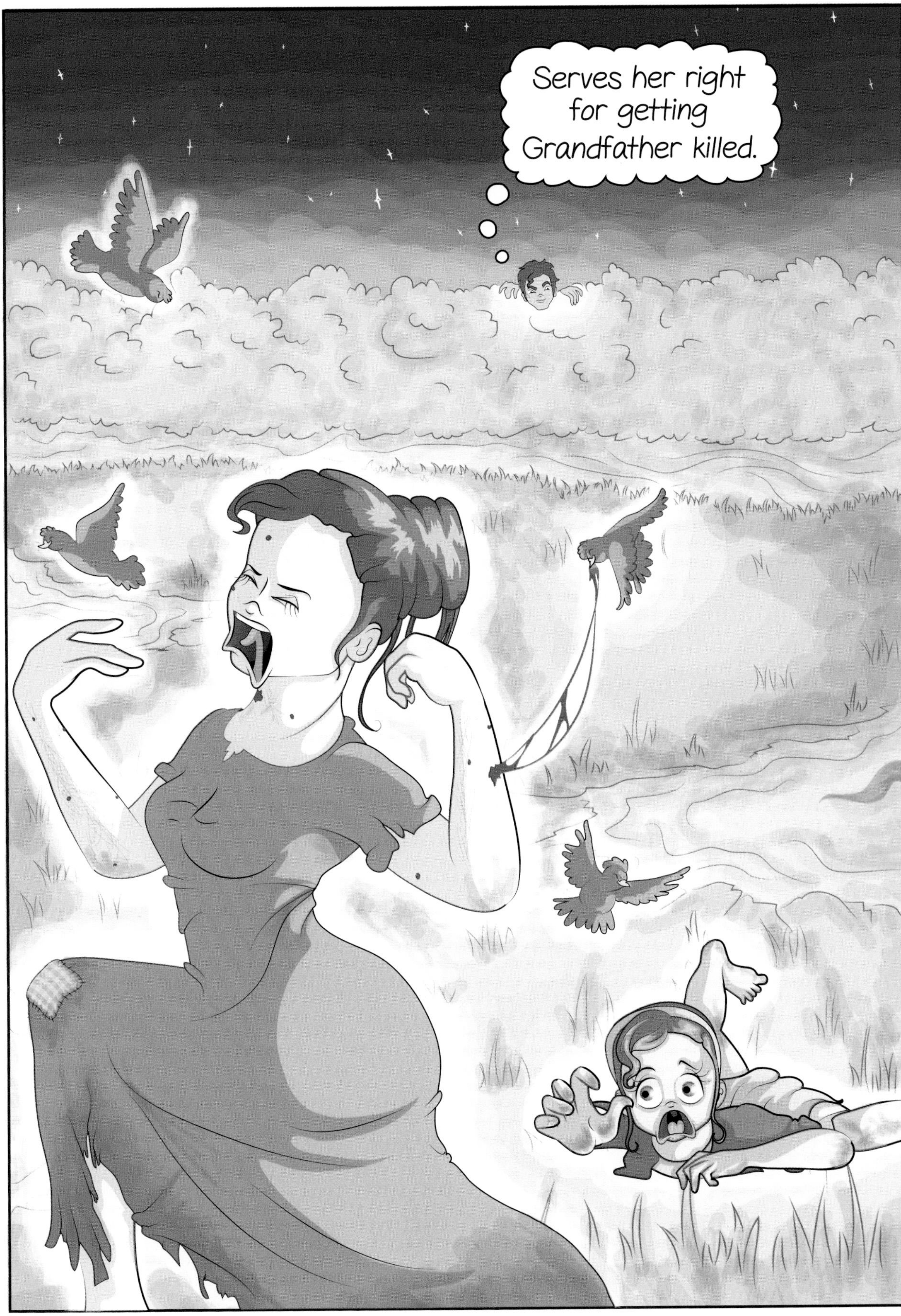
Serves her right for getting Grandfather killed.

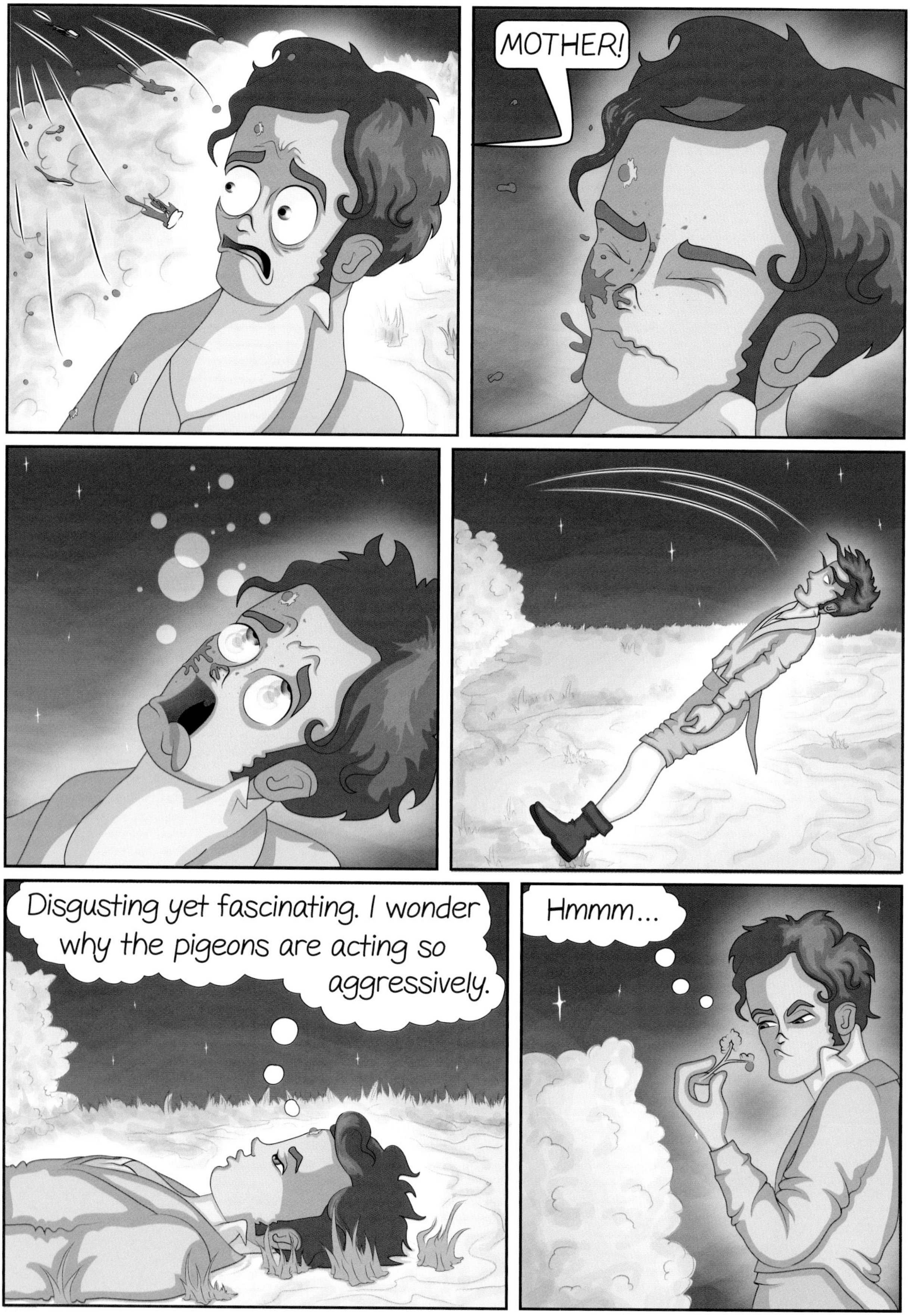
MOTHER!
Disgusting yet fascinating. I wonder why the pigeons are acting so aggressively.
Hmmm...

Forty minutes later, back at the house, also still back in 1809.

CLAVICEPS RABIDUS IS A PECULIAR FUNGUS THAT STRIKES GOOSEBERRIES ON VERY WET YEARS PRECEDED BY UNUSUALLY DRY YEARS. CAUTION! GOOSEBERRIES TAINTED BY THE CLAVICEPS RABIDUS CAUSE VIOLENT MADNESS RESEMBLING DEMONIC POSSESSION. NO CREATURE IS IMMUNE TO ITS EFFECTS. MERCIFULLY, THIS AFFLICTION IS ONLY TEMPORARY.

R-I-I-I-P!

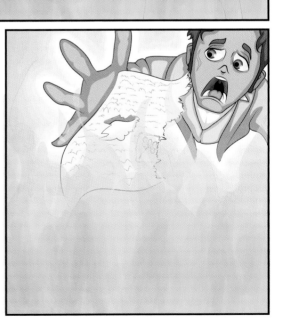

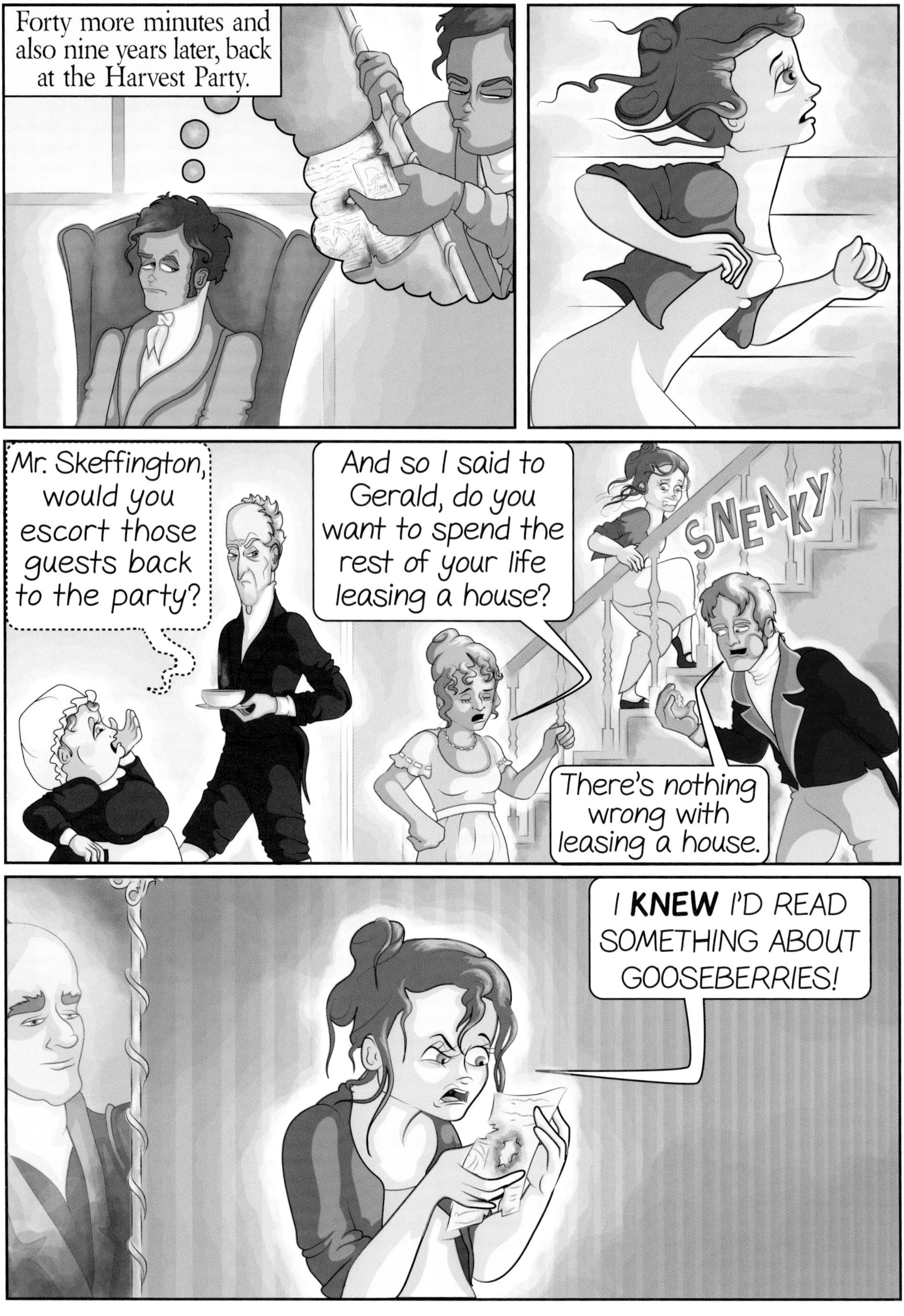

Forty more minutes and also nine years later, back at the Harvest Party.
Mr. Skeffington, would you escort those guests back to the party?
And so I said to Gerald, do you want to spend the rest of your life leasing a house?
SNEAKY
There's nothing wrong with leasing a house.
I **KNEW** I'D READ SOMETHING ABOUT GOOSEBERRIES!

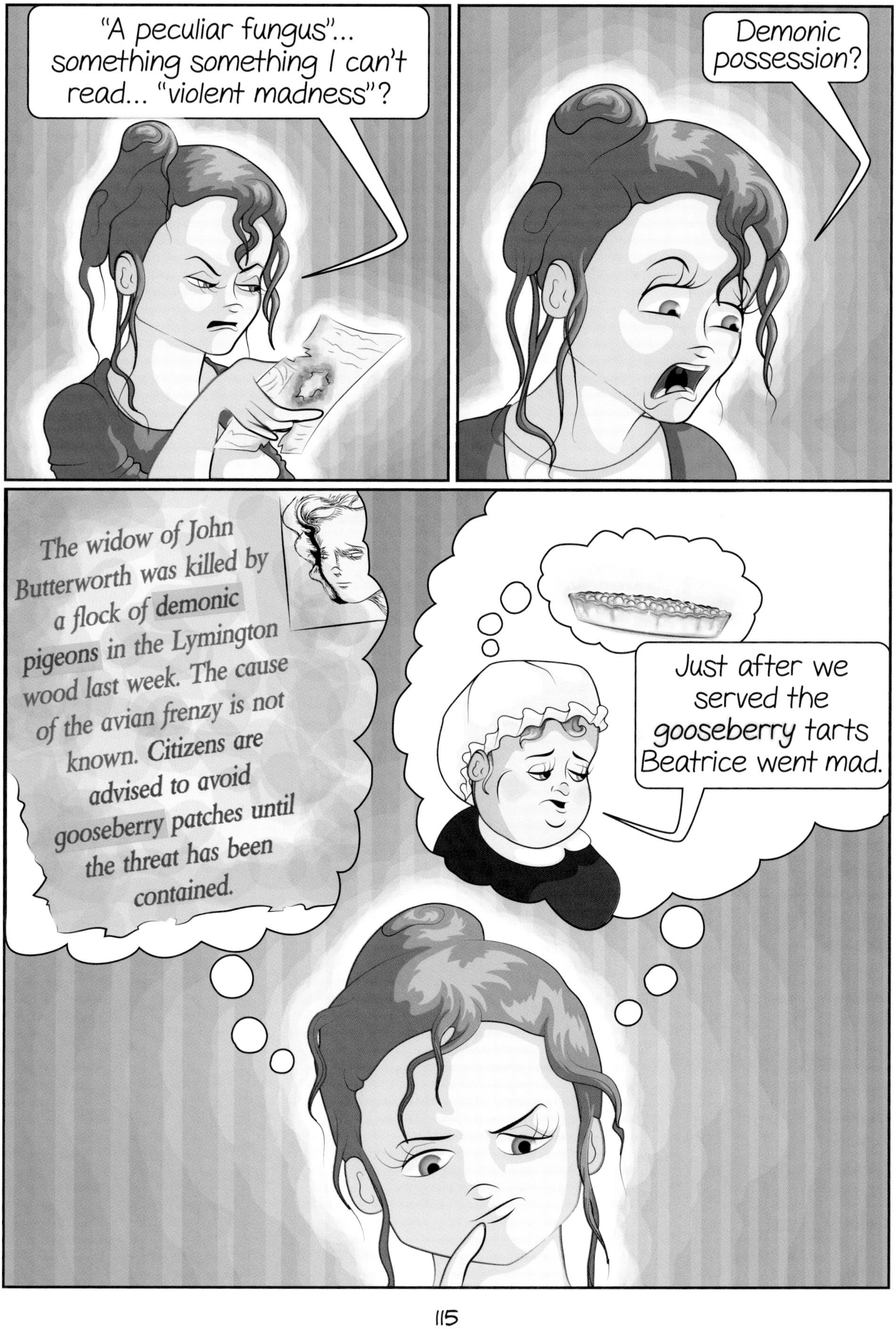
"A peculiar fungus"... something something I can't read... "violent madness"?
Demonic possession?
The widow of John Butterworth was killed by a flock of demonic pigeons in the Lymington wood last week. The cause of the avian frenzy is not known. Citizens are advised to avoid gooseberry patches until the threat has been contained.
Just after we served the gooseberry tarts Beatrice went mad.

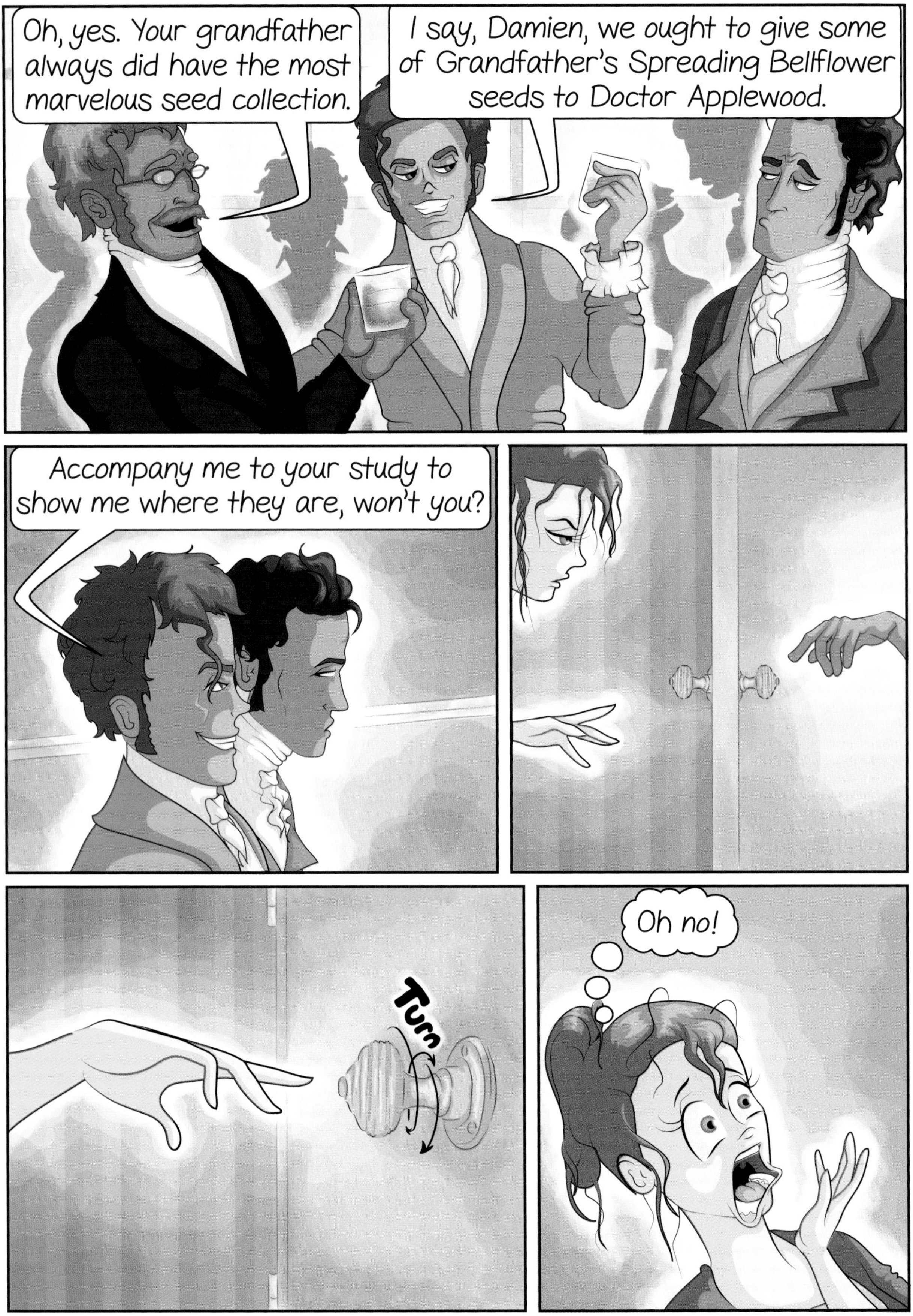
Oh, yes. Your grandfather always did have the most marvelous seed collection.
I say, Damien, we ought to give some of Grandfather's Spreading Bellflower seeds to Doctor Applewood.
Accompany me to your study to show me where they are, won't you?
Turn
Oh no!

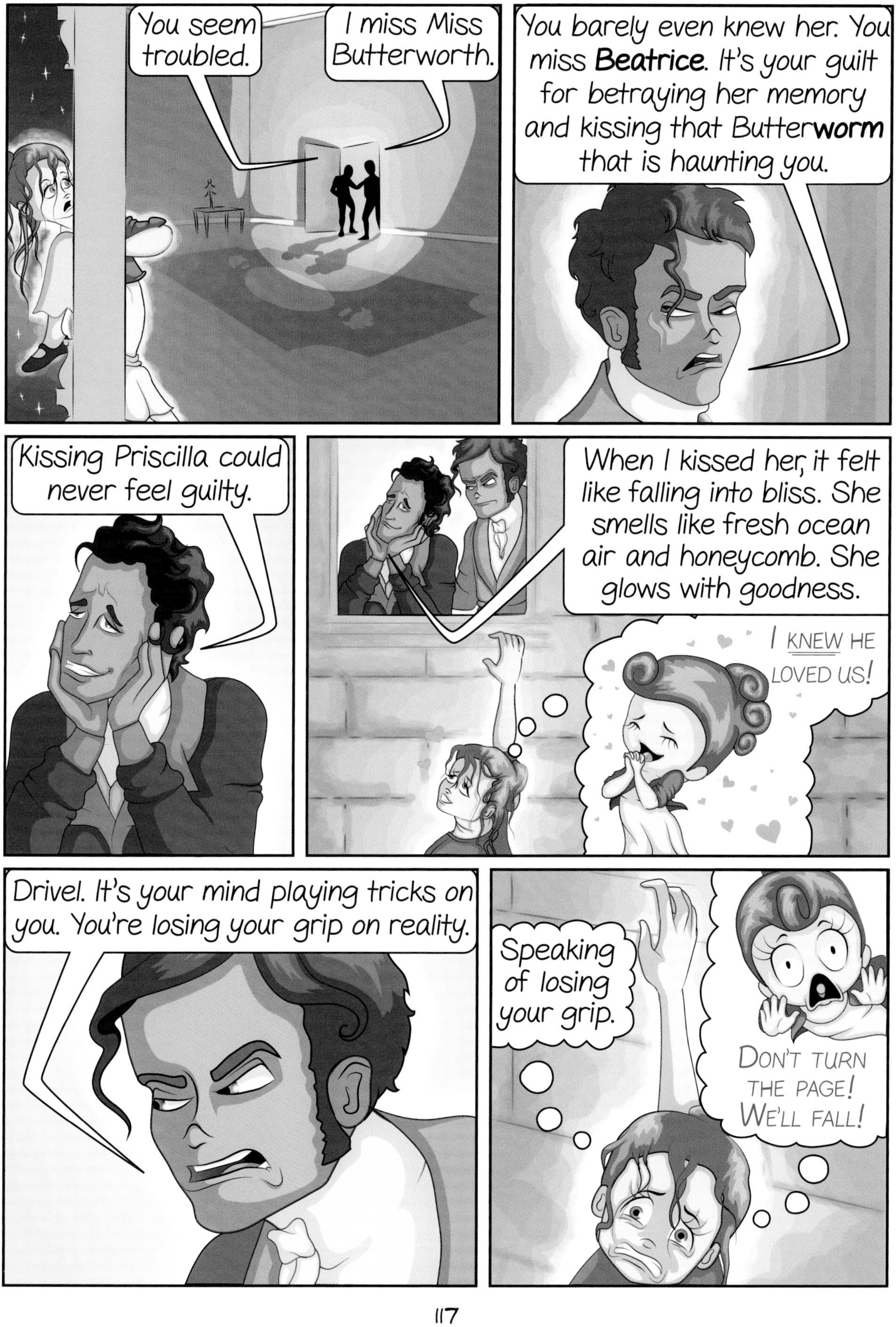
You seem troubled.
I miss Miss Butterworth.
You barely even knew her. You miss **Beatrice**. It's your guilt for betraying her memory and kissing that Butter**worm** that is haunting you.
Kissing Priscilla could never feel guilty.
When I kissed her, it felt like falling into bliss. She smells like fresh ocean air and honeycomb. She glows with goodness.
I KNEW HE LOVED US!
Drivel. It's your mind playing tricks on you. You're losing your grip on reality.
Speaking of losing your grip.
DON'T TURN THE PAGE! WE'LL FALL!

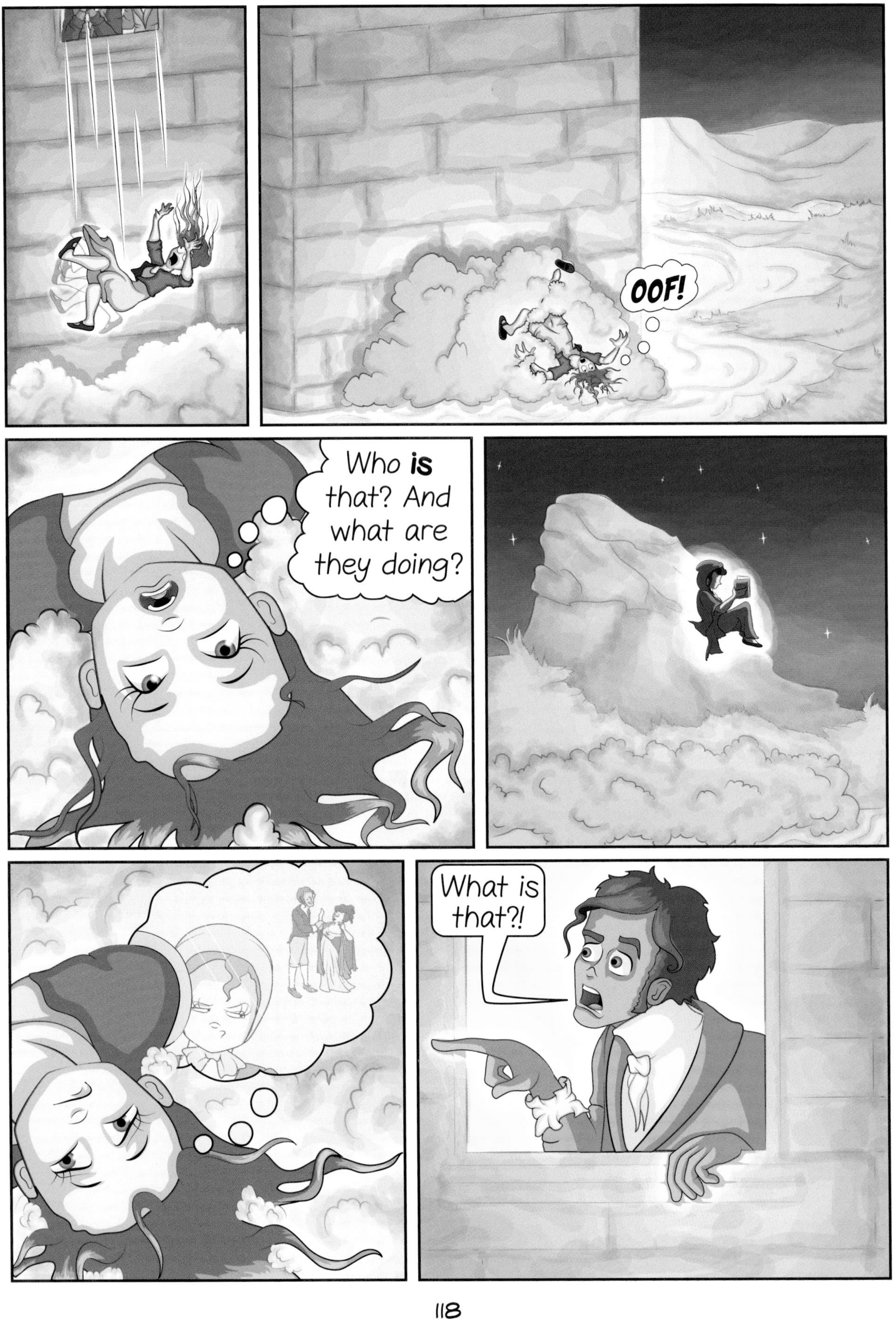
OOF!
Who is that? And what are they doing?
What is that?!

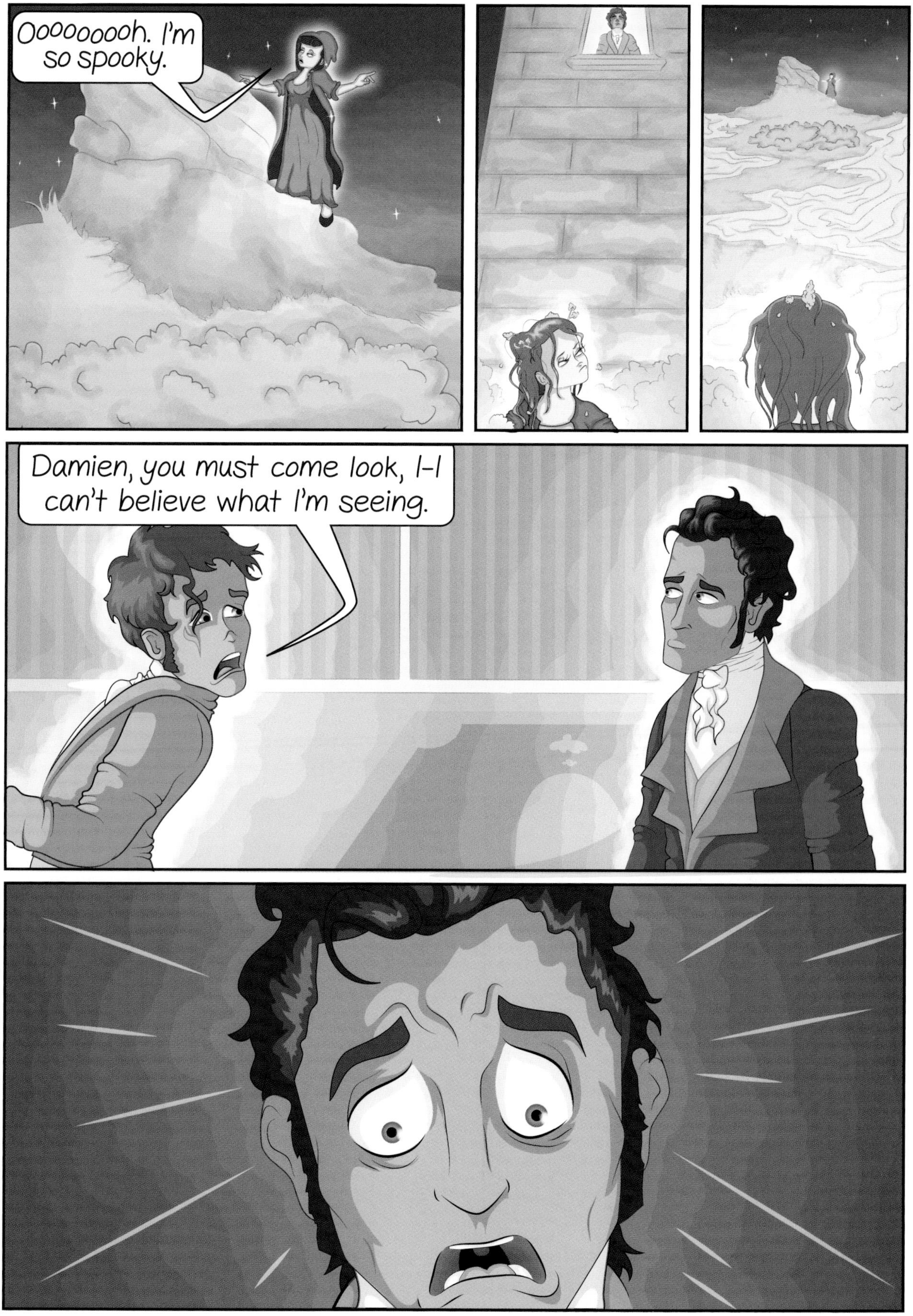
Oooooooooh. I'm so spooky.
Damien, you must come look, I-I can't believe what I'm seeing.

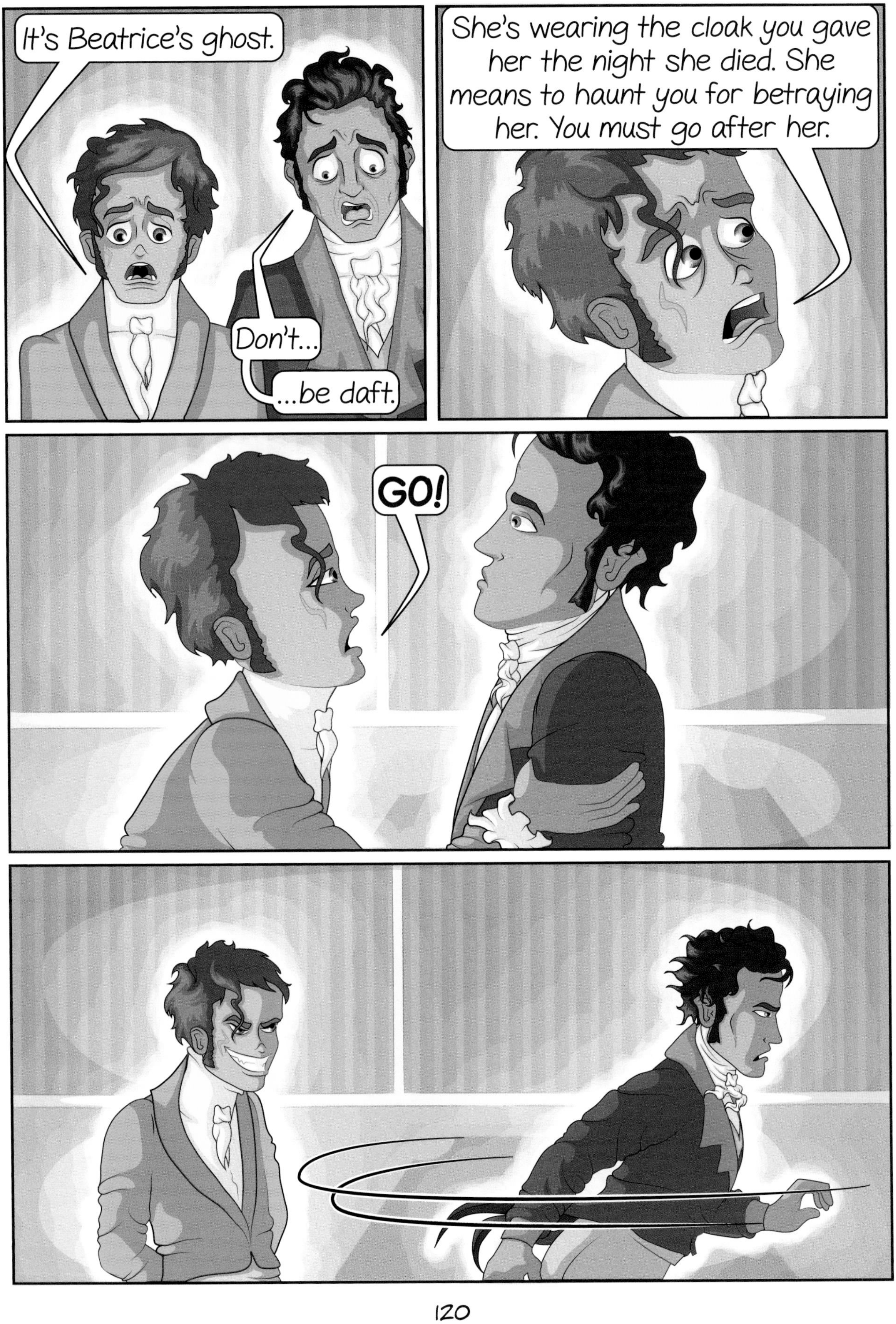
It's Beatrice's ghost.
Don't...
...be daft.
She's wearing the cloak you gave her the night she died. She means to haunt you for betraying her. You must go after her.
GO!

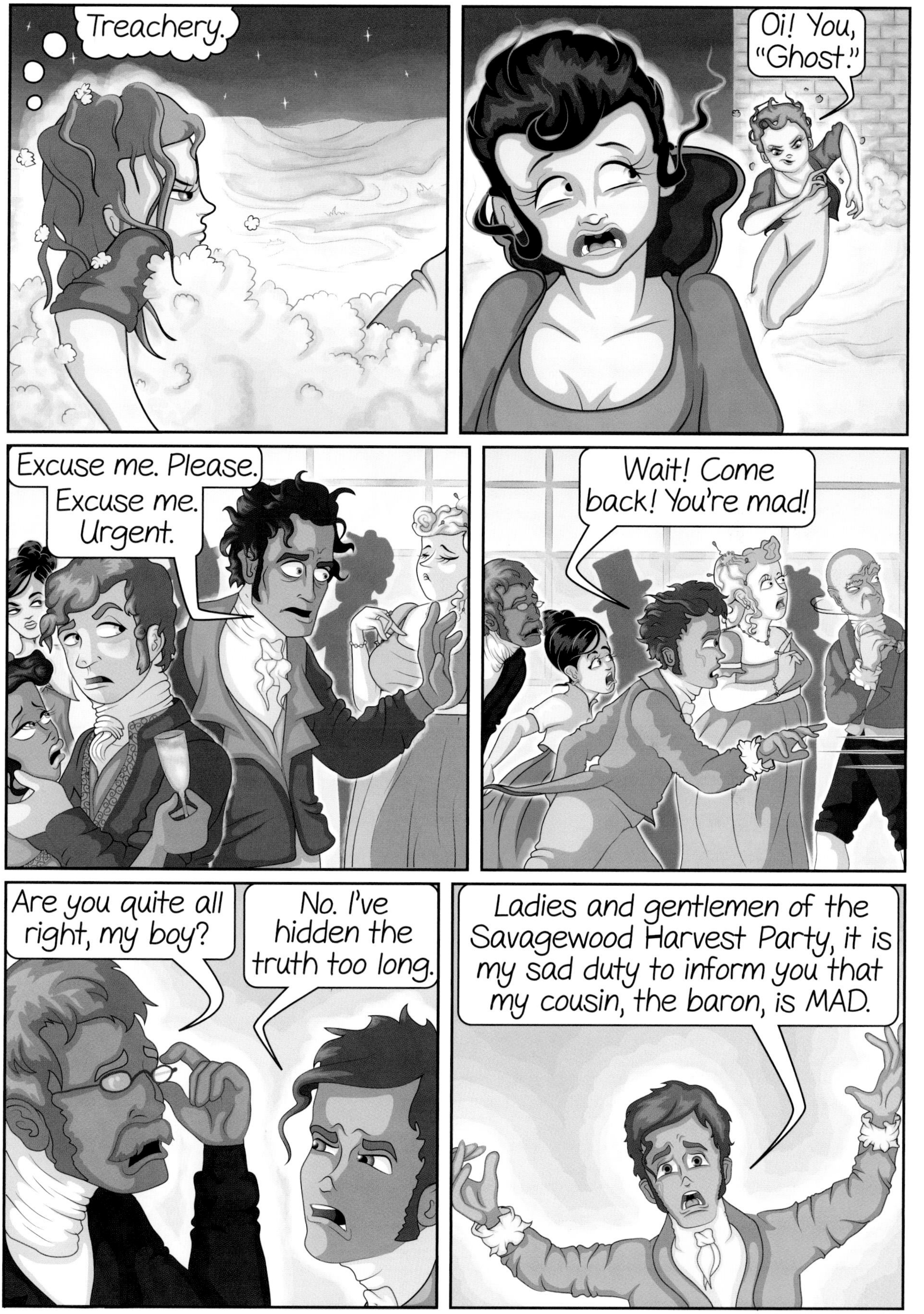
Treachery.
Oi! You, "Ghost."
Excuse me. Please.
Excuse me. Urgent.
Wait! Come back! You're mad!
Are you quite all right, my boy?
No. I've hidden the truth too long.
Ladies and gentlemen of the Savagewood Harvest Party, it is my sad duty to inform you that my cousin, the baron, is MAD.

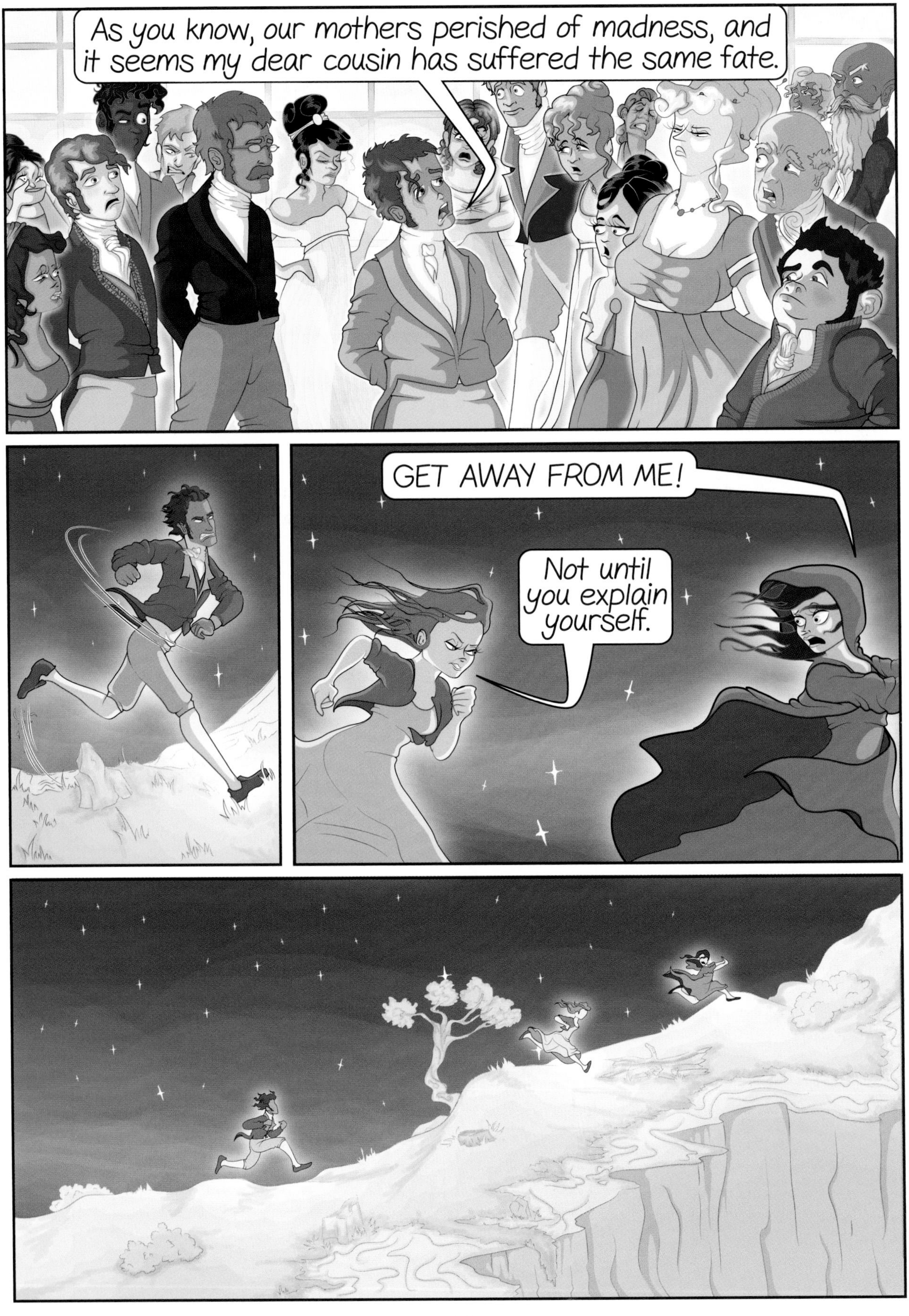
As you know, our mothers perished of madness, and it seems my dear cousin has suffered the same fate.
GET AWAY FROM ME!
Not until you explain yourself.

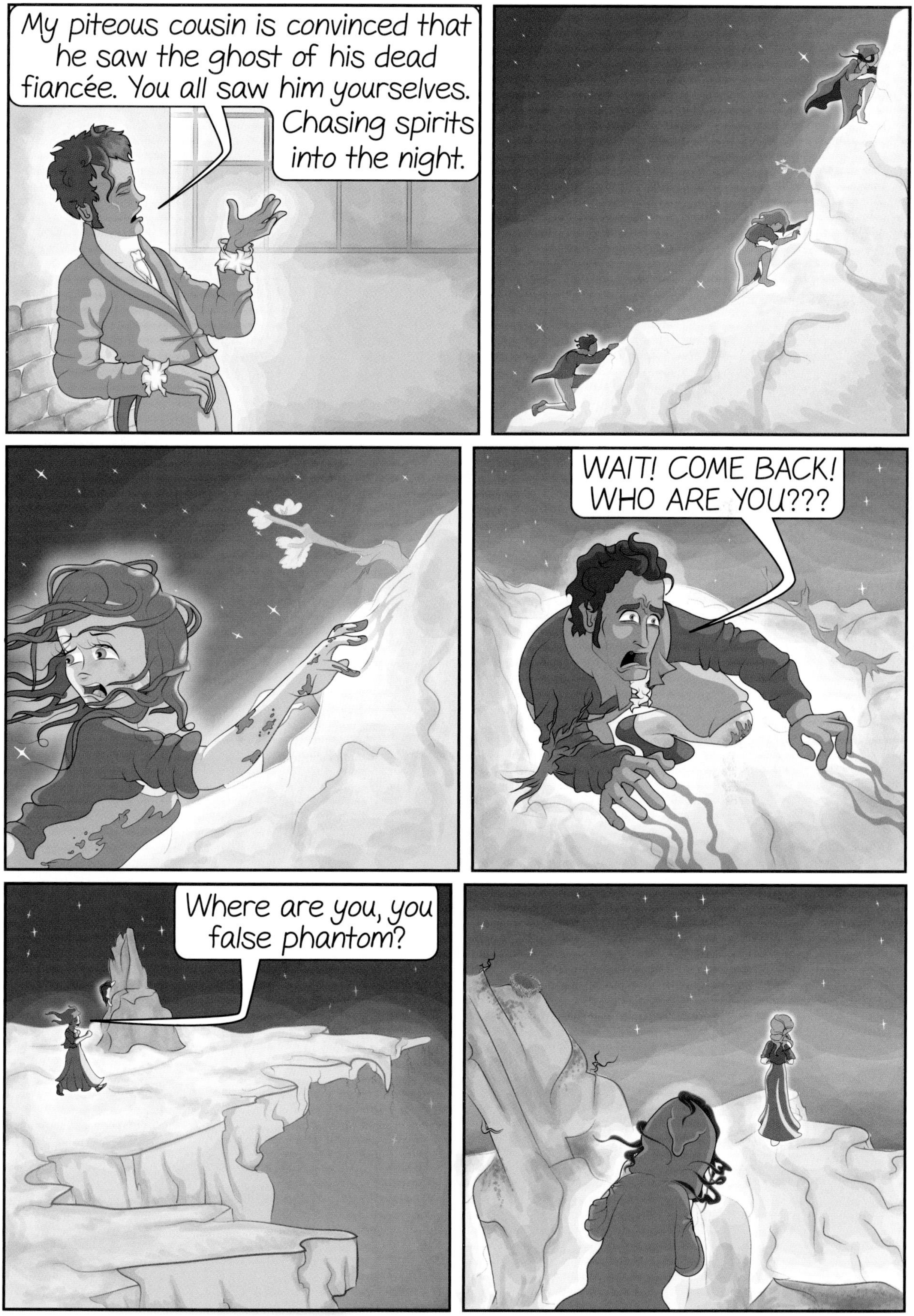
My piteous cousin is convinced that he saw the ghost of his dead fiancée. You all saw him yourselves.
Chasing spirits into the night.
WAIT! COME BACK! WHO ARE YOU???
Where are you, you false phantom?

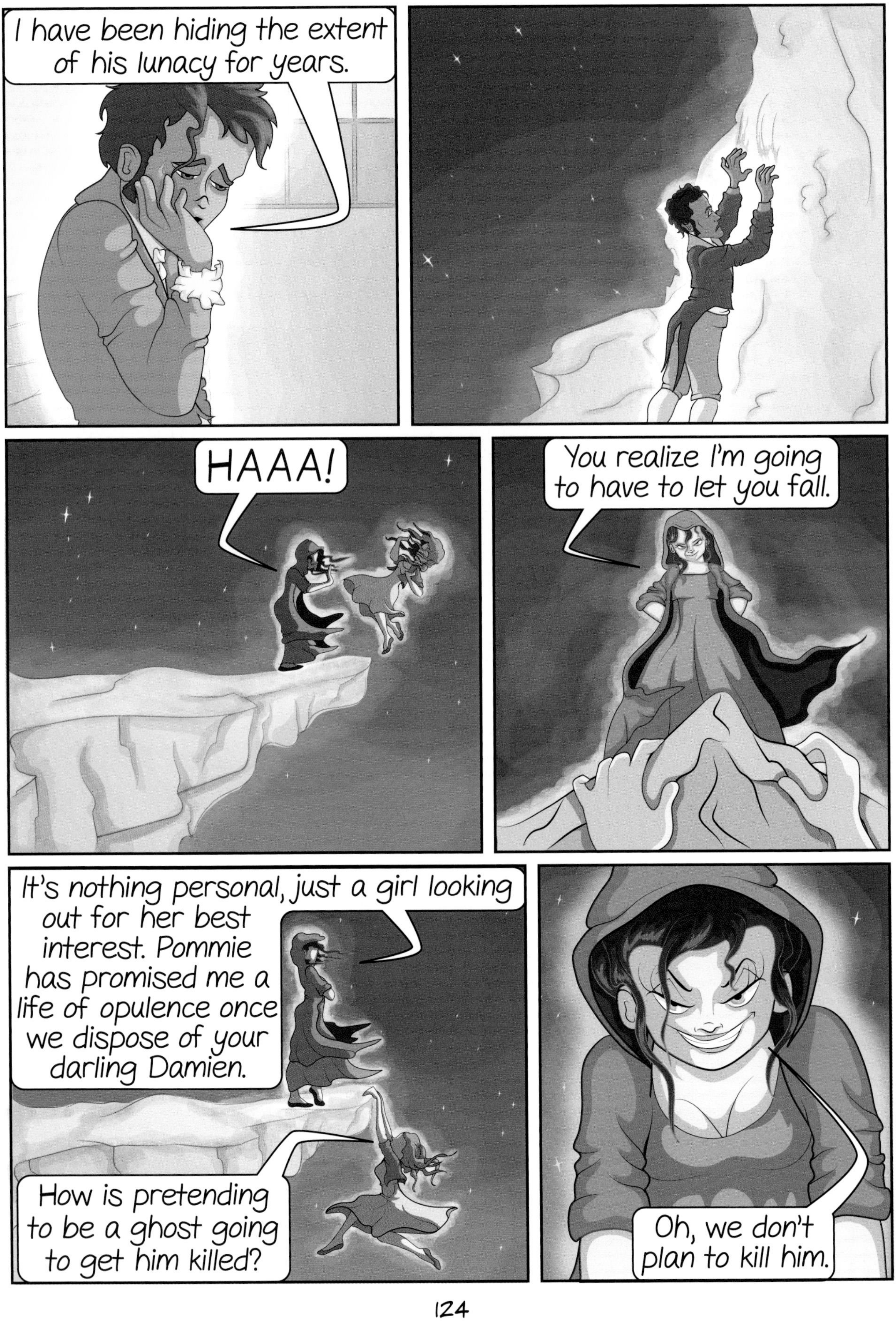
I have been hiding the extent of his lunacy for years.
HAAA!
You realize I'm going to have to let you fall.
It's nothing personal, just a girl looking out for her best interest. Pommie has promised me a life of opulence once we dispose of your darling Damien.
How is pretending to be a ghost going to get him killed?
Oh, we don't plan to kill him.

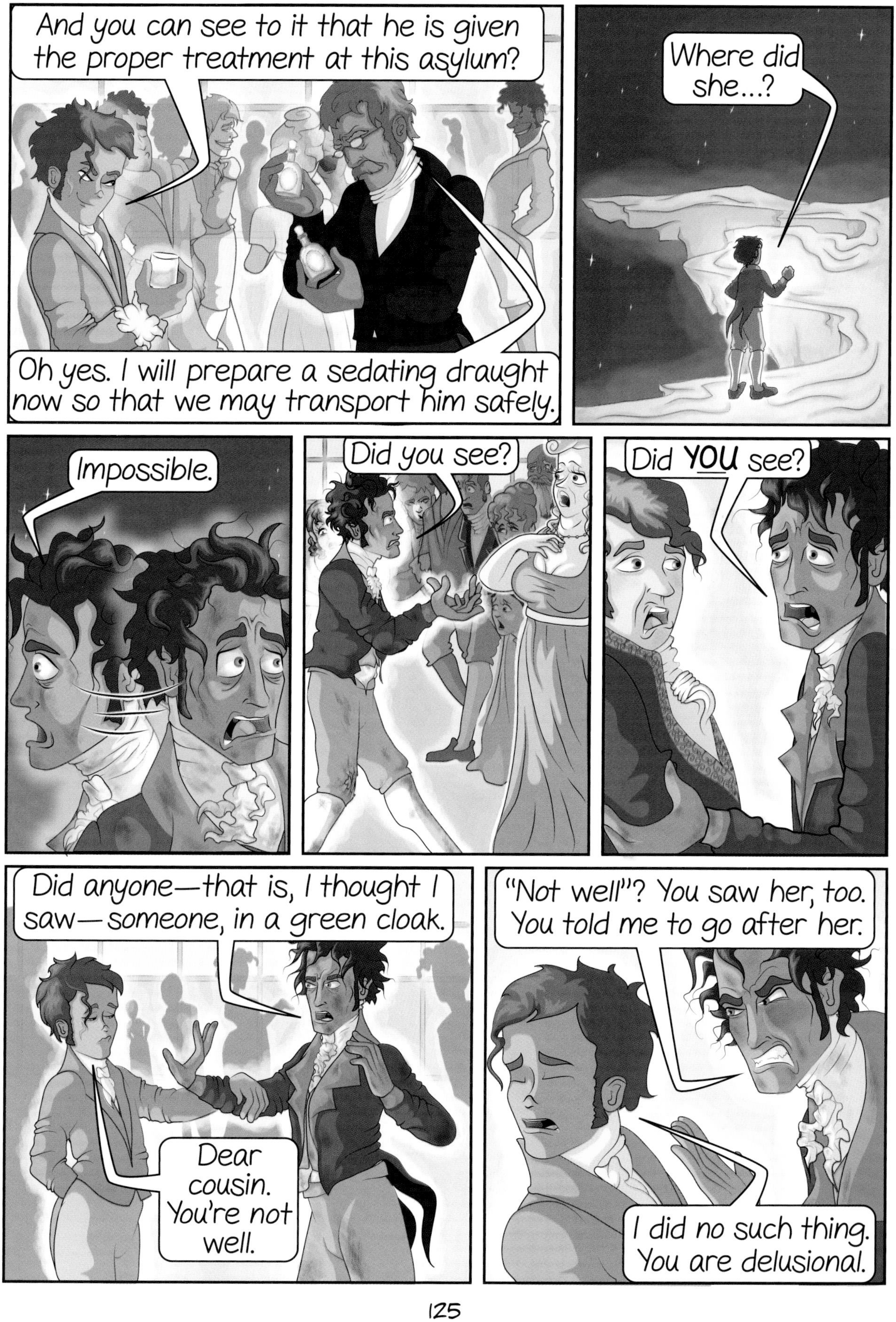
And you can see to it that he is given the proper treatment at this asylum?
Oh yes. I will prepare a sedating draught now so that we may transport him safely.
Where did she...?
Impossible.
Did you see?
Did YOU see?
Did anyone—that is, I thought I saw—someone, in a green cloak.
Dear cousin. You're not well.
"Not well"? You saw her, too. You told me to go after her.
I did no such thing. You are delusional.

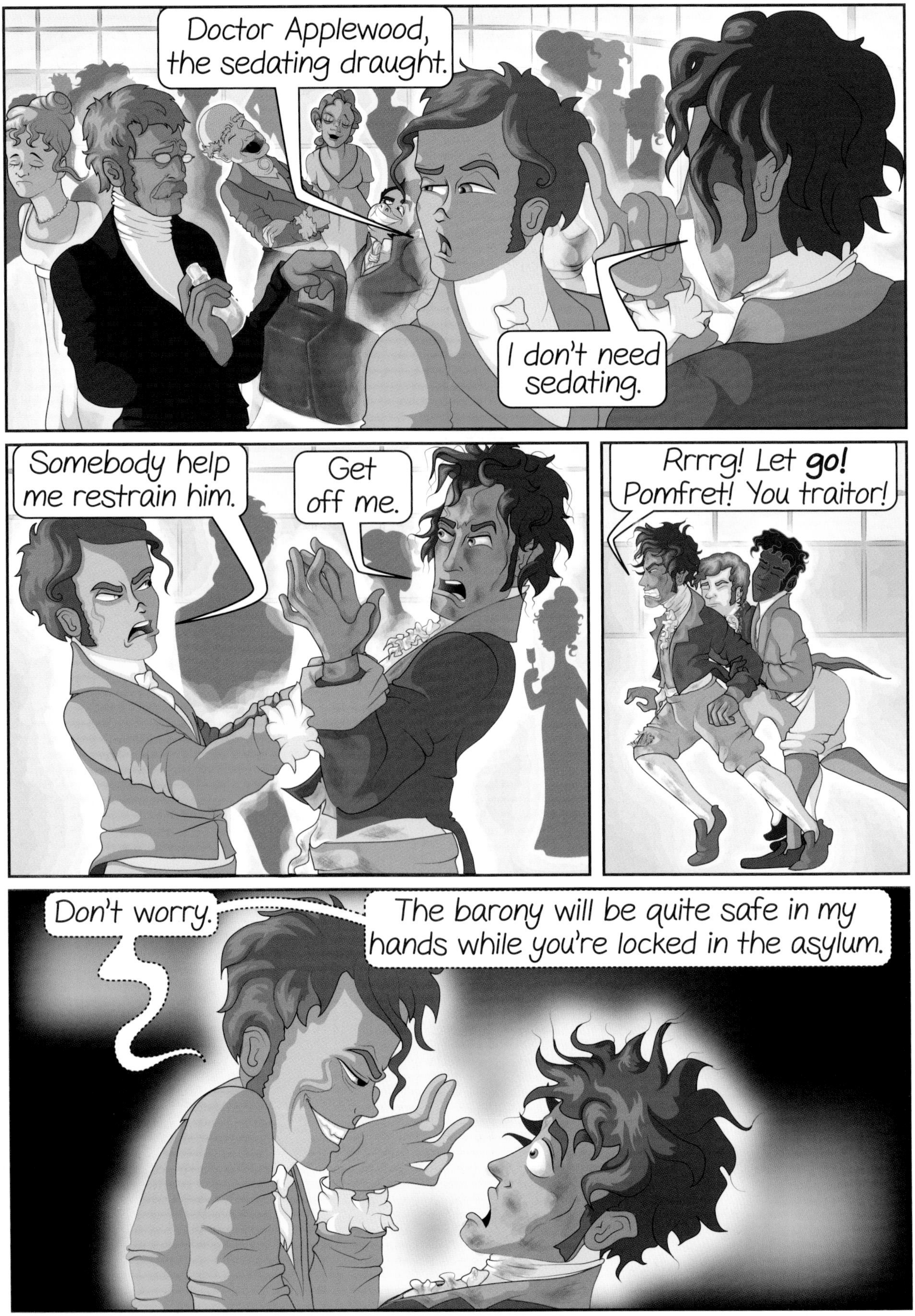
Doctor Applewood, the sedating draught.
I don't need sedating.
Somebody help me restrain him.
Get off me.
Rrrrg! Let **go!** Pomfret! You traitor!
Don't worry.
The barony will be quite safe in my hands while you're locked in the asylum.

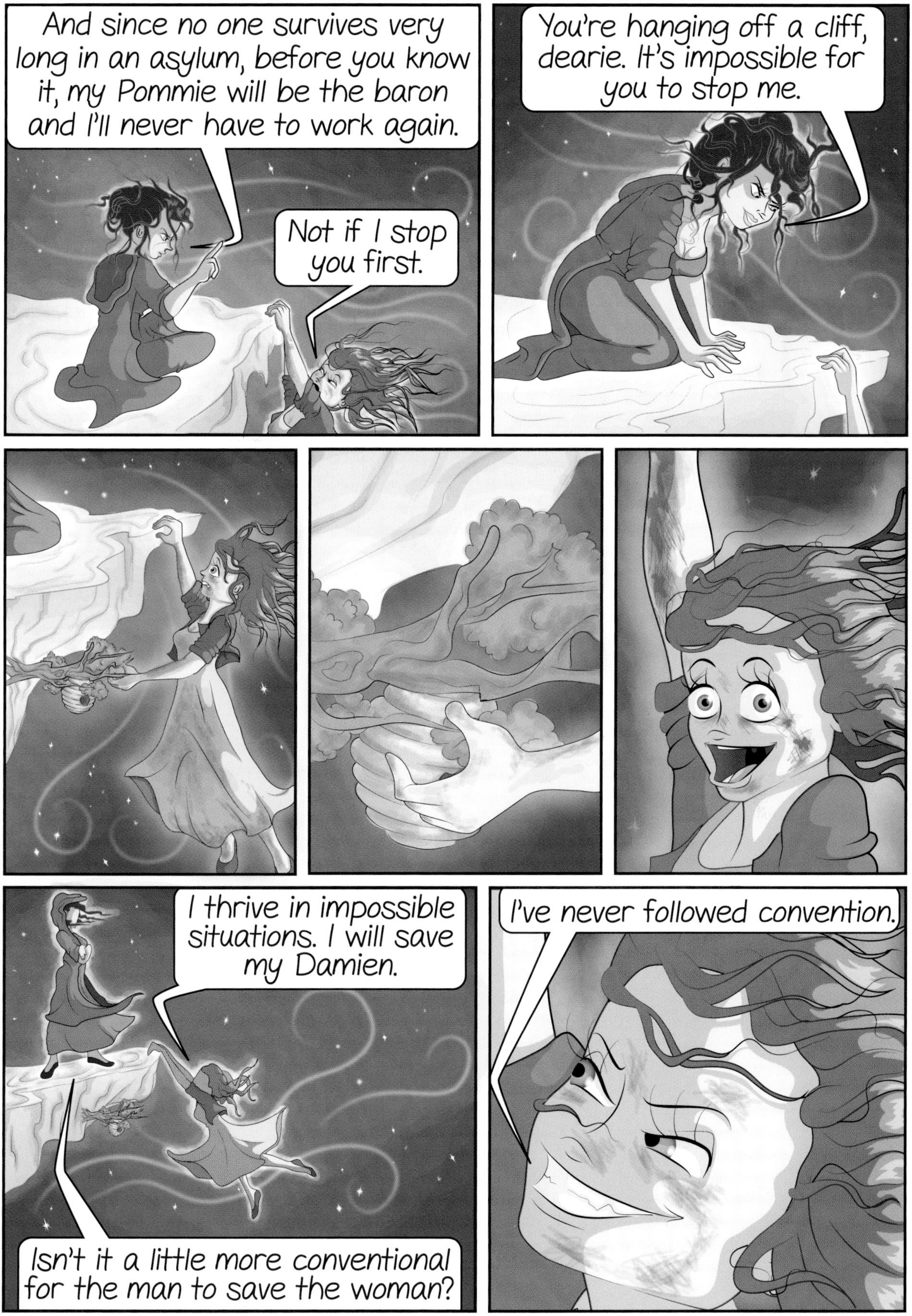
And since no one survives very long in an asylum, before you know it, my Pommie will be the baron and I'll never have to work again.
Not if I stop you first.
You're hanging off a cliff, dearie. It's impossible for you to stop me.
I thrive in impossible situations. I will save my Damien.
Isn't it a little more conventional for the man to save the woman?
I've never followed convention.

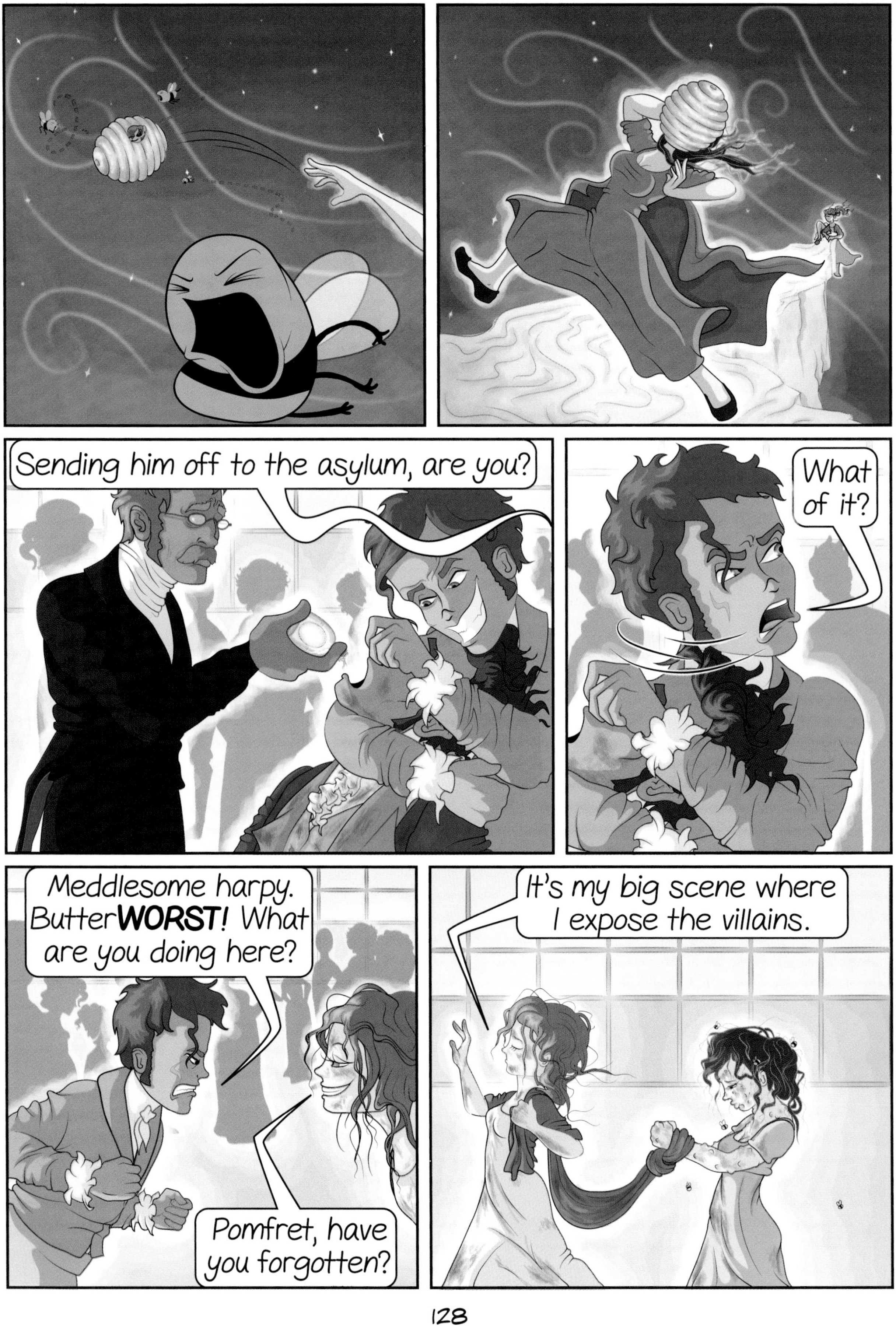
Sending him off to the asylum, are you?
What of it?
Meddlesome harpy. Butter**WORST**! What are you doing here?
Pomfret, have you forgotten?
It's my big scene where I expose the villains.

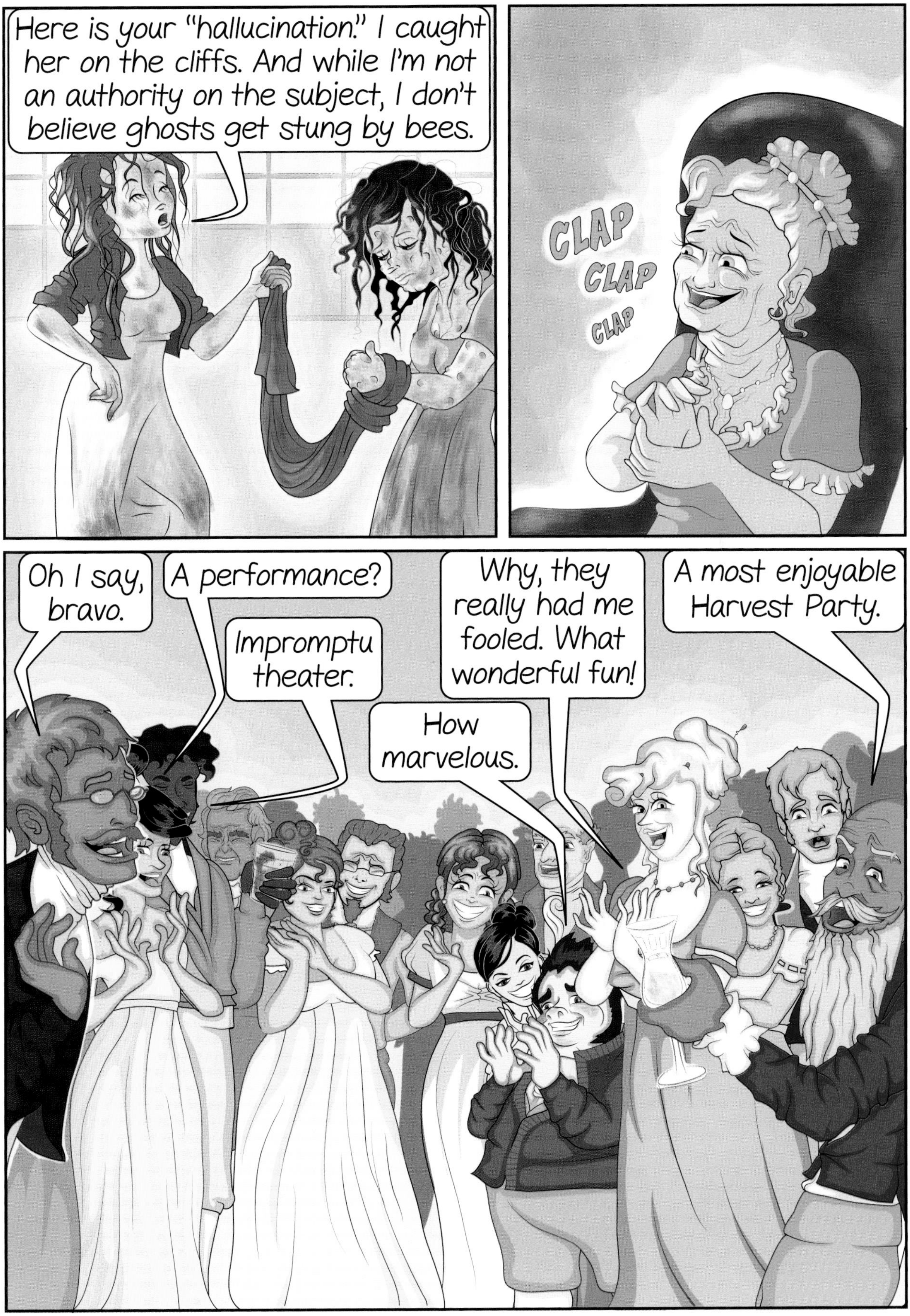
Here is your "hallucination." I caught her on the cliffs. And while I'm not an authority on the subject, I don't believe ghosts get stung by bees.
CLAP
CLAP
CLAP
Oh I say, bravo.
A performance?
Impromptu theater.
How marvelous.
Why, they really had me fooled. What wonderful fun!
A most enjoyable Harvest Party.

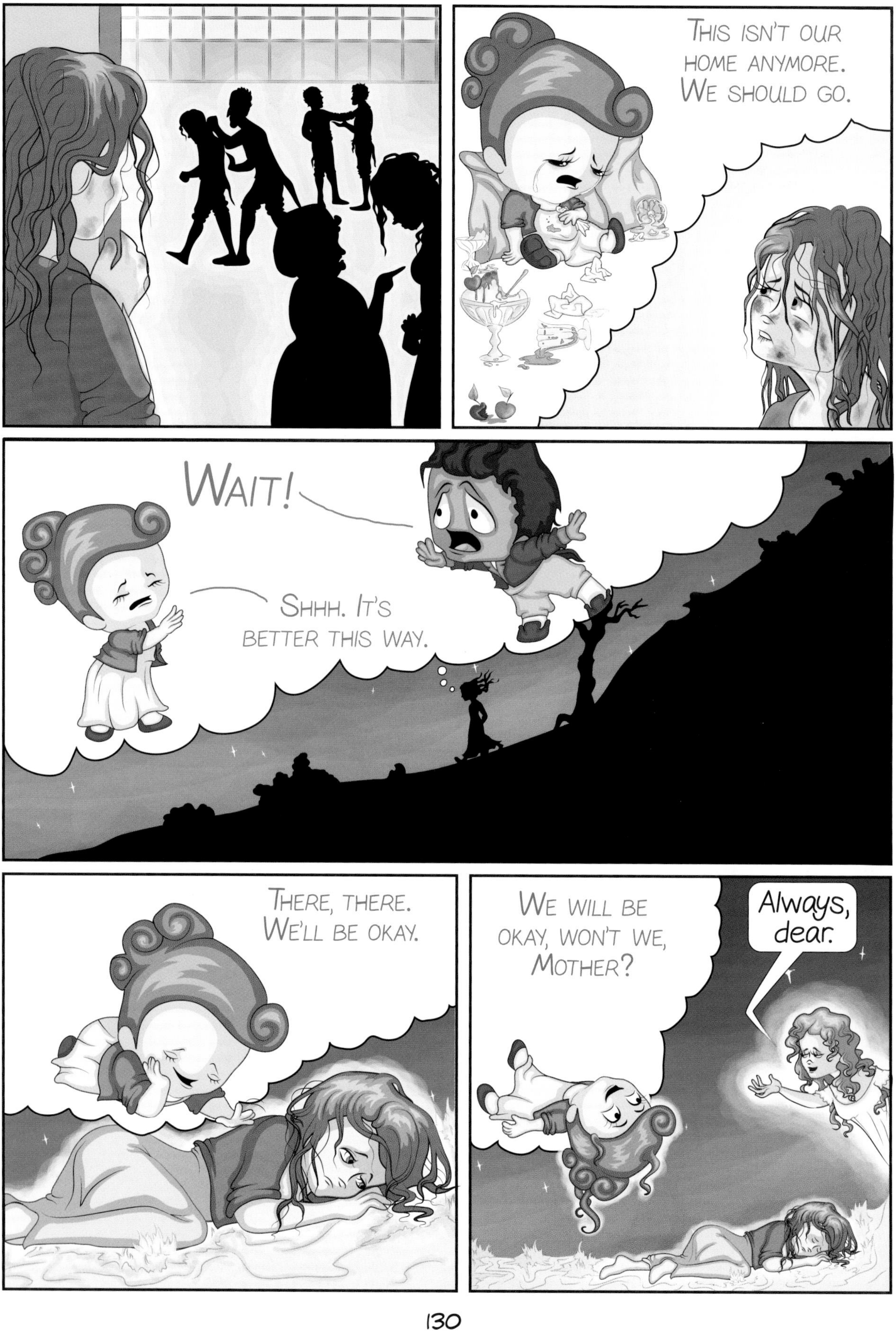
This isn't our home anymore. We should go.
Wait!
Shhh. It's better this way.
There, there. We'll be okay.
We will be okay, won't we, Mother?
Always, dear.

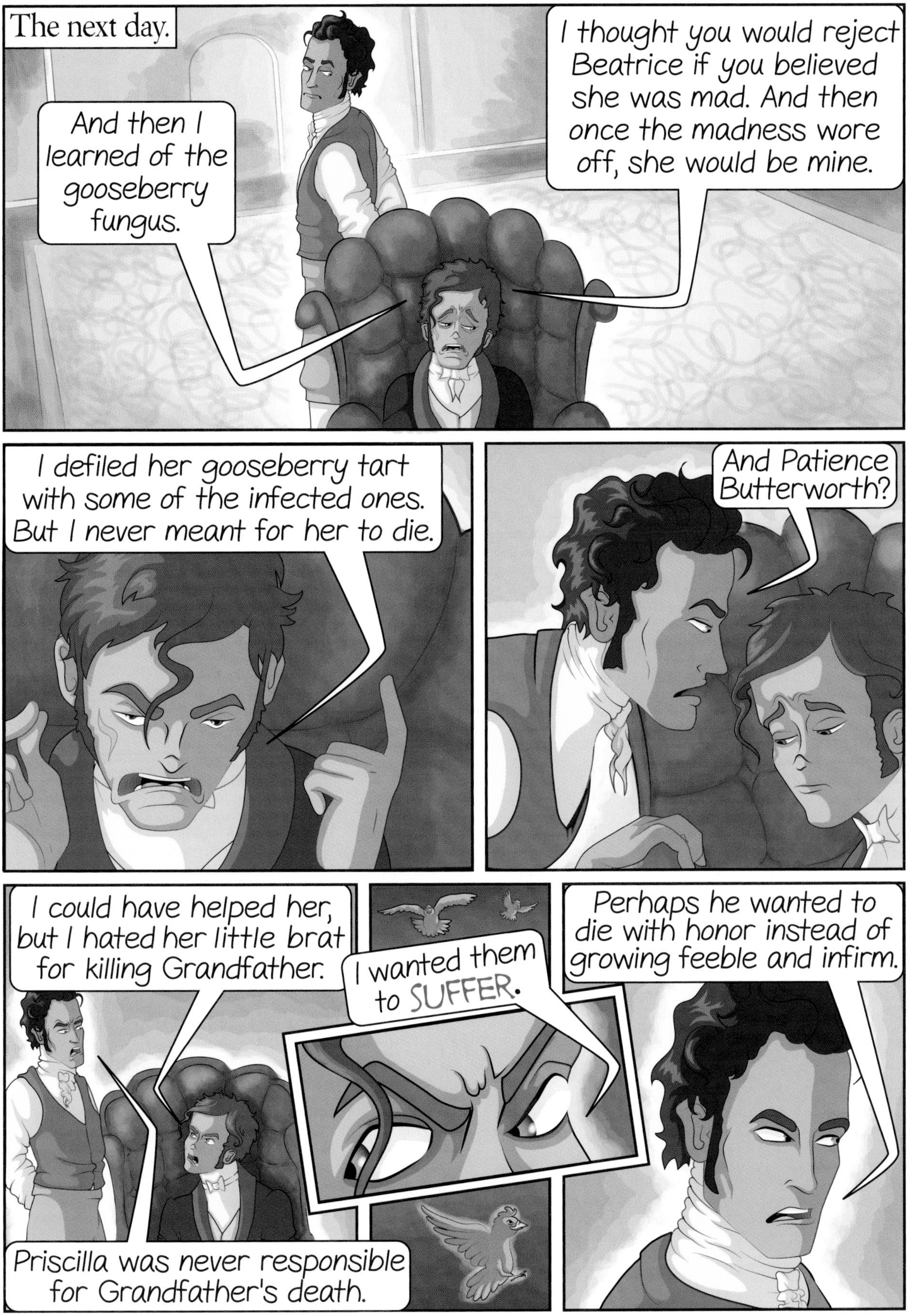
The next day.
And then I learned of the gooseberry fungus.
I thought you would reject Beatrice if you believed she was mad. And then once the madness wore off, she would be mine.
I defiled her gooseberry tart with some of the infected ones. But I never meant for her to die.
And Patience Butterworth?
I could have helped her, but I hated her little brat for killing Grandfather.
Priscilla was never responsible for Grandfather's death.
I wanted them to SUFFER.
Perhaps he wanted to die with honor instead of growing feeble and infirm.

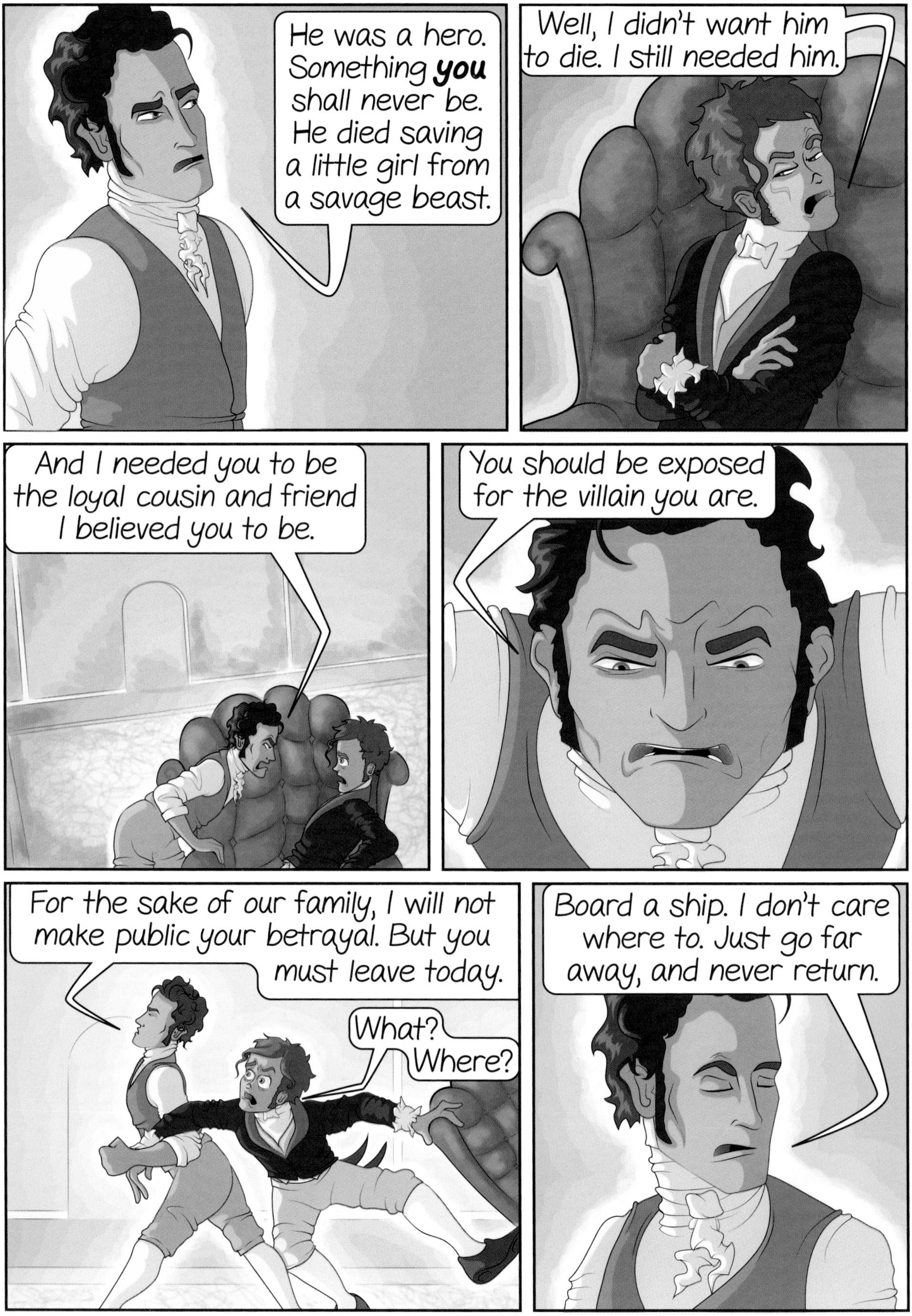

He was a hero. Something **you** shall never be. He died saving a little girl from a savage beast.
Well, I didn't want him to die. I still needed him.
And I needed you to be the loyal cousin and friend I believed you to be.
You should be exposed for the villain you are.
For the sake of our family, I will not make public your betrayal. But you must leave today.
What?
Where?
Board a ship. I don't care where to. Just go far away, and never return.

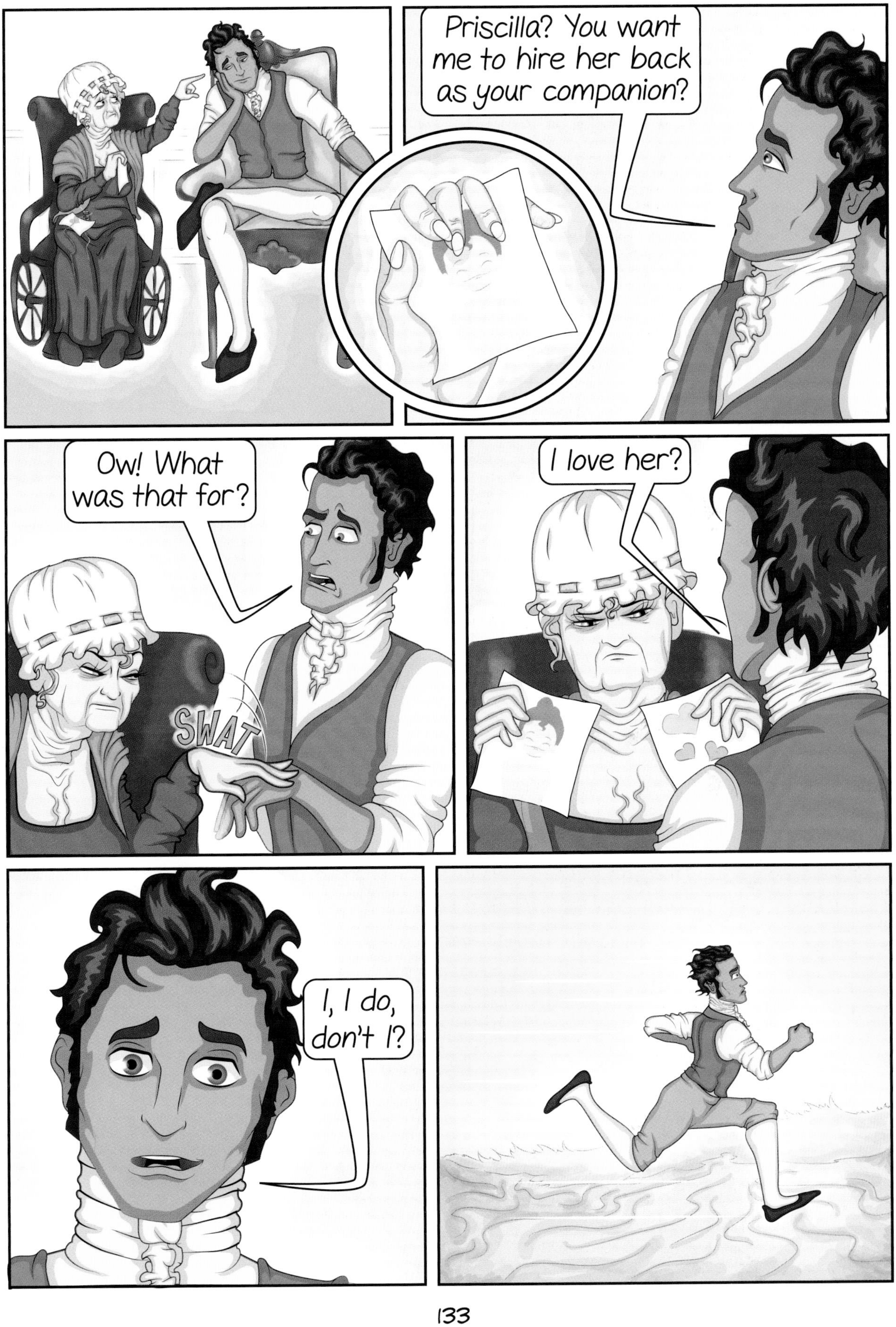
Priscilla? You want me to hire her back as your companion?
Ow! What was that for?
SWAT
I love her?
I, I do, don't I?

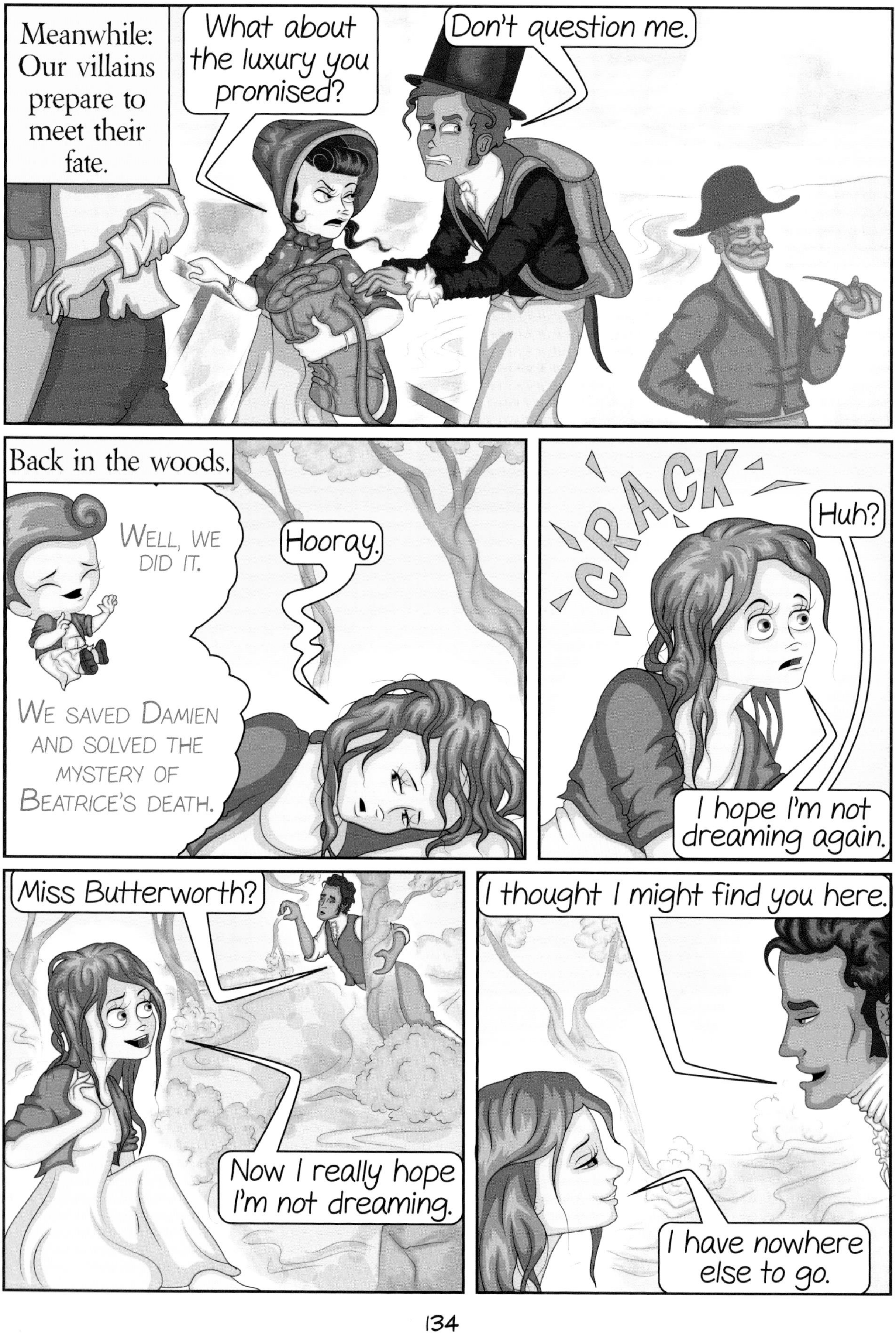
Meanwhile: Our villains prepare to meet their fate.
What about the luxury you promised?
Don't question me.
Back in the woods.
Well, we did it.
We saved Damien and solved the mystery of Beatrice's death.
Hooray.
CRACK
Huh?
I hope I'm not dreaming again.
Miss Butterworth?
Now I really hope I'm not dreaming.
I thought I might find you here.
I have nowhere else to go.

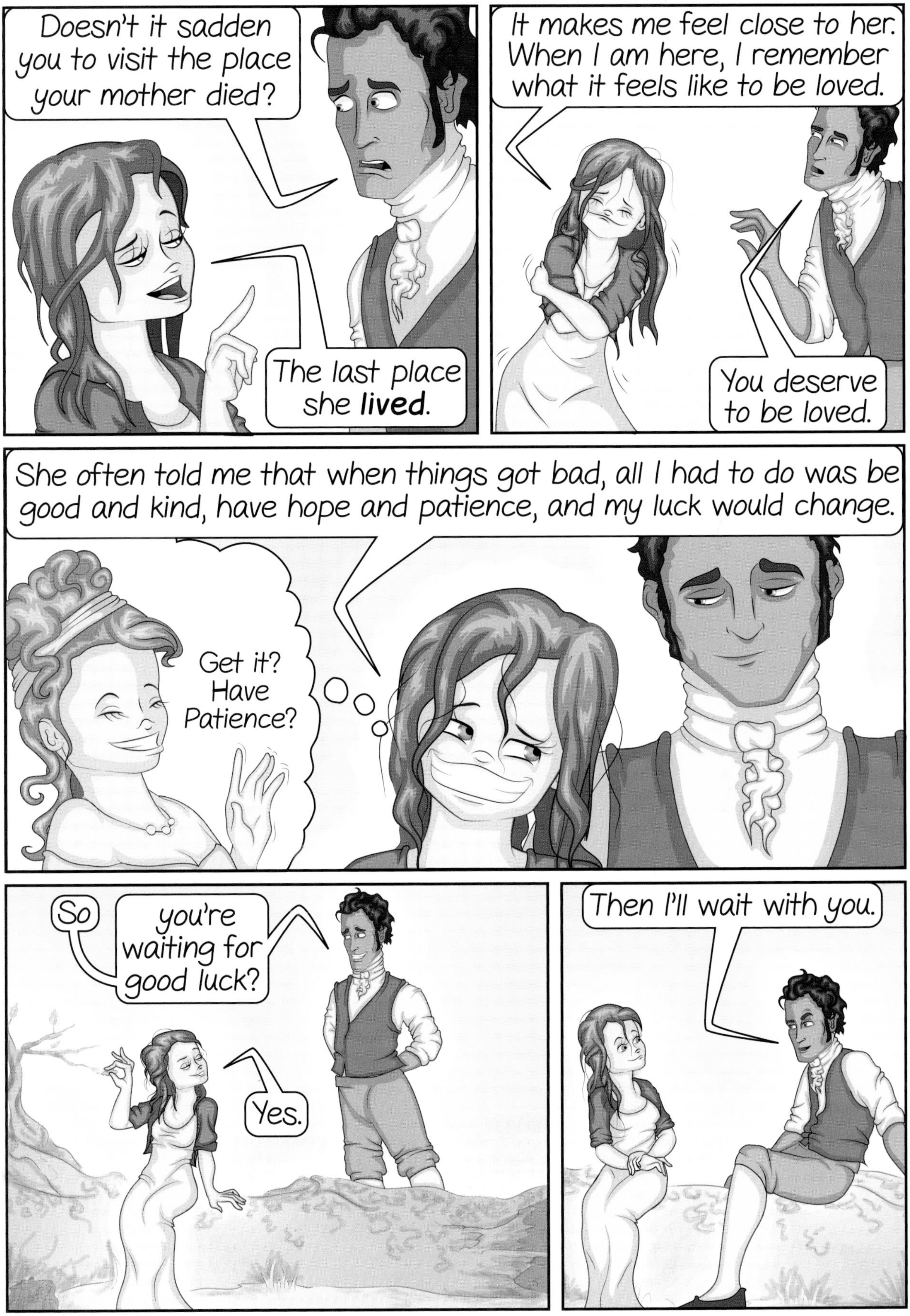
Doesn't it sadden you to visit the place your mother died?
The last place she **lived**.
It makes me feel close to her. When I am here, I remember what it feels like to be loved.
You deserve to be loved.
She often told me that when things got bad, all I had to do was be good and kind, have hope and patience, and my luck would change.
Get it? Have Patience?
So
you're waiting for good luck?
Yes.
Then I'll wait with you.

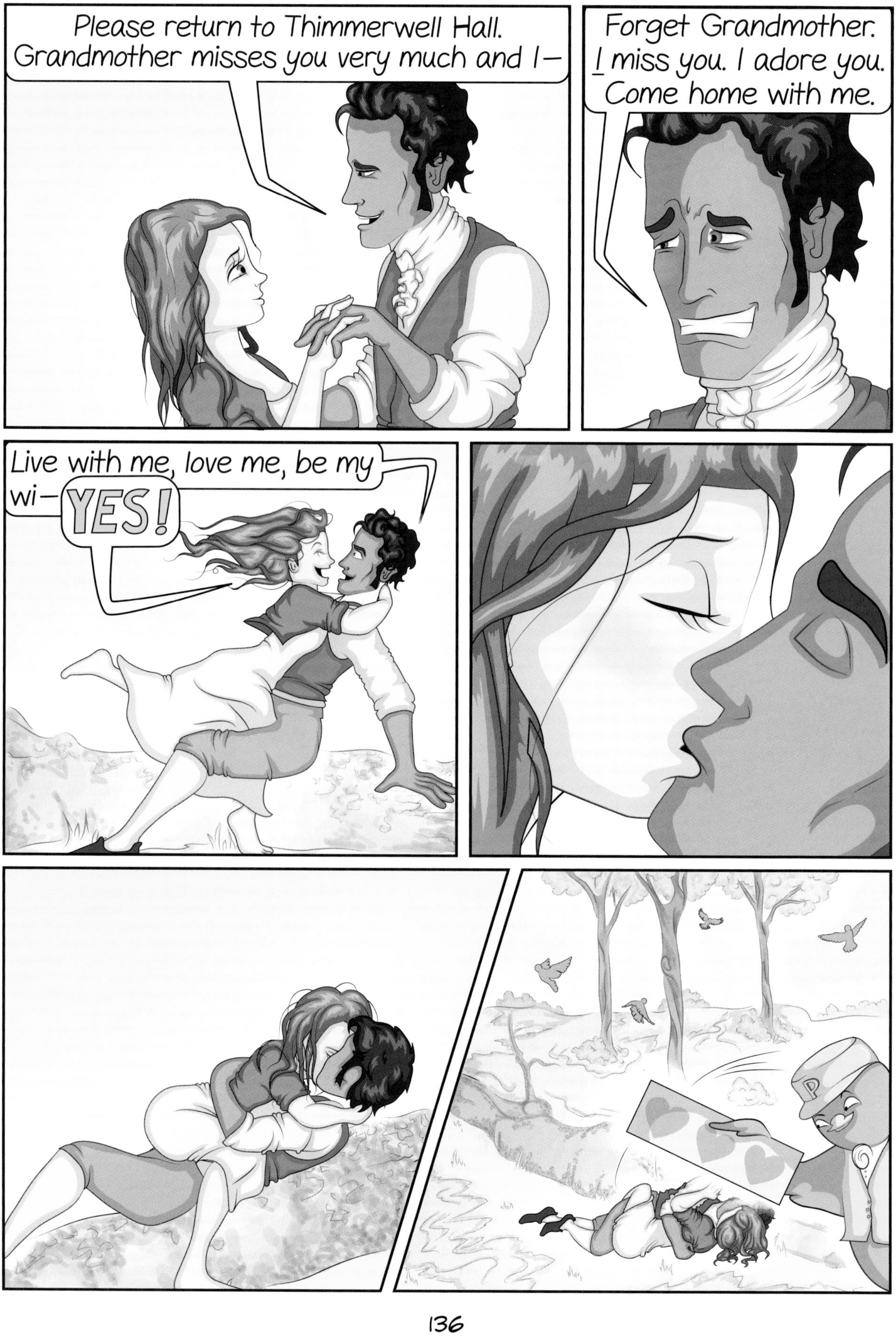
Please return to Thimmerwell Hall. Grandmother misses you very much and I—
Forget Grandmother. I miss you. I adore you. Come home with me.
Live with me, love me, be my wi—
YES!

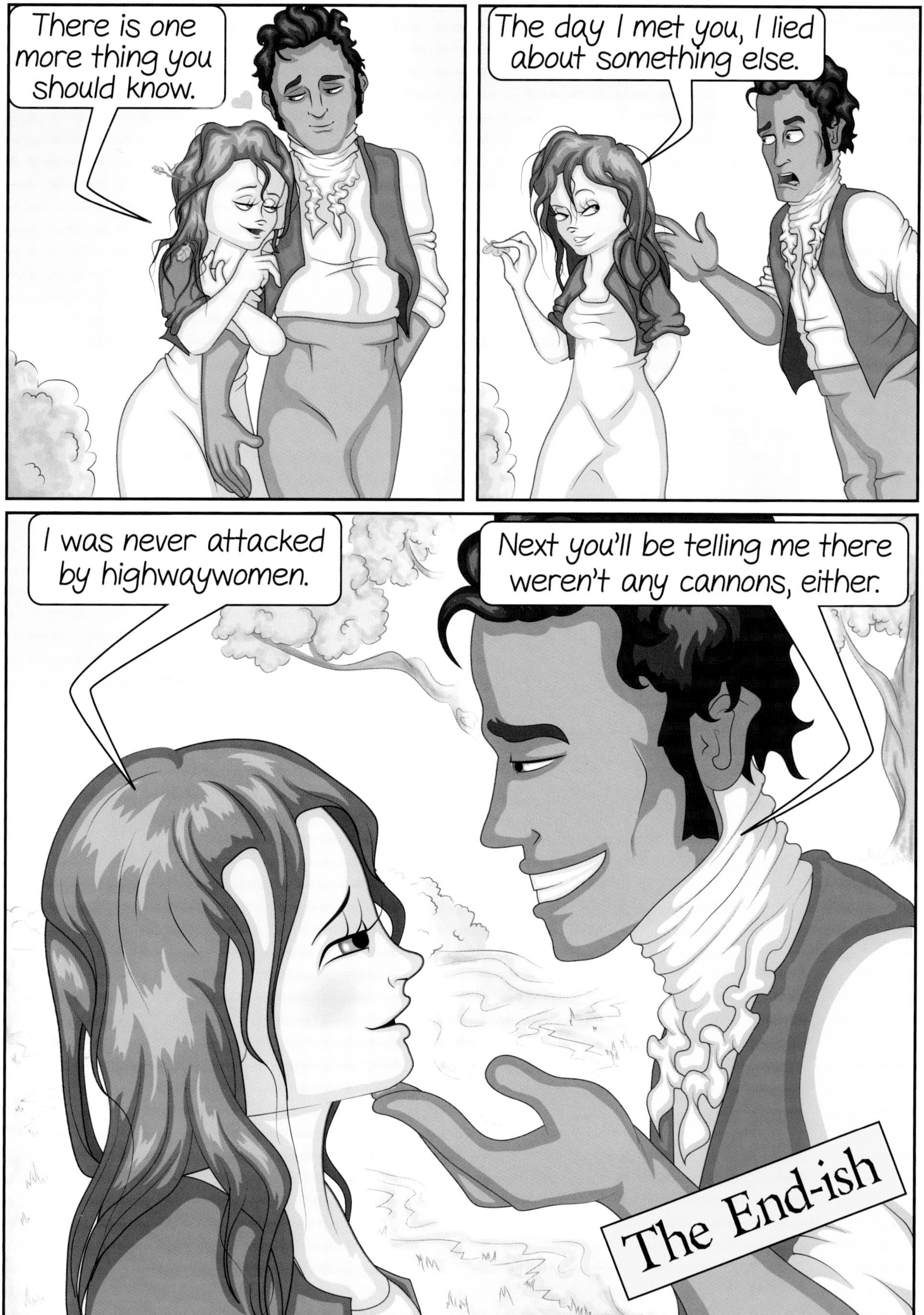
There is one more thing you should know.
The day I met you, I lied about something else.
I was never attacked by highwaywomen.
Next you'll be telling me there weren't any cannons, either.
The End-ish

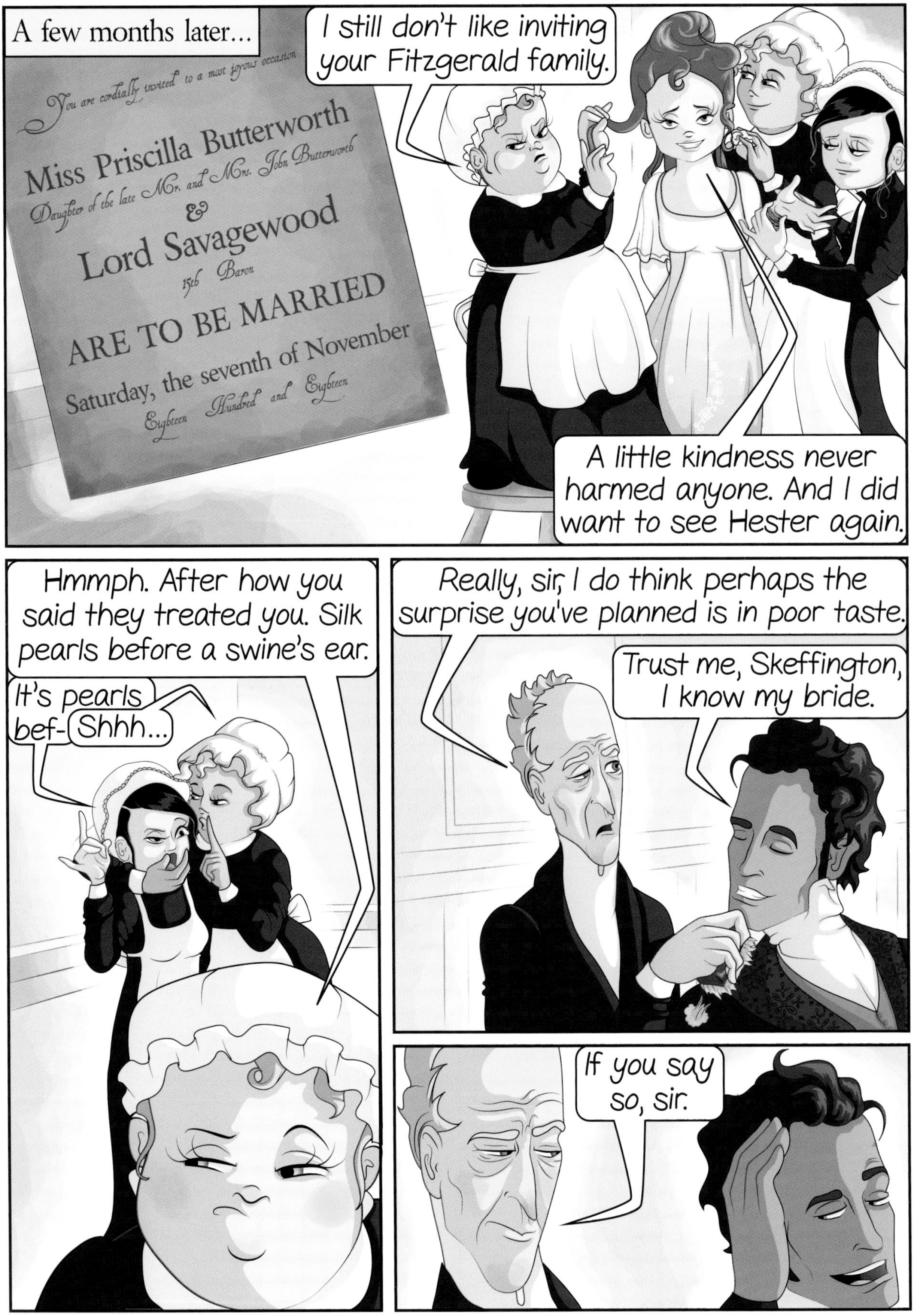
A few months later...
You are cordially invited to a most joyous occasion
Miss Priscilla Butterworth
Daughter of the late Mr. and Mrs. John Butterworth
&
Lord Savagewood
15th Baron
ARE TO BE MARRIED
Saturday, the seventh of November
Eighteen Hundred and Eighteen
I still don't like inviting your Fitzgerald family.
A little kindness never harmed anyone. And I did want to see Hester again.
Hmmph. After how you said they treated you. Silk pearls before a swine's ear.
It's pearls bef-
Shhh...
Really, sir, I do think perhaps the surprise you've planned is in poor taste.
Trust me, Skeffington, I know my bride.
If you say so, sir.

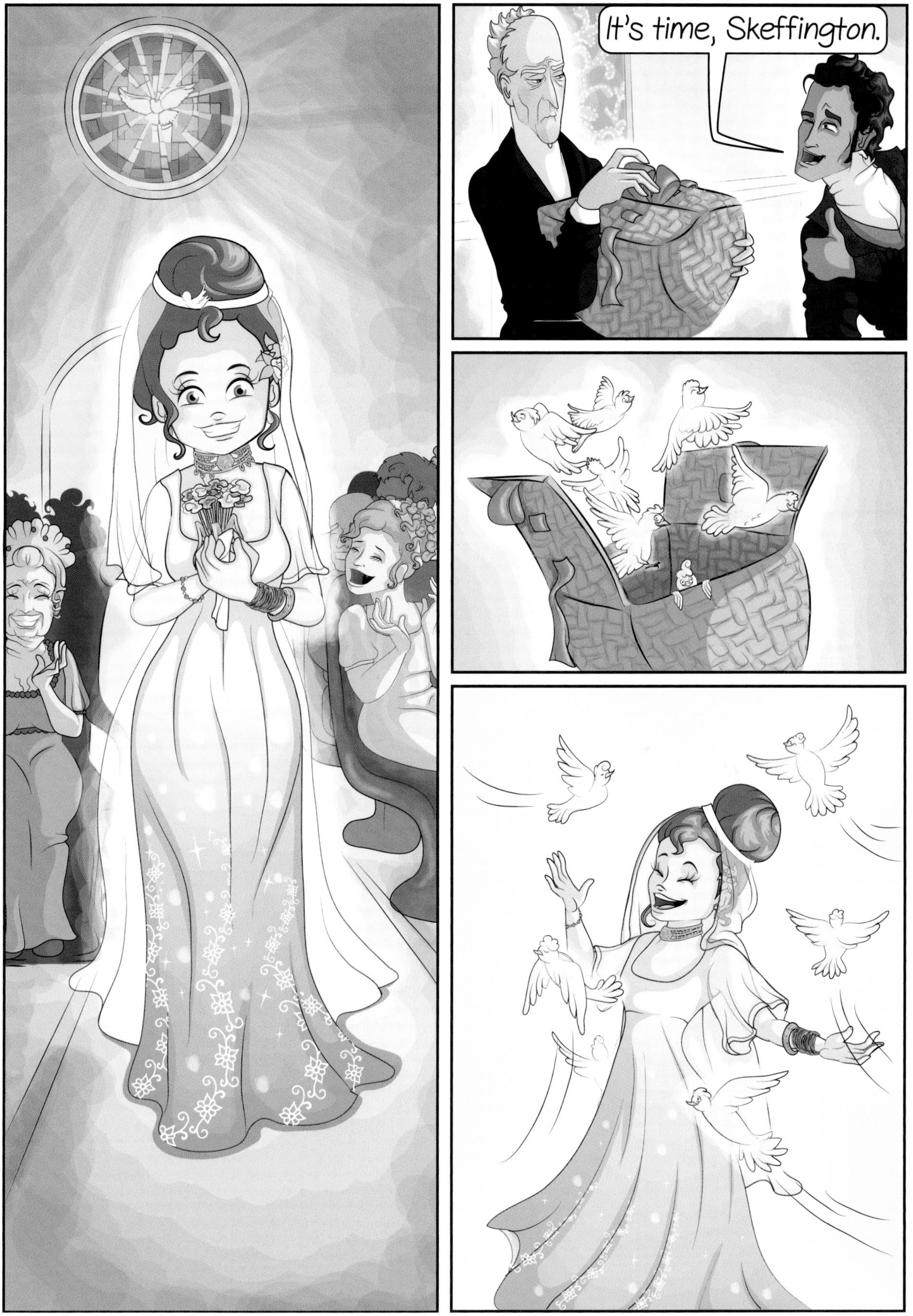
It's time, Skeffington.

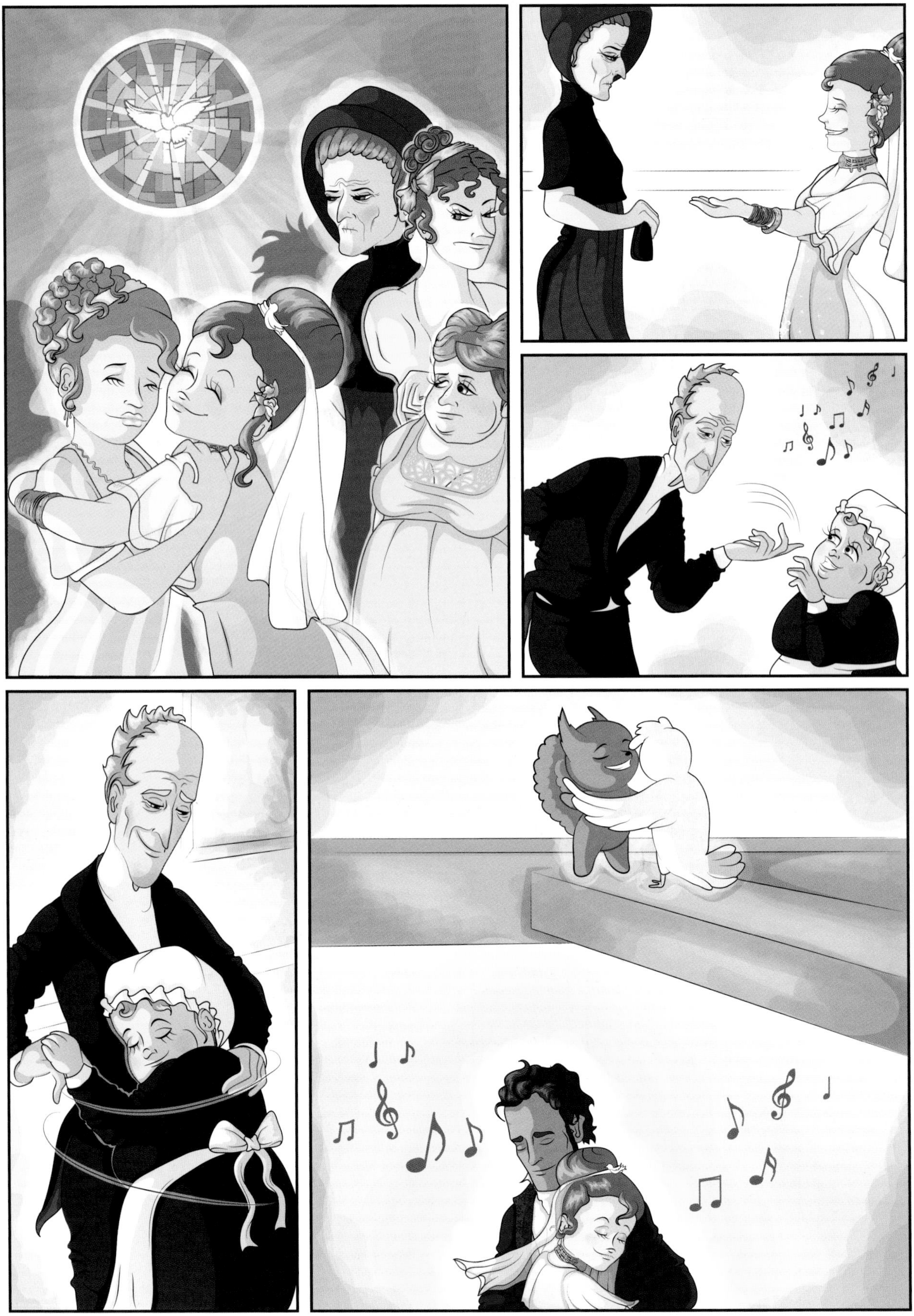

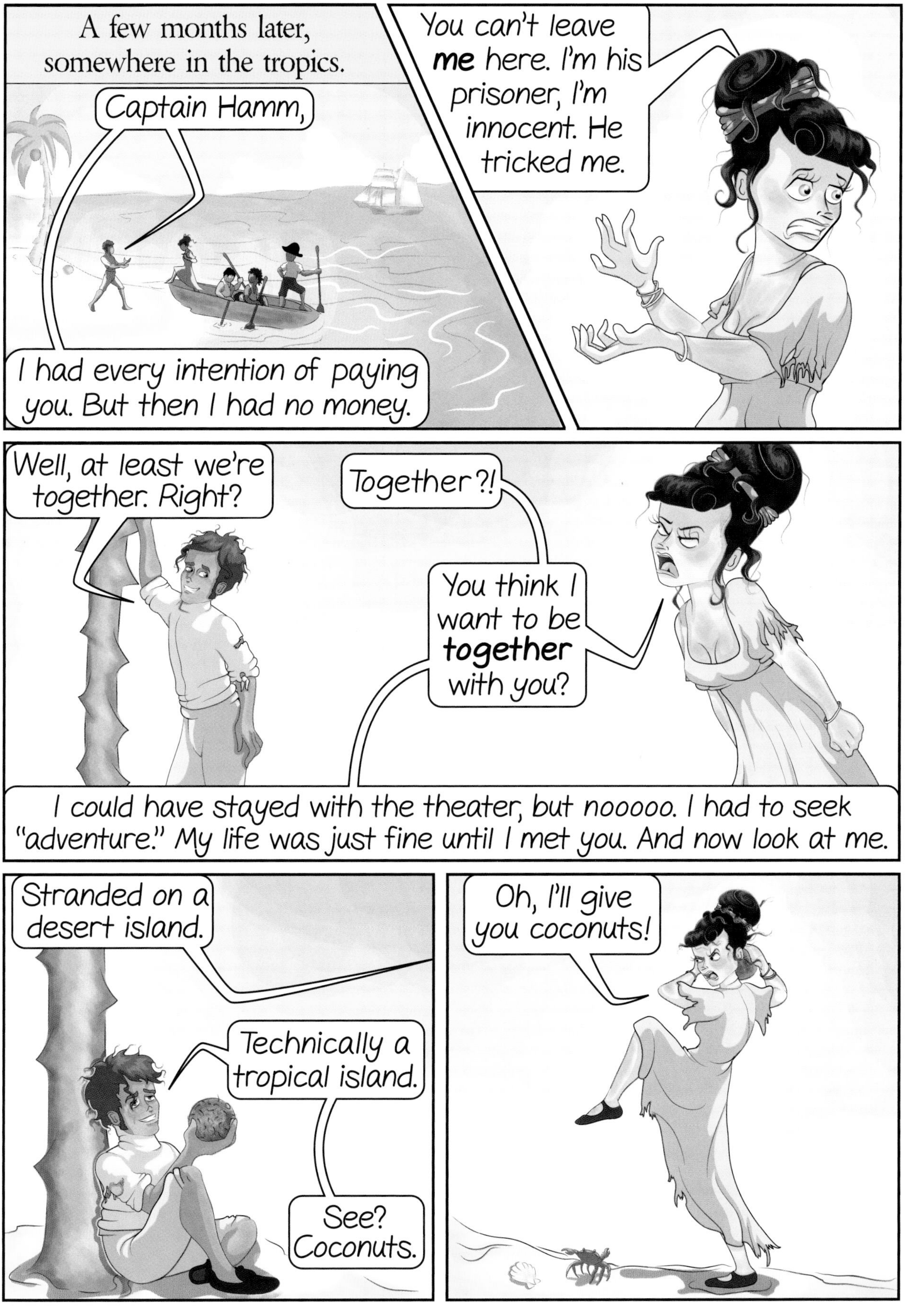
A few months later, somewhere in the tropics.
Captain Hamm,
I had every intention of paying you. But then I had no money.
You can't leave **me** here. I'm his prisoner, I'm innocent. He tricked me.
Well, at least we're together. Right?
Together?!
You think I want to be **together** with you?
I could have stayed with the theater, but nooooo. I had to seek "adventure." My life was just fine until I met you. And now look at me.
Stranded on a desert island.
Technically a tropical island.
See? Coconuts.
Oh, I'll give you coconuts!

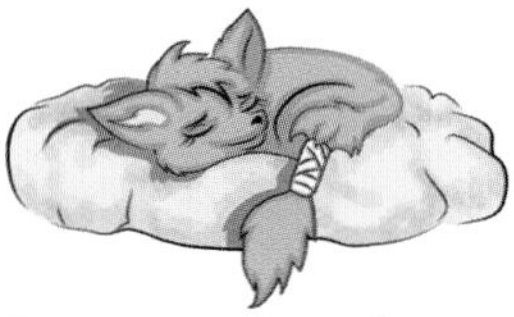

# Acknowledgments


Susie Asher
Steven Axelrod
Robin Barletta
Pam Barricklow
Abi Bowling
Mireya Chiriboga
Judyth Collin
Emily Cotler
Sonali Dev
Jennifer Hart
Lyssa Keusch
Vedika Khanna
Matt Langley
Shelby Peak
Nisha Sharma
Liate Stehlik
Diahann Sturge
Erika Tsang
Mikhail Twarogowski
Jenn Zapf

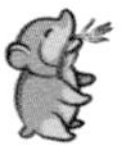

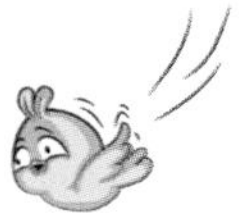

Thank you. This one took a village.
I am so lucky to have this village.
~JQ

# About the Author

JULIA QUINN is the #1 *New York Times* bestselling author of countless historical romances, including the Bridgerton novels, which were recently adapted into a Netflix original series. She is a graduate of Harvard and a dropout of Yale, and she loves to travel, despite recurring nightmares about arriving at borders without a passport. She once took her younger sister to England, and while they were able to clear immigration without incident, they now both have nightmares about JQ's attempt to navigate Hyde Park Corner in a rental car.

# About the Illustrator

VIOLET CHARLES does her best drawing at four a.m., drinks herculean quantities of herbal tea (blueberry, please), and loves her husband and dog . . . not always in that order. She is a California–to–Rocky Mountains transplant, speaks passable Swedish, and enjoys cartoon ducks, etymology, anything pink, and the death metal music genre. She is the cartoonist behind the webcomics *Bridget over troubled Waters* and *Violets Aren't Blue*.

She is Julia Quinn's younger sister.

# In Memoriam

On June 29, 2021, Violet Charles—my beloved baby sister and the illustrator of this book—was killed by a drunk driver in a crash that also took the lives of our father and her beloved dog Michelle. Violet's husband died five months later of injuries sustained in the crash.

I received the news in the middle of the night. "Why would someone be calling this late?" you think, and strangely, your brain doesn't go to the worst until the person on the other end of the line just says it: "I'm so sorry. I'm so sorry."

Over and over, I heard those words. My heart became hollow, then it was crushed under the weight of grief. I knew such sadness was possible, but I had never felt it myself.

As I slowly coped and grieved, it became clear to me that the best way to honor Violet was to make sure *Miss Butterworth and the Mad Baron* was published with all the excitement and fanfare that it deserved. Violet had worked on the project tirelessly—I know the cover indicates that the book was written by me and illustrated by her, but she did a huge portion of the writing and just about all of the plotting. *Miss Butterworth* was my idea, but it was her baby. For her not to see *Miss Butterworth and the Mad Baron* released into the world of readers is the cruelest joke imaginable.

Here are a few of the many wonderful things about Violet:

- She was easily the funniest person in our family, and that's saying a lot.
- She was incredibly smart and wildly clever, but she couldn't punctuate for crap, and I had to go over every word bubble in this book with a fine-toothed comb. (And if there is still a typo, please don't tell me. I assure you, I do not want to know.)
- She was convinced that Tom Kha Gai (Thai coconut chicken soup) could cure the common cold.
- She loved things that were tiny and cute, and that meant that we had the most darling individual desserts every Thanksgiving.
- She called her nieces and nephews "niblings," because really, shouldn't there be a word for that?
- She was kind. And she was fair. She thought deeply about the things that were important to her, and she also thought deeply about the things that were important to the people she loved.
- She was remarkable.
- I miss her.

~ Julia Quinn

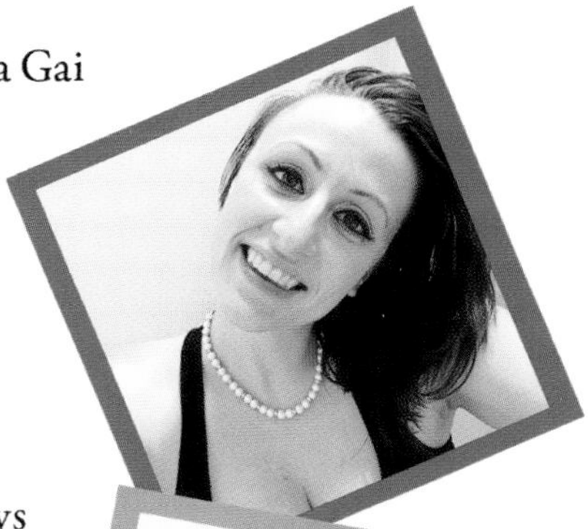

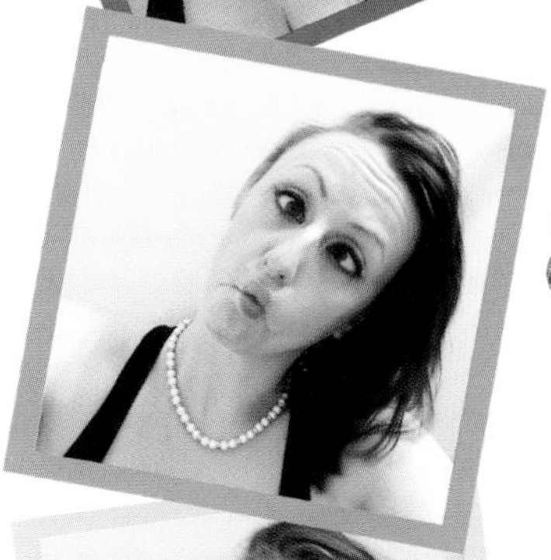

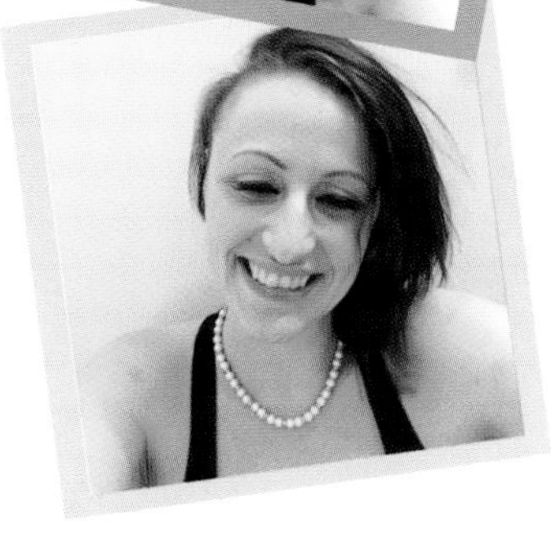

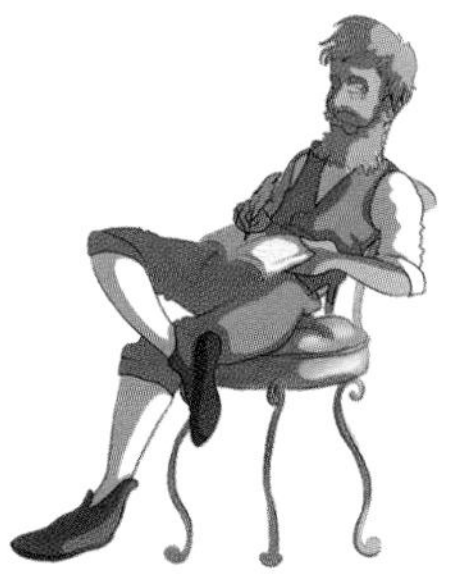

# Colophon

THIS BOOK was illustrated almost entirely using Adobe Illustrator. It was laid out in Adobe InDesign. The fonts are Austtina and Serlio on the cover, Austtina and Garamond Premier Pro in the front and back matter, and GelPen and Berylium for (most of) the story. The paper is 80# Sterling Ultra White.

MISS BUTTERWORTH herself first appeared in Chapter 3 of *It's In His Kiss* (seventh in the Bridgerton Series) and later appeared in both the Bevelstoke and Smythe-Smith series. More information can be found at JuliaQuinn.com and MissButterworthandtheMadBaron.com.

NO PIGEONS were harmed in the making of this book.

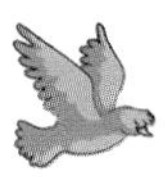

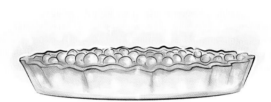

This is a work of fiction. Names, characters, places, and incidents are products of the author's imagination or are used fictitiously and are not to be construed as real. Any resemblance to actual events, locales, organizations, or persons, living or dead, is entirely coincidental.



HarperCollins books may be purchased for educational, business, or sales promotional use. For information, please email the Special Markets Department at SPsales@harpercollins.com.

FIRST EDITION

Library of Congress Cataloging-in-Publication Data has been applied for.

ISBN 978-0-06-295859-4

22 23 24 25 26 LSC 10 9 8 7 6 5 4 3 2 1